# VOICES
# OF EIGHTEENTH-CENTURY
# BATH

# VOICES
# OF EIGHTEENTH-CENTURY
# BATH

An anthology of contemporary texts
illustrating events, daily life and attitudes
at Britain's leading Georgian spa

**Compiled by Trevor Fawcett**

**RUTON : 1995**

**To**
**Adrian, Jon and Kari**

First published in the United Kingdom in 1995
by RUTON, 25 Northampton Street, Bath, and
produced by R. Milsom & Associates 01454 850033

ISBN 0-9526326-0-8

# CONTENTS

*The cover and page illustrations have been redrawn by
Barbara McLaughlin after two Bath caricatures by
G.M.Woodward, both of them engraved by Isaac
Cruikshank and published in 1796: ' The Cabinet
Council' and 'A Group at Bath'.*

❦ ❦ ❦ ❦ ❦ ❦ ❦ ❦ ❦ ❦ ❦ ❦ ❦ ❦ ❦ ❦

# *INTRODUCTION*

Eighteenth-century Bath was always good copy. No other English centre outside London attracted so much attention, was more written about and marvelled over. Rich and poor, famous and obscure, people flocked to the spa for their health, for pleasure and dissipation, to mingle with their peers and social betters. They came too out of simple curiosity, for the markets and shops, to do business of many kinds, or in search of adventure, profit, employment, and even charity. Some merely passed through or stayed a single season; others returned time after time or took up residence for good - for after all, as Mrs Piozzi enthused in 1788, there was no place 'where one lives so *well* for so little Money, no Place where so many Beauties meet, no Place where there are such Combinations of Gayety and such Opportunities of Snugness'. No place either, by that date, which had mushroomed so fast, where so many sick and infirm hopefully resorted, where lodgings and organised diversions and service industries so flourished, where disparities of wealth showed so blatantly and which offered to view such a cross-section of the nation.

Bath spoke indeed with multiple voices, a representative sample of them captured in this volume - at times as vividly as if transcribed from some Georgian tape-recorder. We listen to land developers and shopkeepers, country parsons and waggon-owners, school-teachers and pupils, criminals and antiquaries, physicians and bluestockings. We hear the composer Haydn, the artist Gainsborough, the politicians Wilkes and the elder Pitt, Lord Chesterfield and David Garrick, John Wesley and Jane Austen, Wedgwood the potter and the future George IV. Private letters, diaries, memoirs, newspaper reports, advertisements, Corporation records and guidebooks are among the contemporary sources drawn on to present a rounded view of a time and a place.

Many of the extracts chosen are entertaining in their own right, and each of them illuminates some aspect of eighteenth-century Bath. They have been grouped under eighteen broad headings and arranged chronologically within each section so as to give some idea of historical changes during the period. As far as possible the spelling, punctuation and capitalisation of each quotation (however idiosyncratic) follows the original source, though paragraph breaks have been dropped and are indicated by a double slash (//). Editorial omissions are signalled by dots (...), additions are enclosed within square brackets, and dates before September 1752 cited in new style. It should be noted that references given in abbreviated form after many quotations are printed in full at the end of the book.

Care has been taken in the selection of 'voices' to ensure that - however individual and even discordant they may sound in solo performance - the final outcome is a balanced chorus on eighteenth-century Bath. The whole context may be explored further in various published accounts of the Georgian spa, including the appropriate chapters of *Bath: History and Guide* by Trevor Fawcett and Stephen Bird (pub. Alan Sutton, 1994).

## THE DEVELOPING TOWNSCAPE

*For the first quarter of the century Bath's physical growth remained slow, confined to new houses (a few with striking Baroque façades), a row of shops, the first modest Pump and Assembly Rooms, and some extension and modernising of older properties. Still walled round, it was an attractive small country town. Only when the increasing pressure of visitors began to demonstrate just how profitable building development might be did successive waves of expansion on the peripheries gradually transform the spa. And even then, it took the elder John Wood's visionary insistence on Classical splendour to save Bath from merely humdrum schemes, and to create the fine Georgian terraces and spectacular set-pieces that so dazzled contemporaries from the 1730s onwards, above all Queen Square and later the Circus and Royal Crescent. Henceforth supply generated demand, demand encouraged supply. Elegant lodgings and improved amenities drew yet more visitors (and well-to-do residents), which in turn emboldened others - among them Bath Corporation itself and the Kingston and Pulteney estates - to emulate Wood with their own speculative projects. Only periodic lapses of business confidence, mostly at times of national danger, caused the flow of credit to dry up. In the second half of the century, stimulated by the intense rivalries of projectors, architects and builders, a uniquely impressive architectural townscape, harmonious in its Classical idiom and universal use of local stone, spread across the hillsides and meadows, even invading the old city centre as new public buildings arose there too and cluttered streets were widened. Beginning in the 1750s the excitement of visitors as they wandered through Bath and its suburbs is increasingly evident. Well-proportioned terraces, crescents and squares in the smarter districts were enhanced by clean, broad pavements and, at night, decent street-lighting. Certainly there were squalid areas and back-street eyesores, but by 1790, when the building frenzy reached its highest pitch, these could be overlooked and the whole urban scene described in extravagant superlatives: Bath had become the most elegant city in Europe. Only a few dissenting notes, chronicled in the following extracts, disturbed the chorus of approval.*

### 1. 1705 A small place with shaded walks and new houses

At the east end of the abbey are the groves, planted with rows of trees: here the company usually meet, and in the adjoining gravelled walk are the raffling-shops, with a bowling-green behind them. From the groves and walk you have a pleasant prospect of the river and adjacent hills. The city is but of small circumference, it may be about a mile and a half; it has but one parish church [*within* the walls] besides the abbey, but is graced with many new buildings: I observed one belonging to a citizen, the front of which house was adorned with four orders of pilasters, one in each story, viz. the Doric, Ionic, Corinthian, and Composite, with a handsome balustrade, all of stone; the windows were sashed and the mouldings very neat and proportionable to the structure. I never see any private building that pleased me more than this, it being exactly regular and strikes the beholder with an agreeable grandeur.

*Gale, Tour, p.23*

### 2. 1725 Built of local limestone and sited in a hollow

Bath stands low being almost surrounded by hills, & makes no considerable figure till you come up to it, there are gates at it's Entrance, here are two Churches only and a Chapple. The Abby Church is large & handsome and built like a Cathedral, tho' tis not one, there is a fine Organ, and in the outward Isles several good monuments, the other Church and Chapple are of inferiour note. The Town is paved with a flat stone and the Houses are built with the same sort of stone plentiful in this Country, and are three or four storys high, and generally sash'd and look very handsome. The Town is populous though not large, and has a neat [Guild-]hall adjoining to the Market Cross very handsome and built with freestone...

*Diary of a Tour, pp.113-14*

### 3. 1700-26 On the eve of Palladian correctness

In the Progress of these Improvements Thatch'd Coverings were exchang'd to such as were Tiled; low and obscure Lights were turn'd into elegant Sash-Windows; the Houses were rais'd to five and more Stories in Height; and every one was lavish in Ornaments to adorn the Outsides of them, even to Profuseness: So that only Order and Proportion was wanted to make BATH, sixteen Years ago, vie with the famous City of *Vicenza*, in *Italy*, when in the highest Pitch of Glory, by the excellent Art of the celebrated *Andrea Palladio*...

*Wood, Essay, 1742-3, vol.1 p.92*

### 4. 1730 John Wood I gets off to a bad start with Chandos Buildings

...it is the Opinion of almost every one who has seen them & especially who have lodged in them that no two houses have been worse finished and in a less workmanlike manner by any one who pretended to be an Architect & had any regard for his own Reputation or the Interest of the Person who was his Benefactor & imployed him [i.e. Lord Chandos himself].

*BCL, Chandos MS (microfilm), Duke of Chandos to John Wood I, 29 Aug 1730*

### 5. 1732 Queen Square in progress: Wood's first urban masterpiece

The Workmen who have been a long Time employ'd in erecting a new Square in Barton Grounds, on Saturday laid the first Stone of the Chapel to be built for the Use of the Inhabitants, in the Presence of many Persons of Distinction, who contributed largely towards the said Work, which, with that of the Square, goes on with all possible Expedition; and the latter will far exceeed any publick Building of that Kind in England, and outdo every Thing in Bath, both for Air and Situation.

*Gloucester Journal 11 Apr 1732*

### 6. 1741 Sir William Pulteney frets to his steward about his Bathwick estate

If you have been at Bathwick I take it for granted you have spoke to all ye Tenants there, & that they have paid their rents; there is one Hull at the Spring gardens [an embryonic pleasure garden], that I know not how to deal with, he has never yet paid a farthing of rent, & yet I am told complains of me, as a hard land Lord. There is another Gardiner ... exactly in the same circumstances; & Mr Wiltshire I am told, complains that he does not know who to apply to for taking ye ground he wants...// I am inform'd Mr Allen [Ralph Allen] talks of making soon a Bridge over ye River, which must certainly affect my Estate very much, & I hope you will consult how to turn it to ye best advantage... // You know how much... these Estates of mine have been neglected, & misused; it will require your utmost vigilance & care to put them upon a right foot, & if my coming down should be judged necessary to enable you to do this, I am ready to do it as soon as the Elections are over.

*BrRO, AC/JS/57/15 (e), Pulteney MS, Sir William Pulteney to Jarret Smith, 30 Apr 1741*

### 7. 1747 A paved promenade

There is one Thing that I can't pass over, which is the handsome Manner of their Paving the Publick Walks. You may walk from the End of the *Parade*, quite to the *Pump-Room*, on a fine Pavement; so that, let it be ever so wet, the Walk is not dirty. Indeed, the Pitching in the Streets here is better than in most Places of the Kingdom, and far preferable to the Metropolis.

*Draper, Brief Description, pp.13-14*

### 8. 1750 Bath's expansion begins to attract permanent residents

The town is well built of hewn free stone, and great additions have been made without the walls of late years, as of all Queen's square to the north-west, mostly inhabited by persons who live constantly at Bath, and the whole consists of very fine buildings, and since that a great pile of buildings... called the North and South Parade, being terminated to the east by the river.

*Pococke, Travels, vol.1 p.154*

### 9. 1752 John Wood I makes an offer for the Ham on the Kingston estate

Since you were here we have lost Mr Gay whose Lunacy has for many years put a Stop to all Improvements on the Ambery and Barton Farm. That Estate is now clear of all the settlements and Entails with which it has been clogged for more than 60 years and according to the talk of the Town Scheme upon Scheme are to be Executed on it, one of which Sir John Cope mentioned to me just before he left Bath and named the Duke of Bedford for his Author. Should Building revive this way it will be of great Prejudice to our Being on the other side of the City [i.e. on the site of the Parades] and therefore am willing to strain the Matter as far as possible on my side to Encourage my lord Duke [Kingston] to a speedy Accommodation... I will give his Grace £400 a year for the Ham exclusive of what Mr Marchant [a lessee on the estate] would Reserve and £200 a year shall Commence directly the other £200 a year seven years after...

*BL, Egerton MS 3516, John Wood I to Mr Shering (Kingston's agent), Bath 18 Dec 1752*

### 10. 1755 *Property rights and parochial attitudes*

... this Day fortnight [i.e. a fortnight ago] I was accidentally passing through the [Abbey] Church and saw the Door leading into the Abbey Garden open and the Churchwardens were there with workmen who were digging and searching, when I demanded what they were at they told me they were searching how far the foundations of the Church extended and that they claimed ten feet all round the Church as their property. I then told them they had no business there without a legal Authority which I know they had not and therefore I insisted on their moving off the Premises, they then told me they would not and the workmen who were John Ford and Robert Smith said they stood on the Church and not the Duke's [Kingston's] land and they would maintain it, and moreover the Churchwardens gave me notice to take away the mortar stuff that is against the Church within the Month or they would seize it as their property. However I made the workmen fill up the Hole they had Dug and would not let them Dig further... // Tis amazing that such a Malignant temper should subsist in the minds of these Bath People, who have such Oportunities everyday of civilizing themselves, that they are so blind to conviction and so untouched by Experience as not to perceive of how great advantage to the Town the improvements within these twenty years have been, and how great they may be. The other day I saw a Team of horses drove into a Brook as soon as the Leader entered he begain drinking and as soon as he had quenched his thrist he began trotting on unregardful of his fellow Labourers; just so is our Bath Man, his Views are so mean and contracted and his Spirit so low mean and groveling that for a little private advantage he would not care if all his species suffered.

*BL, Egerton MS 3516, John Wood II to Mr Shering (Kingston's agent), Bath 1 Oct 1755*

### 11. 1755 *No tipping and no bill posting*

WHEREAS several Persons have made it a Practice to throw Soil and Ashes into the triangular Piece of Ground before the *Grand Parade;* and likewise into the narrow Strip of Ground before the *South-Parade*, to the great Injury of

our Estate, and to the endangering the Wall, which is built and supported at our Expence, as a Boundary between our Land and Mr.*Marchant's* Garden, - THIS THEREFORE IS TO DESIRE all Masters and Mistresses of Families, inhabiting the *Parades, Duke, Pierepont,* and *Orchard* Streets, to command their Servants not to offend in like Manner for the future, for we are resolved to prosecute, to the utmost Rigour of the Law, all and every Person that shall throw any Dirt in either of the said Pieces of Ground..., and we do likewise forewarn all Persons from sticking up Play-Bills, Advertisements, &c. on the Gate-Piers, and Obelisks of *Queen-Square,* for we will prosecute any Person that shall so offend, or shall otherwise deface the said Piers, Obelisks or Ballustrades of the said Square. Jen.Wood, Jo Wood [John Wood I's widow, John Wood II].
*Bath Advertiser 1 Nov 1755*

### 12.  1757  Water Supply for the Circus: Wood versus Atwood

Mr.Attwood [Thomas Warr Atwood] shewed me a letter from you [Thomas Garrard, landlord of the Barton estate] in which you promise him to be a Sharer in the Water scheme, I am very sorry you made that promise & am afraid you did not thoroughly consider it, nor its Consequences - Mr.Attwood is far from being a freind to our buildings, his Connections with the Corporation biasses him entirely a different way, and if you do not keep the whole to your self but will let it in Shares, and do not then shew a preference to the Builders on our own Ground... it will give them such Umbrages that I dread the Consequences, & I beg you maturely to consider it as a point of the greatest moment. Mr.Attwood I have observed in all the Conversations I have had with him, has always endeavoured to throw Rubs in our Way... I have no objection to employ Mr.Attwood as a Plumber even in preference to one of the same trade who has built on the Ground, if he be not an Adventurer, but if he is tis certainly absurd to employ him.
*BCL, AL 1682, John Wood II to Thomas Garrard, Bath 30 Jul 1757*

### 13.  1759  Will the Circus ever be completed?

This is... a city, in my opinion, more worth seeing than any I was ever at, the great Metropolis excepted. Twice I have been there before, but 'tis infinitely improv'd by the building the circus, and the whole street [Gay Street] by which 'tis approached from the square. They seem to fear the former's ever being finished, its progress is so extremely slow; nine houses only are yet erect'd. There is intended to be three times that number, and the openings between give a fine view of the country. Those that are complet'd give one an idea of the elegance of the whole, they being in magnificent taste in the Doric, Ionic, and Corinthian orders...
*Powys, Diaries, p.50, entry for Aug 1759*

### 14.  1763  Modern comfort and splendour

Proud squares, parades, circus, buildings, and streets daily arise. Houses are sold far above their cost before they are roofed in. Masons and carpenters, who formerly mortgaged story by story, are now men of property... Turkey carpets

now cover the best floors. The rooms are wainscotted. The doors are adorned
with brass locks and hinges; tongs, pokers, shovels, grates, and fenders are all
of polished iron, or brass. Down-beds, soft blankets, fine linnen, damask
curtains, mahogany tables, chairs, cabinets, and costly mirrors, furnish every
room. The servants garret is now as good as the masters bed-chamber was
thirty years ago, and all at the old price of ten shillings a room, and five for a
garret during the season. The entry doors are spacious, the stairs magnificent.
*Sutherland, Attempts, p.119*

### 15.  1767  The spread of houses and lodging-house 'cats'

I believe Sir it would astonish you to see how the new Buildings are extending
in all points from the old center of Bath, The Pump Rooms - We almost reach
Lansdown & Claverton-down, north & south, but not quite to Bristol & London
for East & West. I think verily the End of some of our *Master* Builders will be
to meet some of their Marylebone Friends near a certain Ditch. It does not
appear to me that many of the new Houses are occupied by Genteal Families
newly residing in Bath, but only that the Lodging-House *Cats* are endeavouring
to draw more Talons upon us, by having Houses in all quarters.
*Gainsborough, Letters, p.135, Thomas Gainsborough to Richard Stevens, M.P., Bath,*
*13 Sep 1767*

### 16.  1768  London outclassed in urban design

Believe me, *Bath* greatly exceeds *London* in regularity of building, and in
being proportionately a much finer city: the most criticising eye must allow
that the Circus is truly beautiful, and ornamented to that just degree of elegance,
which... lies between *profusion* and *simplicity*.
*Young, Tour, p.153*

### 17.  1769  Hewn stone, regular plan, and pretty countryside

This place (Bath) surprised and pleased me extremely at first. It was so new a
sight to see a town built of hewn stone, instead of ragged and dirty brick, and
streets and parades on a regular plan, and above all the circus, instead of the
confused heap of buildings of all shapes and sizes which compose every other
town in England. The neighbouring country is very pretty - hills of some height
with cultivated valleys running among them, the principal one (which leads to
Bristol) watered by the Avon. There are many fine trees in the hedge-rows; and
some woods clothing the sides of the hills.
*Gray, Correspondence, vol.3, p.1087, Norton Nicholls to Thomas Gray, Bath 27 Nov*
*1769*

### 18.  1775  Siting the new Guildhall: a critic speaks out

The Buildings and Markets being now laid out so prejudicial to their beauty
and interest, arises from Mr.Attwood's very capital blunder in building the
Hall to the Market Place and great thoroughfare, where the shops for businesss
should have been, and the shops fronting the country, where there is no
thoroughfare, out of the way of business, and where, from its contiguousness

to the Prison, and the uncommon beautiful Prospect for the large Room, the situation was mark'd out as plain as possible for the Hall. Independent of the misapplication of so much valuable ground; the dining Room in this Hall, instead of having an open view of the country, will now have an agreeable view of Mr.Attwood's notorious lead roof [on a new market building], and the raw meat in the shambles.

*Bath Journal 21 Aug 1775, letter from 'A Citizen'*

### 19.  1787  *The speculative boom still in its infancy?*

We hear with pleasure that Mr.Symons has lett the ground for twenty-seven houses in Camden-place [later Camden Crescent], and that Mr.Spackman has nearly lett the whole ground that is to form the New Crescent [Lansdown Crescent]. A very grand plan, we also learn, is drawn of new streets, a circus, and square, to be built in Bathwick meadows; which for elegance and convenience will at least equal any buildings in this city. A range of 30 capital houses {Marlborough Buildings} is also erecting west of the [Royal] Crescent. // Bath, as a city, is certainly only in its infancy; for being a central point, abounding with all the luxuries of life, all the amusements for the gay, or the rational society for the aged, and healing waters for the deceased [i.e. diseased], who can wonder that all the opulent, who are not obliged to reside part of the year in London, should prefer such a residence; or that single gentlemen or ladies of small fortunes should retire to such a place, where they may live as reasonable as in a village in Yorkshire?

*Bath Chronicle 8 Mar 1787*

### 20.  1787  *The other face of Bath*

... BATH... , as a city, is like a Frenchman's shirt - the ruffle is very fine, but the body very coarse. Place a man in his sleep in the Crescent, and he might upon waking conceive himself in an amphitheatre, erected by the same workmen who built the Temple of Solomon; but instead of this, place him in one of those blind alleys - for there are no other communications - which separate the old town from the new, and fancying himself in Field-lane or St.Giles's [London slums], he would immediately search for his pocket handkerchief. In short... all is either splendidly dull or dirtily vulgar.

*Dibdin, Tour, pp.33-4, letter ix, 21 Oct 1787*

### 21.  1787  *Mrs Piozzi tires of crescents*

Bath is a pretty Town, so the People call it a *Great City* & then I affront them by laughing: they are building two new Crescents on Lansdown; very stupid never to change the form of Architecture... they will have all the same stuff over and over again till one is weary on't.

*Piozzi, Thraliana, vol.2 p.697, Bath, Nov 1787*

### 22. 1789 The fastest growing place in the kingdom

A very good row of houses are almost finished from the extremity of this [the Royal] Crescent leading up towards Lansdown, where near the summit of the hill is also erecting another new Crescent, parallel with the other, called Lansdown-place, with a large chapel, &c. just below... Betwixt this and the royal Crescent, a most admirable plan is projected for immediate execution, which is to consist of another Circus, several handsome streets, parades, groves, &c. and when finished will render this part one of the completest spots in Europe. In short these elegancies daily seem to spring up here by enchantment; for on the opposite side, called Beacon-hill, we see a third Crescent [Camden] in great forwardness, the principal story of which displays much Corinthian splendor, one of these columns appearing between each window. A plan is also drawn by Mr.Baldwin for immediately erecting in Bathwick meadows, belonging to Mr.Pulteney, on the other side his beautiful bridge. These, together with the abovementioned, are calculated to be no less than 1600 houses. What an unparalleled spectacle will this city be when the present plan is finished.

*Shaw, Tour, pp.294-5*

### 23. 1790 John Wesley foresees Bath's last days

I took a view of the new buildings. There are at present none like them in England. They have not only added a second crescent, with two beautiful rows of houses, near Ludstown [Lansdown], but a whole town on the other side of the city, which is swiftly increasing every day. And must all these fine buildings be burned up? Yea -

> Earth and heaven destroyed,
> Nor left even one in the mighty void!

*Wesley (J.), Journal, vol.8 p.46, entry for 3 Mar 1790*

### 24. 1791 The pastoral charm of the Royal Crescent

There is a sameness in the Circus, which may not perhaps be perceived by those who view it merely as a fine piece of architecture, but must be felt by others who are doomed to reside in it. The effect is not so in the Crescent; there is, to use an expression of Gray's, something so *rus-in-urbe-ish* in the whole of it, that I would chuse a house in that edifice, when compared with one in the Circus...

*Clarke, Tour in 1791, pp. 144-5*

### 25. 1791 Dusty, stifling, showy, inconvenient, and with a Scottish feel to it

Bath is a town about twice as large as Aberdeen, and situated in the bottom of a deep and narrow valley, overhung with steep hills on every side; so that there is hardly such a thing to be felt there as a fresh breeze. The soil is white chalk [actually *limestone*], which on the surface of the ground is pounded, by the feet of animals, and the wheels of carriages, into a fine powder, which, in dry weather, is continually flying about; and, drawn in with the breath, proved most offensive to my lungs, though they are not easily affected; in wet weather it covers all the level and narrow streets with a deep mire. The heat of the place is, as you will readily suppose, very great; and the air much more close and stifling than that of London. Some of the streets are, in respect of architecture, very elegant, if they be not too gaudy, and too much ornamented; but, on the whole, it is an irregular and very inconvenient town. Being all built of free-stone, (an uncommon thing in England,) it has more the air of a Scotch town than of an English one... and it put me more in mind of Edinburgh than any other place I have seen...

*Forbes, Life of Beattie, vol.3 pp.114-15, James Beattie to Miss Valentine, 27 Jul 1791*

### 26. *1793 Picturesque light and shade*

The general aspect of Bath depends more for its characteristics on the hour of the day, and the state of the atmosphere, than almost any other city. In a clear morning, half an hour after sun-rise, and when the smoke of the town, which is always the greatest at the time of lighting fires, is dispelled, the eastern part of the town appears to great advantage, particularly Camden-place, and Beacon-hill: the light partially connects itself with the lower town, till it reaches the cathedral; it is then intercepted by Claverton-downs; and the remaining part of Bath, towards Widcombe, is enveloped in shade. When the sun has risen above the summit of the opposite down, the effect of the light then becomes general, and disperses without forming any subject for a picture. // An evening scene is productive of much more brilliant effect: the Crescents are then seen to the utmost advantage; their situation, their concave form, which catches a variety of light, and their tone of color, are then peculiarly adapted to the pencil. In the month of January, when the air is frosty, and the sun is dropping from the horizon, there is an effect of light and shadow on these buildings, and on the Circus, that is not to be described with the pen.

*Ibbetson et al., Picturesque Guide, pp.102-3*

### 27. *1794 Haydn's impression of Bath*

Bath is one of the most beautiful cities in Europe. All the houses are built of stone; this stone comes from the quarries in the surrounding mountains; it is very soft, so soft, in fact, that it's no trouble to cut it up into any desired shape; it is very white, and the older it is, once it has been taken away from the quarry, the harder it gets. The whole city lies on a slope, and that is why there are very few carriages; instead of them, there are a lot of sedan-chairs... But too bad there are so few straight roads; there are a lot of beautiful squares, on which stand the most magnificent houses, but which cannot be reached by any vehicle: they are now building a brand new and broad street [Great Pulteney Street]. // N.B.Today, on the 3rd [August], I looked at the city, and found, half-way up the hill, a building shaped like a half-moon [Royal Crescent], and more magnificent than any I had seen in London. The curve extends for 100 fathoms, and there is a Corinthian column at each fathom. The building has three 3 floors. Round about it, the pavement in front of the houses is 10 feet broad for the pedestrians, and the street is wide *a proportione*; it is surrounded by an iron fence, and a terrace slopes down 50 fathoms in successive stages, through a beautiful expanse of green; on both sides are little paths, by which one can descend very comfortably.

*Landon, Haydn in England, p.266, Josef Haydn's notebook, Aug 1794*

### 28. 1799 Bath compared with London

This Place is more beautiful than ever - finer Streets, Newer Squares, London looks dirty and *Commercial* to it; Bath is the head Quarters of Pleasure and Gayety; our Stone Buildings give it such an Air of Cleanliness...

*Piozzi, Letters, vol 3 p.59, Hester Lynch Piozzi to Margaret Owen, Bath, c.12 Feb 1799*

### 29. 1799 Plaudits for the street lighting

The dimness of the [oil] Lamps in this city, has often occasioned severe remarks in the public papers; we are now pleased to have an opportunity of saying, that at no period were the streets of Bath so well lighted as at present; the glass burners occasion a brilliant and steady light in the spacious streets and open places; whilst the patent burners [Argand lamps] give a perfect illumination to all the narrow lanes and avenues, where they have been judiciously retained.

*Bath Herald 14 Dec 1799*

### 30. c.1800 A Neoclassical view

When I say that Bath is the most elegant of cities, I ought, perhaps, to qualify the expression by observing, that it is rather the elegance of the buildings themselves, than of their distribution, that is to be admired. It is an assemblage of beautiful edifices; but there is nothing of that plan and commodious intersection of streets, which ought to be supposed, when we speak of them as forming a superb city. The parades are delightfully situated; the great Crescent, the lesser ones, the squares, and the Circus, are fine piles of building; and the town-hall is a magnificent structure, bearing some resemblance to the Vatican at Rome. The whole city is built with a cream-coloured stone; and its architects deserve considerable praise. The new streets are commodiously wide, and of great extent. The most beautiful is that called Great Pulteney Street... It is built in a uniform manner... and the several orders of architecture having been preserved through the whole, the effect is magnificent in the extreme.

*Mavor, British Tourists, vol.6 p.273*

*ᴺᴋ᷊ *ᴺᴋ᷊ *ᴺᴋ᷊ *ᴺᴋ᷊ *ᴺᴋ᷊ *ᴺᴋ᷊ *ᴺᴋ᷊ ᴺᴋ᷊ ᴺᴋᵏ ᴺᴋᵏ ᴺᴋᵏ ᴺᴋᵏ ᴺᴋᵏ ᴺᴋᵏ ᴺᴋᵏ ᴺᴋᵏ

## TRANSPORT

*Bath's unprecedented expansion depended quite crucially on the roads and waterways that served it and that also tapped into a whole nationwide network of communications - for these were the arteries that transported the materials it was built from, carried the myriad goods consumed there, bore the daily traffic of the neighbourhood, and above all brought the influx of visitors from near and far that were its lifeblood. It was this realisation that lay behind a series of Corporation-sponsored Acts of Parliament (from 1707 onwards) to improve the steep, stony approaches to the city. Yet it took many decades of turnpike legislation before road surfaces became less dangerous and journey times reduced dramatically. Even the much-frequented Bath-London road, always busy with coaches, waggons, carts, riders, pedestrians, and droves of animals (not to mention highwaymen), continued to be dangerous in places well through the century, especially during bad weather. On the west side of Bath the notoriously poor roads to Bristol made the long-intended Avon Navigation an increasing necessity. When the six locks by-passing the ancient river weirs finally opened to traffic in late 1727, the boost to Bath's economy must have been immediate. Timber, tiles, pennant paving stone, glass, agricultural produce and other bulky and heavy cargoes could now be conveyed by water to the quayside below the old bridge directly from Bristol and beyond - from the reaches of the Severn, South Wales, Ireland, and from distant places overseas. An extensive British market far beyond Bath similarly opened up for local limestone from the Combe Down quarries as it arrived in quantity at the Dolemeads riverside on Ralph Allen's innovative railroad. Around the end of the century the advantages of water transport would be further demonstrated by the new canals, especially in cheapening the cost of coal - an important commodity at Bath and hitherto laboriously brought in by trains of pack animals.*

*As Ralph Allen perceived in connection with postal routes, Bath was a natural hub of communications; regular waggon and coach services plied from the inns, and in the season and on market days the city centre was often congested with vehicles. Providing horse and livery stables was a business itself at Bath, yet the most characteristic mode of transport depended not on horses but* human *muscle-power: bath chairs and sedan chairs and eventually invalid wheel-chairs as well.*

### 31. 1700 The rocky road to Bath

Having Din'd [at Sandy Lane], we proceeded on our Journey, but with a great deal of difficulty; for the Road was so Rocky, Unlevel, and Narrow in some places, that I am perswaded the *Alps* are to be passed with less danger... but we were jolted so Cursedly, that I thought it would have made a dislocation of my Bones; we all complained, but could find no Remedy; nor would I advise any who have been sufferers in *Venus* sports, to Adventure the Fatigue of a Coach to the *Bath*, least it dis-joint a Member or two. At last when our Patience was almost worn out, we agreed to light rather than endure it any longer; but our Chariotier inform'd us, we were almost at our journey's-end, which we presently found to be true... // Being come to the *White-Hart*, our long wish'd-for Port, we refreshed our selves with much Joy, after our tedious Mortifying-Journey...
*Ward, Step to the Bath, 1700, pp.154-5*

### 32. 1702 On a ride from Oxford the last stretch proves the worst

When we came to the edge of Landsdown, we saw Bath so near and plain that we thought to get in presently, but when we came to the bottom the road was so bad, deep, dirty, &c. that it was past 9 ere we got in.
*Yonge, Journal, entry for late May 1702*

### 33. 1707 The first Turnpike Act to improve local roads

...And whereas the greatest part of the...[highways near Bath] being all of them Ancient Roads for Coaches, Carts, Waggons and other Carriages, by reason of the great and many Loads and heavy Carriages of Goods and other things which are Weekly drawn through the same... and being almost in every Place... very Ruinous and Impassable, insomuch that it is become very Dangerous to all Persons, Horses and Cattle that pass those Ways... That for the Surveying, Ordering, Repairing, and Keeping in repair the said Ruinous Places... Seven or more... Justices... shall... Appoint Surveyors... And for Defraying the Charges... the said Justices... shall... appoint... Collectors of... Sums of Money, in the Name of Toll, to be paid for all such Horses, Carts, Coaches, Chariots, Calashes, Chaises, Caravans, Waggons, Wains, or any other Carriage... and for Sheep, Lambs, Droves of Oxen, or Neat Cattle, or Pack-horses, as... shall be lead, pass, or be driven in or through the said... Ways...
*Acts of Parliament, 6 Anne c.42, 1707*

### 34. 1716 A recalcitrant young coachman

While we were in the church [of St Mary Redcliffe?] the coachman came to us and told us we must make haste and go on, else we must lie by the way short of Bath to-night. This was so insolent that we could not bear, and I scolded at him and Mr.Powell took him by the collar. When we came to the coach the young fellow was very insolent and when Mr.Powell had spoke to him called him 'rascal', upon which Mr.Powell struck him with his whip. The father of the young fellow now... began to be calm and willing to appease us and said his son was in drink. However, the young fellow was so sullen and impudent that we were almost afraid to let him drive the ladies to Bath, but he did it very well.

*Ryder, Diary, p.243, entry for 25 May 1716*

### 35.  *1726  Snowbound on the Bath-London road*
*Bath, Dec.*10. Last Monday the Coach was set fast in the Snow, and forced to stay all Night on the Downs beyond Marlborough; the Horses were taken out, and put into a Stable at Marlborough, and the poor Passengers left to make the best of themselves in the Coach all Night.

*Farley's Bristol Newspaper 24 Dec 1726*

### 36.  *1729  The prospect of a miry journey back to Yorkshire*
My sister Mary proposes staying only six weeks from the day we got here; and indeed I believe it will be absolutely necessary for us to leave this place then on account of the roads. We have had almost continued rains ever since we came, that I really dread the roads cross the country, but much more staying here... At present this country is all in a sea, and every little brook hardly passable...

*HMC 42 Carlisle, p.61, Lady A.Irwin to Lord Carlisle, Bath 24 Sep 1729*

### 37.  *1730  Travelling times to London begin to improve*
BATH and BRISTOL Two-Days COACHES, // For LONDON. // THIS is to give Notice to all Gentlemen and Ladies, That the said COACHES will begin to FLY on Monday the 6th Day of April next, and set out every Monday, Wednesday, and Friday Morning, by One oClock from the White-Hart-Inn in Broad-street, Bristol, and the Bell-Inn in Bath; for the One-Bell-Inn in the Strand, the Bell-Sauvage on Ludgate-Hill, the Sarazen's Head in Friday-street, and the Three Cups in Bread-street, London; and return from thence again the same Days as above, for Bath and Bristol. // *Note*, The Three Days Coaches go to and from the same Inns.

*Farley's Bristol Newspaper 4 Apr 1730*

### 38.  *1734  Ralph Allen has difficulty shipping Bath stone*
... I have made use of all the different methods which I cou'd conceive to fix a ship to carry your stone, and am greatly concern'd that it is not yet in my power to acquaint you a Vessel is secured; upon the question I've offer'd not only to advance the freight but likewise have given an expectation of a protection for the seamen belonging to that ship; and besides the Persons usually Imploy'd at Bristol I've ever since my return from London constantly dispatch'd others from hence that I can confide in, to assist me, and am now hourly in hopes to succeed.

*BCL, AL 385, Ralph Allen to Lord Leicester, Bath 1734*

*39. 1735 Goods liable to toll at each lock on the Avon*

... Goods and Merchandizes navigated on the... River Avon, between... Bath and Bristol; to witt... Fine Stone, Pitching Stone for Streets, Gravel & Marble, Cornish Tiles & Bricks... all kind of Coal... Freestone... Timber of Oak and Elm... Fir... Ten feet Deals... Wood Laths, Liquor of all kinds, Bottles[,] Pitch, Tar, Brass, Copper, Iron, Lead, Tallow, Cheeses, Butter[,] Salt, soap, Grocery Wares of all kinds, Oysters, Dyers wares[,] Tobacco Pipe Clay, Fullers Earth, Earthen Ware, Woollen & Linnen Manufactures, Leather, Raw Skinns, Hides, Yarn, Hemp, paper, Grain of all kinds, Wheat, Pease and Beans... Barley... Oats & Malt... Wool, hair[,] feathers, Hay, Straw, Cotten in Baggs, Flax, hops, household Goods & Tanners Bark...

*BRO, Avon Navigation, Copy of the Agreement [to extend the navigation], 1735*

*40. 1739 How to control the sedan chairmen*

To prevent Impositions, and to reduce the *Chairmen* to a little better Order than they are in at present, it is humbly hoped, that all offences shall be punishable *on the Oath of the Party agrieved;* that the *Chairmen* shall stop as often as the Person they carry requires, provided the Person they so carry don't go out of the Chair, nor detain them above one Quarter of an Hour in every Six-penny Fare; that when a Chair is called from any Stand, the first on that Stand to come, except another is called by Name or Figure: That no Chairman shall presume to carry his Chair so near any House, Wall, or Pallisade, as to prevent or obstruct a convenient Way for Foot-Passengers; and that the Fares of Chairs shall not be confined to the Limits of the City, but extend to all the neighbouring Parts, after the Rate of Six-pence for every half Mile; that the sick Stranger [i.e.visitor] may be carried at a reasonable Rate into a Region free from the Smoak and Smell of the City; since the Invalids [may wish to] take the Benefit of the fresh Air in fine Weather, when the Gay and Healthy... choose to walk... and the *Chairmen* [are] destitute of any other Employ.

*Case in Relation to the Hire of Chairs, 1739*

*41. 1744 Notice of the Bath-Bristol wherry run*

S.TOMKINS'S // BATH and BRISTOL WHERRIES. // WHEREAS one very great Discouragement to Persons going by Water in the abovesaid *Wherries*, has been the Tediousness of the Passage, &c. chiefly occasion'd by setting out too late from *Bath*, as have been the Custom. - In order therefore to remove that Objection, and to render the Passage agreeable and expeditious, as well as cheap, I propose my *Wherries* setting out exactly at Eight o'Clock every Morning... and carry Passengers at *One Shilling* each, (Lockage included) by which Means we shall arrive in *Bristol* about Noon, and have sufficient Time to carry out Orders, and prepare our Freight for the next Morning; which I hope will induce Shopkee[pe]rs and others to send their Goods and Parcels by Me, when they can be certain of having their Returns the next Day, which could seldom be done, by not leaving *Bath* 'till Ten or Eleven o'Clock, as usual. - My *Wherries* are neatly fitted up, for the Accommodation of Passengers, &c. and as I have no other Affairs upon my Hands, shall constantly attend the

Business myself, with able Hands to work each of the said *Wherries*; one to set out every Morning, as above, from the Sign of Admiral *Vernon*, near the Brid[g]e, *Bath;* and the other from the *Golden-Boy*, in Swan-Lane, Castle-street, *Bristol*; at which Places Goods and Parcels are taken in, and Passengers agreeably treated, // *By their humble Servant,* // S.TOMKINS.
*Bath Journal 11 Jun 1744*

### 42. 1751 The Garricks suffer a bad journey
We got here [to Bath] Fryday Evening by Seven o'Clock; Yr Sister [in-law, Mrs Garrick] was much jolted for ye ten last Miles, and bad Roads they are, tho not dangerous...
*Garrick, Letters, vol.1 p.160, David Garrick to his brother George, Bath 31 Mar 1751*

### 43. 1754 A poor job of turnpiking the great road to Bath
At the first erection of turnpikes, the road makers *ex professo*, who perhaps were yeomen-like farmers, and gentlemen's bailiffs, made a very poor figure in their undertaking, witness, amongst others, that great road from *London* to *Bath*; it errs and blunders in all the forms; its *strata* of materials were never worth a straw; its surface was never made cycloidal; it hath neither good side ditches, nor foot paths for walkers; no outlets were made for water that stagnates in the body of the road; it was never sufficiently widened, nor were the hedges ever cleared: Of course, 'tis the worst public road in *Europe*, considering what vast sums have been collected from it.
*Gentleman's Magazine, vol.24 for 1754, p.348*

### 44. 1757 Bath well sited to oversee cross-country mails
And since the great produce of the Bye and Cross Letters principally arises from the Correspondence carried on between the Outports and Chief Manufacturing Towns in the distant parts of the Kingdom it has always appeared to the Memorialist [Ralph Allen] most reasonable to fix the place for the Principal Management of this Concern in the Country, rather than London... and several concurring Circumstances induce the Memorialist to think Bath or that Neighbourhood preferable to any other place for the Residence of the principal Officers... as being the Center of the Great Cross Road as well as the Bristol Road, also adjoyning to the Western Road and at no considerable distance from the Chief Circulation of Bye Letters on the Chester or Northern Roads.
*BCL, AL 1501 (photo), Ralph Allen, Memorial to the Treasury, 1757*

### 45. 1761 Two sorts of sedan chair
A large number of sedan-chair men - at present over a hundred - find sufficient subsistence, and charge a moderate fare; for a distance of 500 yards, sixpence; for an English mile, one shilling... Few people, or scarcely any, use carriages in the town, except to take a drive; many who do not live far off, or do not use the waters, go on foot in fine weather. For going to the waters there are specially made sedan chairs, which are quite small and low, bowed at below so as to

give room, and with very short poles, for the purpose of carrying the people straight out of their beds, in their bathing costume, right into their baths.
*Kielmansegge, Diary, p.121, entry for Oct/Nov 1761*

### 46. 1761 Ralph Allen's industrial tramway

The stone [quarried on Combe Down] is brought in a remarkable way down the hill towards the town. On each side of the road, iron, two or three inches broad, in the shape of carriage-ruts, is laid down; the stones are put into low but strong trolleys, with broad iron wheels, with an outer rim projecting in such a way that they cannot slip out of the iron ruts; the horses attached to the trucks have consequently nothing more to do than to put them into motion, as afterwards they run down by themselves with great speed, so that the horses can hardly keep their proper place in front. But the trolley can be stopped at any moment by means of a spring attached to it, which causes an iron bar to catch into the wheel.
*Kielmansegge, Diary, pp.132-3, entry for Oct/Nov 1761*

### 47. 1763 Lord Chesterfield's wintry passage

I arrived here... last Sunday; but after the worst day's journey I ever had in my life; it snowed and froze that whole morning, and in the evening it rained and thawed, which made the roads so slippery, that I was six hours coming post from the Devizes, which is but eighteen miles from hence; so that... I might as well have walked on foot.
*Stanhope, Letters, vol.6 letter 2276, Lord Chesterfield to his son, Bath 24 Nov 1763*

### 48. c.1764? A petition about the lane from Bathwick hamlet

That the Inhabitants of the said Parish carry the whole Produce of their Gardens and other Grounds to the said City [of Bath], and bring from thence most of the Dung and Soil used for manuring their said Gardens and Grounds. That the said Lane is for the greatest part of the year so very ruinous and founderous, and in many places so narrow, that your Petitioners cannot pass the same with Broad wheels, and it is very difficult to pass even with narrow wheels. That the Turnpike stands near the end of the said Lane, between that and the City, and from the badness of the said Lane, your Petitioners are under a necessity of using narrow wheels, whereby they are not only obliged to pay the additional Toll of one half more than the usual Toll, but are also deprived of the benefit of the several Exemptions from Toll... tho' they make use of the said Turnpike Road but for the space of two Furlongs.
*BrRO, AC/JS/104/5, Petition to Parliament of Bathwick Inhabitants, c.1764?*

### 49. 1765 By post-coach to London in a day

*This is to give Notice,* // That the POST-COACH, // *Hung on Steel Springs, with four Horses and two Postillions,* Which lately went in Two Days, will now go in ONE. // Sets out from the Grey-Hound Inn in the Market-Place, Bath, and the White Horse, Fleet-Market, London, every Night in the Week

(except Saturday) at Two o'Clock, and arrive[s] at each Place about Five in the
Evening. // [N.B.] To carry only Four Inside Passengers, each of which is to
pay THREE-PENCE per Mile, and be allowed 14 lb. Luggage, for all above to
pay Three-Halfpence per Pound. This Post-Coach goes thro' Devizes, Andover,
Overton, Basingstoke, Blackwater, Staines Bridge, &c. // [N.B.] The
Proprietors are determined to spare no Expence to render the Post-Coach as
complete as any in England.
*Bath Chronicle 30 May 1765*

### 50.  1777  Kingswood colliers raise the dust

Sett off [from Bristol] on horseback for Bath; fine roads, sun excessively hot
and scorching, almost choaked by the dust which arose in clouds, by the
Carriages and horses we met and overtook in great numbers... at $^1/_2$ past 4
o'clock departed [from Bath] having been in town since 10 o'clock; designing
to return by way of King[s]wood were discouraged by the Colliers who to give
us a specimen of their disposition having suffered me to pass on a few rods,
soon put on their horses, galloped before, and raised such a cloud of dust as
almost suffocated me; on this my Company thought it best to leave the road to
the Colliers and pursue that over the bridge, returning by the same way of
Keynsham &c. that we went.
*Curwen, Journal, vol.1 p.380, entry for 17 Jul 1777*

### 51.  1778  The need for riding lessons

J.DASH, late Usher, Assistant, and Rough-Rider to the Riding-School in the
City of Bath, begs leave to inform the Nobility, Gentry, and others, that it
having been reported that he had quitted this city, and intirely dropped
Instructing in the art of Riding; and as many Ladies and Gentlemen have
complained they are incapable of managing their horses on the road,
notwithstanding they have been taught at a Riding-School: This is to acquaint
them, that he still continues to give Lessons to make them proficients in that
art...
*Bath Chronicle 30 Apr 1778*

### 52.  1780  Diverse travellers

Took a Ride to Bristol - sun shone sweetly - roads dry... Met & passd a variety
of objects, such as, a Lord, a Badger, a Coach & six [,] a dungcart & one - Post
chaises & four - Knife Grinders - Officers, Mole catchers - Parsons and Coal
horses - Rabbits, wildfowl, & Methodist preachers. All these, and much more
did I meet with or See, or pass in my Peregrination... I heard *Colliers* on their
Horses after selling their bags of Coal, dispise a Grand equipage for which
they were forcd to give way, & damn the Owners, with all the pride of a
Conscious... superiority.
*BCL, B920, Edmund Rack, A Disultory Journal of Events at Bath, entry for 14 Feb
1780*

### 53. 1782 John Wilkes battles to Bath through wind and snow

Here I am... after combating all the unexpected fury of the elements... The roads are just passable, but the efforts of four strong horses could scarcely drag the light post-chaise, in which I was, with little baggage... It snowed... all Thursday night, and the entire following day, and the wind was very high; so that I scarcely remember a worse travelling day. This morning was a clear sunshine, but it froze intensely, and this afternoon the flakes descend in great abundance. I never saw a more shivering landscape, and I passed waggons and post-chaises laid low, not in the dust, but in the snow, and absolutely deserted by men, cattle, &c.

*Wilkes, Letters, vol.2 pp.236-7, John Wilkes to daughter, Bath 23 Mar 1782*

### 54. 1784 Palmer's record-breaking flying mail

The New Mail Coach has travelled with an expedition that has been really astonishing, having seldom exceeded 13 hours in going to or returning from London. It is made very light, carries four passengers, and runs with a pair of horses, which are changed every six or eight miles; and as the bags at the different offices on the road are made up against its arrival, there is not the least delay. The Guard rides with the Coachman on the box, and the mail is deposited in the boot. By this means, the inhabitants of this city and Bristol have the London letters a day earlier than usual, - a matter of great convenience to all, and of much importance to merchants and traders.

*Bath Chronicle 12 Aug 1784*

### 55. 1789 A caravan link with Cheltenham

A Desire to accommodate the numerous Companies that frequent Cheltenham during the season, has induced CHARLES HEMMINGS, Poulterer, of Wade's-Passage, Bath, and JONATHAN WILDEY, Poulterer, near the New Butter-Market, Cheltenham, to establish a CARAVAN Between BATH, GLOUCESTER, and CHELTENHAM, as a cheap, safe and expeditious conveyance of passengers and parcels... // By this conveyance C.Hemmings will have the further satisfaction of furnishing the Nobility and Gentry at Bath with Pigeons and Asparagus, during the early season, at more reasonable prices than as yet they have ever been supplied in the Bath Market.

*Bath Chronicle 14 May 1789*

### 56. 1791 Turnpike improvements in the suburbs

... the Commissioners of the Turnpike-roads... last year expended an additional thousand pounds in widening and improving the different approaches to this city; and a proposal... has been made by the builders concerned in *Grosvenor-Place*, to remove the present turnpike-house on the London road, and erect a new one in a better situation, and we hope upon a more *elegant design*; after which a row of posts and chains are to be continued all the way to Lambridge, which will have a very fine effect on the principal entrance into Bath.

*Bath Chronicle 15 Sep 1791*

### 57. 1798 Canalization and cheaper coal

We have the pleasure to congratulate the publick on the important information, that five vessels loaded with coal were conveyed on the Somersetshire Coal Canal to Dunkerton, from Camerton works on Monday. Mr.Pickwick, of the White-Hart, brought the first two loads to Bath the same day with the same team [of pack animals]. In the course of three weeks, or a month, we understand, a wharf will be opened, for handling of coal on the Wells road, near Dunkerton, about $3\frac{1}{2}$ miles from this city, from whence a team can bring two loads a day with great ease. This will make a reduction of eight shillings per load in the carriage only.

*Bath Chronicle 4 Oct 1798*

### 58. 1799 Parking problems

*To the Medical Gentlemen of Bath,* // Who keep CARRIAGES. // GENTLEMEN, // The Inhabitants of the lower end of the MARKET-PLACE, paying heavy Rents for the sake of Situation, and already labouring under great and unavoidable Inconveniences from their being no Carriage road for the conveyance of Coals and other necessaries, to the Grove, Parades, Church-Yard, &c. beg leave respectfully to observe, that they are much inconvenienced by the front of their Houses being lately become a perpetual stand for your Carriages, insomuch that their Shops are, for that part of the day, the most advantageous for their respective trades, nearly hid from the sight of the Public eye: They therefore request you will direct your Coachmen to take their situation on the Market side of the street... // They likewise request the PRINCIPAL BREWERS will order their Draymen to observe the same rule, by unloading at the avenue leading to the Grove, instead of the paved foot-way... and, they are sorry to observe, that unwarrantable insolence is too frequently the return for gentle remonstrance from Servants of each description.

*Bath Herald 15 Jun 1799*

### 59. 1800 Further extension of the waterways

On Tuesday the Committee of Management of the Kennet & Avon Canal, proceeded from Sidney-Garden up the Canal to Monckton Comb, a distance of five miles, which, with its various bridges and aqueducts, is now completed in a most substantial manner, to that spot where it is to receive the Somerset Coal Canal.

*Bath Herald 14 Jun 1800*

*ᵗᵃᵗᵉ ᵗᵃᵗᵉ ᵗᵃᵗᵉ ᵗᵃᵗᵉ ᵗᵃᵗᵉ ᵗᵃᵗᵉ ᵗᵃᵗᵉ ᵗᵃᵗᵉ ᵗᵉ ᵗᵉ ᵗᵉ ᵗᵉ ᵗᵉ ᵗᵉ ᵗᵉ ᵗᵉ*

## INDUSTRY, TRADE AND RETAILING

*Promoting a health spa meant playing down sordid associations with 'trade' and manufacturing. All the same Bath was a highly commercial place, a market centre, an unrivalled focus for the luxury and fashion trades, and a significant producer of specialist commodities in its own right. In a city whose urban fringes often resembled a shifting building site the quarrying, stone-carving and construction industries had a dominant role, and Bath products and expertise in this field were valued throughout the region. Good business was likewise to be had for upholsterers, cabinet-makers, ironmongers and braziers, and others responsible for the fitting out and furnishing of buildings. Engineering, coach-building and brewing, all well-established (like furniture- and wheelchair-manufacture) before 1800, would develop further in the nineteenth century. The old textile industry had long since migrated to the surrounding villages (including Twerton, which also boasted a brassworks), but the clothing trade was of paramount importance, employing numerous shoemakers, tailors, hatters, dressmakers, staymakers, and milliners, who worked to customers' orders or to meet the increasing demand for ready-made garments. The most visible token of commercial life were the shops, outstanding in range and quality and, like the provisions market, among the chief sights and diversions of Bath; some of the showrooms even outdid those in London - at least according to Josiah Wedgwood who himself established a retail outlet here for his Staffordshire wares. At the opposite end of the scale stood the cheap all-purpose chandlers' shops, the pawnbrokers, the street-vendors and door-to-door salesmen. Competition was rife at all levels of retailing, as various examples of sharp practice, cheating, exploitation of staff, and ingratiating advertisements amply testify. Financial transactions still carried risk for both buyer and seller, but the steady increase in banking facilities, while also not risk-free, must have been of general benefit. The Corporation controlled the provisions market, the price of bread, and licences to sell alcohol, but its attempt in the 1750s to preserve freemen's trading monopolies by supporting the revival of the traditional 'companies' or guilds ultimately failed. Masters' cartels operated in some trades and these bitterly opposed any incipient trade-unionism. Otherwise Bath was subject to the unrestricted play of market forces.*

### 60. 1719 Stone carvers in demand

(23 Apr 1719) Tom Parfit and I went [from Wells] to Bath to see the Manner and Proportion of the Battlements of a new House ... in Trim-Street... Later, I sent for Mr.Harvey, the Stone-Cutter, and Discours'd with him; and agreed to give for his Son's Cutting a Coat of Arms in my Brother Farewells Tomb-Stone 40s; And I was to send an Horse for him to Wells, and to supply him with Diet and Lodging; If he did it within a month from this time.

(4 Nov 1725) ... I went to Mr Greenway's, that I might speak with him about Vases which I had a mind to put on the Top of mine House [at Wells], instead of the Rails & Ballisters now decay'd.

*Morris, Diary, pp.69 and 124*

### 61. 1725 Handsome, well-patronised shops

... the streets though narrow have many handsome shops which are well accustomed by the great resort of nobility & Gentry to this place... The Chief walk for the Ladyes and Gentlemen, is one pav'd with freestone reaching from the east end of the Abbey... on one side are Limes planted, on the other very handsome Toy [fancy gift] shops like those in London.

*BCL, MS B914.238, Diary of a Tour by Three Students from Cambridge, 1725, pp.114 and 118*

### 62. 1732ff A constant supply of stone from Combe Down

He [Ralph Allen] carried on so great a work with a carriage road from the quarries to the river, and a Stone-Yard in Dolemead, and a crane to load block stone which was sent away yearly 1800 Tons; and on the hill for taking the stone out of the quarry was four horse cranes, and one to lay the stone down to square it... and then the carriage road being finished the next place was to erect shades [sheds] in the stone yard near the river for workmen to work the several sorts of stone for any building in Bath... All the time Bath Garden work was going on (which was the Parades) four carriages were going the hill constant, and over the water [i.e. the river]; - four ditto loading on the hill; - two ditto loading block to each to Dolemead; - four ditto spare, if any misfortune should happen: each carriage cost £40... one carriage went down loaded, and drew up the empty one, - an exceedingly good contrivance.

*BCL, MS B926, The Life of Richard Jones, pp.2-4, 13-15*

### 63. After 1737 Collusion with servants and the system of poundage

There is a Juggle carry'd on between some *Tradesmen*, and *Servants*, in this Town, which have been the Source of all the Evils the Freemen complain of; I mean that base practice POUNDAGE... I remember when it was perilous to offer... any such Gratuity... But as Luxury and Effeminacy supplanted the honest blunt Roughness of the *Old English*, this Collusion, in the Year 1720, became Epidemical, and has been in *high Vogue* ever since. Nothing has contributed to the Increase in Shops like this *Legerdemain*; for 'tis as certain to get Custom by a dexterous Management of this Craft, as it is not to succeed in BATH without it... The Tradesman being set up, his early Endeavours are to get good

Recommendations; and in his first Addresses he treats up to the Heighth of
Extravagance, tells of the great Families he has the Honour to serve, and offers
the greatest Encouragement for Custom; which seldom fail. But if, peradventure,
a Family shou'd, by great Chance, arrive in Town, without being thus accosted,
the *Purveyor* [the servant who buys for the family] ... signifies his *Wants* and
his *Expectation* of the customary Usage; the Trader replies, That we may have
no Misunderstanding, do you require DOUBLE or SINGLE POUNDAGE? -
If the Servant happens to be a Novice, the Mechanick must farther explain
himself. Pray, do your Master ever trouble his Head with Tradesmen's Bills? -
Sir, replies the other, My Master... never meddles with such low-life Stuff; if
ever he do look on such a Thing, 'tis only at the Bottom, to see what it comes
to. The Retailer, with a composed Countenance, says, These are Gentry
Tradesfolks may live by, therefore you shall have DOUBLE POUNDAGE,
that is, Two Shillings out of every Pound you lay out with me: I'll take Care to
Make the Bills, and You take Care of the Payment.
*Art of Thriving at Bath, pp.3-7*

### 64. 1742-3 Bath commodities

Our chief Staple Commodity being the Hot-Waters, the Business of BATH, at
this Time, consists in the Cure of Sick and Diseased People; in Letting Lodgings;
and in a Domestick Commerce for Supplying Strangers that Resort to the City
with almost all sorts of Things: In this Trade we have an Abundance of reputable
Tradesmen, who every day strive more and more to furnish their Shops with
Goods, from the best Markets, to be able to retail them upon as reasonable
Terms as the same Sort of Goods can be bought for in the Shops of any other
City in the Kingdom; and in this they so far succeed, that BATH is already
become not only a Mart to its own Hundred [i.e. county division], but to the
Country beyond it for many Miles. // Our principal Commodities are Woollen-
Cloth, Silks, Lace, Toys [fancy goods, jewellery, etc.], Ornaments in Free-
Stone, Block Free-Stone, Deal-Boards, Norway-Oak, Wine, and Coals; but of
the Things ready manufactur'd, few are made at BATH: However, as ingenious
Workmen, as well as such as are concern'd in the Arts and Sciences Yearly
increase, Time will probably raise Manufactures in the City, and establish a
Spirit of Industry in the People, upon just and honest Principles.
*Wood, Essay, 1742-3, vol.2 pp.88-9*

### 65. 1744 A draper and his sidelines

FRANCIS BENNETT, *At the* STAR *in the* Church-Yard, BATH, SELLS all
Sorts of Linnen-Drapery, Woollen-Drapery, and Haberdashery Goods; all Sorts
of Blanketting, Flannels, Swan-skin, and Shags; all Sorts of Teas, Coffee,
Chocolate, and Sugar; with all other Sorts of Grocery Wares; all Sorts of fine
Snuffs, and Cards: All which are sold as cheap as in London, for Ready-Money
[i.e. for cash, not on account]. // N.B. He also furnishes *Funerals* with a new
Pall and Cloaks; and with all other Necessaries, as decent and cheap as in
London.
*Bath Journal 4 Jun 1744*

*66.  1752  Temporarily revived, the craft guilds march with the Mayor*
Last Friday, being the Anniversary of the RESTORATION of King CHARLES
THE SECOND; and the first Rejoicing-Day for the NEW COMPANIES to
make their Appearance, the same was observ'd here in a very *grand Manner*:
The Morning was usher'd in by Ringing of Bells; about Ten o'Clock the Seven
new Companies met at the Pelican, and from thence proceeded, in Order, to
the Guildhall, where they were join'd by the Companies of Taylors and
Shoemakers; and by the MAYOR, ALDERMEN, and COMMON COUNCIL;
and then the *Grand* PROCESSION began, in the following Order to the Abbey-
Church, to hear Divine Service.
1.  The Constables of the City, with their Staves.
2.  The Company of MASONS.
3.  The Company of CARPENTERS, JOINERS, and CABINET-MAKERS.
4.  The Company of TYLERS and PLAISTERERS.
5.  The Company of BAKERS.
6.  The Company of BARBERS and PERUKE-MAKERS.
7.  The Company of GROCERS and CHANDLERS.
8.  The Company of MERCERS and DRAPERS.
9.  The Company of SHOEMAKERS.
10.  The Company of TAYLORS.
11.  The MAYOR, ALDERMEN, and COMMON-COUNCIL.
12.  The MAYOR'S OFFICERS, &c.
Between each Company divers Instruments of Musick were play'd...
*Bath Journal 1 Jun 1752*

*67.  1753  A wine merchant launches a bank*
Mr.ISAAC DE VIC,  //  WINE-MERCHANT, of this CITY,  //  Desires to
inform all Persons,  //  Who have any Occasion to remit MONEY from *London*
to *Bath*, or from thence to *London*,  //  THAT he has Open'd a BANK for that
Purpose, on a Premium of *Ten Shillings* for a *Hundred Pounds*, and in the same
Proportion for any Sums more or less; and that constant Attendance is given at
his HOUSE, near the *North-Parade* - Also, that Mr.*John Stephens*, Banker in
*Princess-Street*, near the BANK in LONDON, will furnish Gentlemen and
Ladies with Bills of Credit on Mr.*De Vic*, at BATH, for any Sums of Money
that shall be paid into Mr.*Stephen's* Hands, in LONDON, which will be an
absolute Security against the Dangers of the Roads, as well as a great
Conveniency to the Company resorting to this Place.
*Bath Journal 19 Mar 1753*

*68.  1754  The right to trade at Bath*
... CHANCELLOR and COMP. [of Duke Street, St James's, London]... ALL
Sorts of Brussels Point, and Brussels Lappet Heads... together with all sorts of
Lace and work'd Ruffles for Gentlemen... We are the Makers of Bath and
Buckinghamshire Laces, of which Ladies may have any Patterns made in a
very short Time. - We likewise make Minuenet Laces.  //  [N.B.] I am constantly
at BATH, during the Season, and I have weekly Remittance here of the newest

Patterns; and Ladies may depend on being well served. I am ready to wait on
them (on the least Notice) at their Lodgings... [N.B.] I hope (notwithstanding
any malicious Insinuations of any... Persons residing, or Traders in this City, to
the Contrary) that the Nobility and Gentry will be of Opinion, I have as great a
Right to trade in this City as any Trader... my Husband being a Freeman thereof:
And I hope they will be farther inclined to think that the Foundation... is for no
other Reason, than because it is not in their Power to sell near so Cheap as me,
as I import all foreign Laces, and am the Maker of the English ones; and their
ill Nature has determin'd me to sell for as small a Profit as possibly I can.
*Bath Journal 11 Nov 1754*

### 69. 1756 Selling at cost price just to keep going

WHEREAS the Custom of Selling at PRIME COST, is, of late, become
frequent in Bath, and as it is the quickest METHOD of paying CREDITORS,
and of Raising Ready-Money for those who have a great Demand for it; and
since, at present, he who expects a Profit on his Goods, has no Prospect of
Business, // BENJAMIN AXFORD, // JEWELLER and TOYMAN, // In
WADE'S PASSAGE, // (Not with a View of getting, but to keep himself
employ'd) will sell off his present Stock at PRIME COST. // [N.B.] The
Public, on examining the Goods, will find the above to be no Deceit, and may
be assur'd, that this is not done with any lucrative View, but only, with a generous
Intent, of LOOSING *as much Money by this Method, as other People.*
*Bath Advertiser 13 Mar 1756*

### 70. 1764 Confidence trick on a pastry cook

On Sunday Evening a Man went to a Pastry-Cook's Shop in Cheap-Street,
and ordered half a Dozen Tarts to be carried to a House on the Burrough-Walls,
together with Change for a Guinea: The Maid was sent with it accordingly; but
was met in the Market-Place by the Man, who desir'd her to give him the
Change, telling her he was going for some Wine, and that she wou'd have the
Guinea on her delivering the Tarts at the House: The Girl very readily gave
him the Money; but to her great Surprize, when she came to the House, she
found the People knew nothing of the Affair, nor had they given Orders for any
Tarts... many Attempts of the same Kind were made on different Shop-Keepers
last Week.
*Bath Chronicle 2 Feb 1764*

### 71. 1764 Any old clothes?

JOHN MATTHEWS, Dealer, // (From *London, Cambridge,* and *Oxford*) //
GIVES most Money for Gentlemen and Ladies CAST-OFF CLOATHS, either
Laced, Embroider'd, Brocaded, or Plain, of any Colour or Kind, from Ten
Shillings a Suit to Ten Pounds... He gives attendance at the Sign of the RAVEN
in the Abbey-Green, BATH. Likewise buys Gold and Silver Lace, burnt or
unburnt.
*Bath Chronicle 29 Nov 1764*

## 72. 1767 High-risk insurance: properties, trades and wares

*Hazardous Insurances* are Timber or Plaister Buildings, and Goods and Merchandize therein, not [themselves] hazardous; or Brick and Stone Buildings, wherein hazardous Goods or Trades are deposited or carried on; such as Apothecaries, Chymists, Bread and Biscuit Bakers, Colourmen, Ship and Tallow Chandlers, Stable-keepers, Inn-holders, Malt-houses, Hemp, Flax, Tallow, Pitch, Tar, and Turpentine.

... *Doubly Hazardous Insurances,* are Thatch'd Buildings, and Goods and Merchandize therein, Timber or Plaister Buildings, wherein hazardous Goods or Trades are deposited and carried on; and also China, Glass, or Earthen Wares, Hay, Straw, all Manner of Fodder, and Corn unthrash'd.

*BCL, Broadsides & Posters 80, Proposals from the Bath Fire Office, 25 Mar 1767*

## 73. 1770 Dressmaking à la mode

MRS.WILLIAMS, MANTUA and SACK-MAKER, in Westgate-Street, Bath, begs Leave to inform those Ladies her Friends, and the Public in general, who may chuse to employ her for the approaching BIRTH-DAY of the QUEEN, that she is returned from London, where she has been (at the Request of her numerous Friends) entirely for the Fashions.

*Bath Chronicle 11 Jan 1770*

## 74. 1771 Orders to a 'chinaman' for the new Assembly Rooms

(18 July 1771) And that Mr B Layton do provide

| | | |
|---|---|---|
| 6 dozn bordered plates at | 17/- | pr dozn |
| 2 Gross of desert do.[ditto] at | 9/- | do. |
| 1 dozn Basons quart at | 36/- | do. |
| 4 dozn 3 pint do. at | 36/- | do. |
| 4 dozn 2 quart do. at | 54/- | do. |
| 36 Cups & Saucers at | $6\frac{1}{2}$ | apiece |
| 60 do. Breakfast at | $6\frac{1}{2}$ | do. |
| 200 Coffee Cups at | 9/6 | pr doz |
| 150 breakfast Basons at | 5 | apiece |
| 100 Jugs for Cream at | 8 | do. |
| 50    do.    do. at | 8 | do. |
| 100 brown Tea Potts at | 12 | per dozn |

(9 Sep 1771) Order'd That Benjn Layton's Bill of Seventy Pounds Two shillings and Ninepence be paid in full... Order'd That Mr Layton do provide Twelve dozen of Jelly Glasses at three shillings per doz, also three dozn of Glasses with handles for Lemonade at four shillings pr dozn, also four dozn of Syllabub Glasses at five shillings pr dozn.

*BRO, Acc.28 no.281 A-F, New Assembly Rooms, Furnishing Committee Minute Book*

75. *1772 The writer Sheridan runs up a bill with a Bath toyman*
Bought of William Evill, In the Market Place

|              |                                                              | £   | s   | d   |
|--------------|--------------------------------------------------------------|-----|-----|-----|
|              | To 1 Pair neat Foyls                                         | -   | 10  | 6   |
| Decr 12 72   | To 1 Pair do  do                                            | -   | 10  | 6   |
| Jany 23      | To one neat Toothpick Case                                  | 4   | 4   | - · |
| June 10      | To one neat Hair Locket                                     | 1   | 11  | 6   |
|              | To 1 neat fancy Ring                                        | 2   | 12  | 6   |
|              | To 2 - do - Seals                                           | -   | 9   | -   |
|              | To setting a Picture in a Case                             | -   | 3   | 6   |
| Augt 25      | To 1 neat Gilt Watch Key                                   | -   | 1   | 6   |
|              |                                                              |     |     |     |
|              | To 1 pair neat Garnet Buttons                             | 1   | 15  | -   |
|              | To Mending Gold Seal                                       | -   | 1   | -   |
| Sepr 9       | To 2 neat German hollow Blades                            |     |     |     |
|              | to Swords with Vellum Scabbards,                          |     |     |     |
|              | neat Steel and Gold Locket & Chape                       |     |     |     |
|              | and mounted to 2 Steel and Gold Hilts,                   |     |     |     |
|              | & Repairing the Hilts - To 1 neat                        |     |     |     |
|              | Morocco Bolt [?] for Swivels                             | 3   | 13  | 6   |
|              |                                                              | 15  | 12  | 6   |

*BCL, Trade Cards, William Evill*

76. *1772 Wedgwood prepares to open a showroom at Bath*
I have been surveying the Bath stone Vases for Piers &c and am rather sorry to tell you that they make them much cheaper than we can do in clay. They sell Vases inriched with fluteings &c quite sufficiently, and large enough for any moderate sized Piers, for 10/6 each, and Necks and balls for 5/, of a tolerable size. // I think all the chance we have in competeing with this Manufacture must be by introducing Bass relief figures upon the Vases, or some ornaments which they cannot execute so well in their coarse-grained stone. // The Stone Vases here are most of them in good stile and very well executed... They make immensely large ones, ornamented in good taste with Vines &c all over, and quite free, larger, and of better forms than our largest black ones, and ask only 50s a piece for them! We could scarcely make them in Clay for so many pounds... // We are now loseing time and *opportunity* sadly in Westgate Buildings for want of something to open. You had better take the Men from Chelsea to pack a day or two than let us want a few crates to complete our assortment. I hope you will send us some enamelled Tea ware, and in short everything to make a complete shew of it, or we had better do nothing, for I think the Toy and China shops are richer and more extravagant in their shew here than in London.
*Wedgwood, Letters, p.124, Josiah Wedgwood to Thomas Bentley, Bath 6 Jun 1772*

## 77. 1780 The start of local porter brewing

*Warren*'s Porter and Amber Brewery, // Near WALCOT TURNPIKE, Bath. // THE principal design in erecting this Brewery was the production of fine Porter; and the Proprietor flatters himself that he shall be able to convince the public, that Porter brewed at Bath will in every respect be equal to what is manufactured in London. But as a considerable time will elapse before the Porter brewed this season can attain to perfection; and as the Brewery is supplied with the river water in its greatest purity, on which account it is peculiarly favourable to the brewing of the most wholesome Ale and Table Beer, those articles are included in the plan; and the favour of the public, in either branch, is respectfully solicited.

*Bath Chronicle 30 Mar 1780*

## 78. 1784 The very latest in fancy goods and perfumery

ORANGE-GROVE, BATH. // [MOORE's] UNIVERSAL TOY-SHOP, // (For Ready Money [i.e.cash] only)... Among the new Articles are the Cestuses, Mulbrowk, Balloon, Gibraltar, and other Fans, pocket-books, boxes, gold-pins, lockets, bracelets, trinkets, ear-rings, tooth-pick cases, purses, Paris irons, combs that will not split... a valuable assortment of penknives and scissars...// PERFUMERY of this year's growth, from abroad, rose pomatum at 1s. per pot... gentlemen's silk bags... hair powder of better quality than any yet sold... toupee irons... the new-invented concave razors, with straps to keep them in order... Moore's new invented card-purses, with Bath mottoes... // The new imported Chymical Ball from Italy, at 1s. each, called the CREMONA VEGETABLE WASH-BALL, for hindering the face and hands from chapping, taking off freckles, and whitening the skin... Wm.Moore faithfully assures his customers... that there is not the least doubt of its being of superior quality to any ball yet sold in this kingdom... // His [other] Shop in Bridge-street is... the best hair-dressers in this city...

*Bath Chronicle 29 Apr 1784*

## 79. 1787 Caveat emptor

Last week several measures with elastic bottoms were seized, by order of the Mayor of this city, from the country gardeners hawking their goods about the streets, being found deficient, and burnt.

*Bath Chronicle 21 Jun 1787*

## 80. 1788 Enlisting public support in the cut-price drapery war

No.26, MARKET-PLACE, BATH, // *THE very flattering Marks of* Public Approbation *which* PRYNN *and* COLLINS *have repeatedly experienced by their* OPPOSITION *to the recent strange mode of purchasing* OLD STOCKS OF GOODS, for the express purpose of SELLING THE SAME AT AND UNDER PRIME COST, *induce them once more to solicit* // THEIR FAVOURS AND PROTECTION; // *And, if it be not too presuming, they request those who are not in immediate want of* LINEN-DRAPERY GOODS, will suspend their purchases till WEDNESDAY next; when they pledge themselves to the

Public to produce FOR SALE, *from purchases made this week in London, a greater* // Variety of CHEAPER MUSLINS, DIMITTIES, and WHITE GOODS in general, // *Than was ever* exposed *in any Warehouse in this City.* // [N.B.] In the mean time the remaining part of THEIR STOCK of PRINTED GOODS will continue selling at a most astonishing Reduced Price, for Ready Money only.
*Bath Chronicle 1 May 1788*

### 81. 1788 A visit to Combe Down quarries

We now entered the adjacent cavern of near 300 yards long, which, from the vast quantity that has been got out for many years to supply the city with its beautiful free-stone, we saw wrought out into various spacious and lofty rooms, and regularly supported by able pillars, left for that purpose... The gentle weepings of the rock in some parts from petrefactions, which, together with a few spars interspersed, reflect the lights of the candles very brilliantly. The former mode of conveying the large blocks directly down the hill to Bath, by machines running on grooves or frames of wood, such as we see in the collieries about Newcastle, is now no more; they carry them in common waggons, to the great detriment of the roads, and inconvenience of travellers.
*Shaw, Tour, pp.300-1*

### 82. 1792 Appeal of the striking journeymen shoemakers

THE JOURNEYMEN BOOT and SHOE-MAKERS of this City, respectfully beg leave to lay their Case before the Nobility, Gentry, and Publick in general. - They have for some time past been without employ, to the great injury of themselves and families, in consequence of many of the Masters having refused to grant their reasonable request, to have the price of their work raised to 2s. for making a pair of Shoes, and 5s.6d. for making a pair of Boots. // That this request is founded in moderation and justice will be acknowledged, when the publick are informed that in London the men are paid 2s.10d. for making a pair of shoes, and 7s.6d. for making a pair of boots. In Manchester, Birmingham, and Liverpool, the price is 2s.6d. for making shoes, and 6s. for making boots; and it is universally known that every article of life is full 25 per cent. cheaper in each of those towns than in Bath. // The publick are at present much injured by the Masters employing ignorant *botching* workmen, who put their work so wretchedly out of hand, that it will not wear a *third* of the time it would if it was well finished; and if the good workmen were in employ, the Masters would not suffer those who now make Gentlemen's Boots to *mend even a pair of old shoes.*
*Bath Chronicle 29 Mar 1792*

### 83. 1792 Feasting the mill workers

At the opening of the Worsted Spinning Mill at Twerton, near this city, on Saturday last, an elegant dinner was given by the proprietors Messrs. Bamford and Cooke, to a party of gentlemen, and to the mechanics, woolcombers, and every other person employed about the mill, upwards of 280 in number. After

dinner the tables were liberally supplied with wine, punch, and strong beer, when the following toasts were given among many others: *Church and King, Mr.Pitt, Success to the Parish of Twerton, the Woollen Trade in all its branches, Success to this undertaking,* (with three times three cheers)... The worsted of the manufactory was considered by the manufacturers present equal in quantity [i.e. quality?] to any worsted in the kingdom.
*Bath Chronicle 1 Nov 1792*

### 84. 1793 Wallpaper - a staple of the upholsterer's business
UPHOLSTERY and CABINET WAREHOUSE, // MARKET-PLACE, Bath. // JOHN STAFFORD respectfully informs the Publick, that he has laid in an immense Stock of Modern PAPER-HANGINGS, // from BOWERS and Co. and other principal manufactories in London; consisting of upwards of two thousand Pieces and Borders of the newest taste... // The Publick will do well to inspect this Elegant Assortment, which is ready to be delivered at the shortest notice, from six pieces to twenty pieces in a set, or any quantity that might be required. // Rooms papered at the shortest notice...
*Bath Chronicle 14 Mar 1793*

### 85. 1793 Financial crisis on the outbreak of war with France
All here is ruin and misery. Two banks broken at Bath; at Bristol things are worse, every hour presents me with some fresh instance of somebody I know undone!
*Walpole, Correspondence, vol.31 p.382, Hannah More to Horace Walpole, Bath 21 Mar 1793*

### 86. 1794 Engineering at Bath: a forerunner of Stothert & Pitt goes under
TO be SOLD by Private CONTRACT, // One 30-inch CARDING-ENGINE, with iron arches and mahogany cylinders - not clothed. // One 28-inch double SCRIBBLING ENGINE, with iron ditto and ditto. // One SPINNING MACHINE - with 40 spindles - one ditto with 80 spindles complete. // A finished AUTOMATON, calculated to work an Engine, without the aid of manual labour. // These articles were manufactured by J. and S.FORD, late of Bath, Bankrupts, and are esteemed excellent workmanship. - Apply to Mr.George Stothert, of Bath, one of the Assignees to the said Estate.
*Bath Chronicle 6 Feb 1794*

### 87. 1795 The favour of royal appointment
THEIR ROYAL HIGHNESSES // THE DUKE and DUCHESS of YORK // / CONDESCENDED // TO HONOUR // JOHN BUTTRESS // WITH THEIR PRESENCE, AT HIS // SILK WAREHOUSE, (in the Abbey Church-Yard) // And have been pleased to appoint him // *Her Royal Highnesses's Silk-Mercer, in Bath,* // WITH PERMISSION // To make use of her Royal Highness's ARMS. // ... THEIR ROYAL HIGHNESSES // HAVE ALSO CONFERRED THE HONOUR ON // JAMES EVILL, // TO APPOINT HIM // THEIR JEWELLER IN THIS CITY, // WITH PERMISSION // To

use their Royal Highnesses' ARMS. // FIELD-MARSHAL // His ROYAL
HIGHNESS the DUKE of YORK, // HAS CONFERRED THE HONOUR
ON // WILLIAM HELLYER, (of the North-Parade) // BY APPOINTING
HIM // HIS TAYLOR IN THIS CITY, // *With permission to use His Royal
Highness's* ARMS...
*Bath Chronicle 10 Dec 1795*

### 88. *1798 The spa's trade in wheelchairs*
DAWSON, *Wheel-Chair Maker*... BEGS leave to inform his Friends and the
Public that he has a very large Assortment of CHAIRS, either for Sale, or to
Lett on Hire in town or country; and as he has declined the Cabinet Trade, he is
enabled to give that attention to the Chair line, which the safety of invalids
requires. // As he intends to accommodate the public with New Chairs on hire
every year, he has several Second-hand ones for sale.
*Bath Chronicle 22 Mar 1798*

## SPA FACILITIES AND TREATMENTS

*Patients were ordered to Bath from every corner of the kingdom. Some, terminally ill, died there; others found scant relief and returned home uncured or were referred to other spas; but many did experience the benefits that sustained the spa's national reputation. Their grateful testimony was reinforced by a barrage of medical propaganda about the effectiveness of bathing and water-drinking, especially when combined with the opportunities for gentle exercise, moderate diversion, and pleasant change of scene and company that Bath also offered. Professional opinion might differ about the natural ingredients of the waters, their potency when drunk cold at a distance rather than taken at the pump, and the value or otherwise of supplementary medication in the way of drugs, but faith in the miraculous, soothing, purifying action of the waters never faltered. The Corporation nevertheless seemed remarkably complacent about its priceless asset. It long resisted advice to improve the various hot baths which remained poorly appointed, open to the elements, and lacking any privacy for bathers - even if the Cross Bath retained some temporary exclusivity. The main Pump Room, despite its mid-century enlargement, could at times barely cope with the crowds of would-be drinkers until it was eventually rebuilt in the 1790s; and the management of the baths and pumps, with the extensive trade in bottled mineral waters, was entrusted to often inexperienced lessees. The Hospital too was left to private enterprise and to charitable funding, and this in spite of the advantages it brought to the city in regulating the numbers of poor patients arriving for treatment. With regard to the resident physicians, surgeons, apothecaries, midwives, dentists and others (as well as visiting practitioners and quacks), who all took advantage of the endless stream of sufferers resorting to the spa, the Corporation had of course no effective control at all, though it always included the medical profession among its own élite membership.*

*89. 1704 Drinking the medicinal waters, a modern fashion*
These Waters then are drunk hot for the most part from the Pump every Morning fasting, or else at Lodgings, as hot as they can procure them; they are drunk hot for the sake of the *Neutral Spirit* that circulates in them, which being somewhat akin to the *Universal Menstruum* or *Alkahest* in our Stomachs, does wonderfully recruit it when lost or broken; and really 'tis strange to see its Operations on weak *Stomachs* and decay'd *Appetites* which are soon restor'd by the drinking these Waters warm... The Custom of drinking these Waters at the Pump and warm, has not prevail'd long, at least has not been made so Universal, for tho' some drank them every Year, yet above 20 Years ago I remember very few came to *Bath* for any thing but the Bathing part.
*Oliver, Practical Essay, pp.214-15*

*90. 1705 Bathing customs*
The situation of the baths is promiscuous, in several of the streets of the city, and surrounded with high buildings, from whence spectators from the windows may view the company when bathing, the surface of the water being entirely open to the heavens; and, during the bathing season, after the patients are retired from the waters, they are let out every evening, and, by the plentiful ebullitions from the springs, the baths are replenished with fresh water by the next morning, before the company comes. // The manner of going in is for the gentlemen and ladies to dress themselves in their proper habits in their own apartments; the first in fine canvas waistcoats of a sandy colour, edged and trimmed with black ribbands or ferreting, and tied down before with strings of the same colour, having on canvas drawers and slippers, and a lawn linen cap; the latter in canvas gowns and petticoats, with pieces of lead affixed at the bottom, to keep them down under the water. Being thus dressed they are brought in chairs, sometimes close covered up in their morning gowns, and are set down in the passages which lead into the bath, shut at each end by a door for more privacy. The descent from the passage or entrance is by stone steps, at which one of the guides attending the bath meets you to conduct you in. The first we visited was the Cross-bath... Two sides of the bath have galleries, one for the spectators, the other for the music. This bath is the most frequented by the quality of both sexes, where, with the greatest order and decency, the gentlemen keep to one side of the bath, and the ladies to the other. No gentleman whatever must presume to bathe in the ladies' district, under a pecuniary mulct, inflicted by the serjeants of the bath: the ladies are supposed to be so modest as not to come near the gentlemen... The ladies bring with them japanned bowls or basons, tied to their arms with ribbands, which swim upon the surface of the water, and are to keep their handkerchiefs, nosegays, perfumes, and spirits, in case the exhalations of the water should be too prevalent. The usual compliment, when any one goes into the bath, is to wish them a good bath; and the company, while bathing, generally regale themselves with chocolate.
*Gale, Tour, pp. 21-2*

### 91. 1709 Bath a magnet for physicians - to The Tatler's amusement

*Letters have been sent to Mr.*Bickerstaff, *relating to the present State of the Town of* Bath, *wherein the People of that Place have desir'd him to call Home the Physicians. All Gentlemen therefore of that Profession are hereby directed to return forthwith to their Places of Practice; and the Stage-Coaches are requir'd to take them in before other Passengers, till there shall be a Certificate sign'd by the Mayor or Mr.*Powell [a puppet master well-known at Bath], *that there are but Two Doctors to One Patient left in Town.*
The Tatler no.77, 6 Oct 1709

### 92. 1723 The Countess of Bristol trusts her apothecary

(13 May 1723) ... Mr. Skrine tells me my Lady Rochester's legs were as bad as mine... and that he quite cured her... with the same medicine he begins with me too night in a glass of the Bath water, and the same in the morning at the Pump.

(15 May 1723) I have begun the pills, which are to do wonders; they made me very sick at first, but Mr. Skrine tells me that must not discourage me, for he will answeir for their succes...

(20 May 1723) ... I am vissibly mended, & hope I shall continue to do so since the thing I most apprehended (which was my legg swelling so immoderately) begins now to abate, as Mr. Skrine assurd me they woud, & tells me he never knew this medicen fail in that complaint...

(25 May 1723) ... I am at last forcd to give over all thoughts of bathing... last Thursday I was worse than ever with it, though I was not in half an hour; for I fell into the most violent hysterick fit I ever had in my life...

(27 May 1723) ... I am really as much better now as I coud hope... I stick... by Mr. Skrine's perscription... though all my friends here tease me to death to have more advice, but I dont think I can have better than one that has had so long experience and practice as he has had of the effects of these waters, which has never yet faild to do me good, nor do I think they woud have lost their good effect now, if I had not been under the necessity of bathing for my legs, which has checkd the progress of the waters towards the cure of my nerves and cholick... and I see daily before my eyes such vast success in those cases that I cant despair...
*Hervey, Letter-books, vol.2, letters 727, 729, 733, 737, 739, the Countess to the Earl of Bristol*

### 93. c.1725? Recommendations to a poor patient

Ye best Docther name is mr. Beath [Bave?] you may Inquire for him near ye Cross Bath and take his advice before you goe Into ye Bath or any thing eles and tell him your Condicson and how Long you have been afflected In your Distemper and he will give you his advice for not[h]ing or [to] any other power [poor] man that goeth there he being thought ye best Docther In that place[;] and if you goe Into ye Bath you are to have a gaied [guide], which will find you Close [clothes] to goe In with for 4d pr. day and a flinen shirt which will cost you 3d a day and if you lodge at Jo:n Rows you may goe unto

ye hot bath which is close by which will safe you 6d a time In a chare hire and
I think that ye hot Bath is as good as any of ye others not But ye may goe to ye
Kings Bath now and then But it will cost you 6 pence a day more [.] ye giude
is to have a flish [flesh] Brush and to Brush ye place afflected when In ye
Bath... and ... I would advise you to be pumpt every time you goe Into ye Bath
200 strokes at a time [;] ye Dry pump is 4d a hundred and the Wett pump: is 2d
a hundred.
*BaRO, Anonymous MS letter, 28/822*

### 94.  1729  A case better suited to Bristol Hotwells
... but the Bath waters, (which I tryed by Dr.Mead's advice), will not do
with me. They put me into such pain upon the account of my disposition to
the stone & gravell, that I was forced to run away to Bristoll for ease, &, I
thank God, found it.
*Stukeley, Family Memoirs, vol.1 p.223, W. Cant to W. Stukeley, 3 July 1729*

### 95.  1734  Dr Cheyne puts his patients' interest before Bath's
... I must beg that you will set apart a day or two to be at Bath before you set
out for Bristol... And you must give it [out] here that you are ordered to
Bristol before you came here and that you see me only to have directions
nearer the spot... for there is such an universal malice against me here for
sending people abroad (as I did my Lady Walpole lately) and to Bristol, that
I have bin threatened with being mobt, and some interested people spread it
that I was sending the P[rince] of Orange there, so that I durst scarce walk
the streets, though there was not the least imagination for it, but on the contary;
for the lower people think it better to let people dy here than send them
elsewhere for their recovery.
*HMC 78 Hastings, vol.3 p.19, Dr G. Cheyne to the Countess of Huntingdon*

### 96.  1736  An effort to persuade Swift to try the spa
If shou'd go from Bath I have reason to think that the remainder of my life
wou'd be very miserable & that I shou'd soon lose the use of my limbs for...
I find nothing but the Blessing of God on these Waters does me any good...
I dayly see such numbers of people *mended* by *them* that I cannot but wish you
wou'd try them as you are sensible your disorders are chiefly occasion'd by a
cold stomach. I believe there is not any thing in this World so likely to cure that
disorder as the Bath Waters which are daily found to be a soverain remedy for
disorders *of that kind*. I know Sir you have no opinion of Drugs and why will
you not try so agreeable a medicine prepared by providence alone... ?
*Swift, Correspondence, vol.4 pp.539-41, Mrs M. Barber to J.Swift, Bath 3 Nov 1736*

## 97. 1737 Professional executioners

Say, florid *Florifer*, if you can tell:
How many Patients you've dispatch'd to Hell?
Say *Harrington* of not inferior skill!
How many Church-yards thy Prescriptions fill?
*Procus* has laid his thousands on the Floor;
And modest *Bostick* his ten thousands more.
Big blust'ring *Cheyné*, not the last in fame,
Tho' the Muse lead up in the rear his Name,
Has sent such Colonies to *Pluto*'s land;
The God was forc'd to beg he'd stop his hand.
*The Diseases of Bath [excerpt], p.5*

## 98. 1737 Tightening the rules on bathing dress

It is Ordered... by this Corporation that no Male Person above the age of Ten years shall at any time hereafter go into any Bath or Baths within this City by day or by night without a Pair of Drawers and a Waistcoat on their bodies And that no Female Person shall... go into any Bath... without a decent Shift on their bodies And that... each Guide shall wear a Cap with a Tassel to it to distinguish them from other People...
*BaRO, Bath Council Minutes, 26 Sep 1737*

## 99. 1738 The daily dose reduced

They used formerly to drink two quarts [of spa water] at Tunbridge and Bath, which would make eighteen pretty good glasses, but not large ones. But our physicians now universally condemn that practice and do not prescribe above a pint.
*HMC, 38, Buckingham, p.241, F.Hare, Bp of Chichester, to F.Naylor, 9 Sep 1738*

## 100. 1740 A bluestocking bored by talk of ailments

The morning after I arrived, I went to the Ladies' Coffee House, where I heard of nothing but the rheumatism in the shoulder, the sciatica in the hip, and the gout in the toe. I began to fancy myself in the hospital or infirmary, I never saw such an assembly of disorders... I wish your Grace would consider Bath water is not Helicon, and affords no inspiration; and that there is no place where one stands in greater need of something to enliven the brain and inspire the imagination. I hear every day of people's pumping their arms or legs for the rheumatism, but the pumping for wit is one of the hardest and most fruitless labours in the world. I should be glad to send you some news, but all the news of the place would be like the bills of mortality, palsy, four; gout, six; fever, one, &c. &c... We hear of nothing but Mr. Such-a-one is not abroad to-day; Oh! no, says another, poor gentleman, he died to-day. Then another cries, my party was made for quadrille to-night, but one of the gentlemen has had a second stroke of the palsy, and cannot come out; there is no depending upon people, no body minds engagements. Indeed the only

thing one can do to-day, we did not do the day before, is to die...
*Montagu, Letters, vol.1 pp.72-3, E. Montagu to the Duchess of Portland, Bath 27 Dec 1740*

### 101. 1742 Warburton is cosseted at Prior Park
I stayed at Widcombe, in the most agreeable retired society with two excellent persons, so very dear to me, till after the Christmas holy-days... My health was then but very indifferent; principally owing to a bilious indigestion, which I had been long troubled with... For this disorder the physicians at Bath advised me to drink the waters. I followed their advice; and the waters were brought hot from Bath every morning for me to drink in bed; which I received so much benefit from, that Mr.Allen [Ralph Allen] would engage me to promise to take the first opportunity of returning to them.
*Nichols, Literary Anecdotes, vol.5 pp.576-7, W.Warburton to Ph.Doddridge, 3 March 1742*

### 102. 1742 A puff for the Chevalier Taylor, oculist extraordinary
They write from Bath, that the Multitude of People that attended Doctor Taylor there, with Defects of Sight, is something so astonishing, that it employs every Body's Attention, every Day some Hundreds endeavouring his Assistance. // On Wednesday last most of the [medical] Faculty, as well as the Gentry there were present at his recovering the Sight of many Persons, and at a Lecture the Doctor gave last Night at the Town Hall, to several hundred Spectators, amongst which were the chief of the Faculty; most of the Gentlemen and Ladies of Distinction there assisted [i.e. were present]. It appears that no less than five Persons, who were born blind, have this Week been recovered by Doctor Taylor.
*The Oracle, or Bristol Weekly Miscellany 18 Sep 1742*

### 103. 1743 Overprescribing - and the tea cure
[Mrs Scawen] says she wishes Dr Oliver dont try too many Medicines which is thought to be his failing. She adds she knew some sent down to Bath in your Condition & orderd to drink Tea &c all made with Bath water & to drink a little glass hot frequently & no Medicines by which they recovered.
*Nuttall, Calendar, letter 841, Ph. Doddridge to M.Doddridge, 12 Jan 1743*

### 104. 1743 Wood's plan for the Pump Room encounters vested interests
There is only one Pump in the *Pump-House* to supply the Company with Water; whereas the present Time requires five or six. The Room too will scarce contain a Third Part of the People: But what is worse than all this, there is no Place belonging to it for People to retire into, when the Waters begin to operate. This the Gentry complaining of, in the latter Season of the Year 1733, was the Reason of my being employ'd to form a Design for making a Chamber over the *Pump-Room*... But Mr. *Richard Morgan* being then Mayor, and his Son then renting *Shaylor's* Coffee-House, he absolutely refused to put the Question to his Brethren [on the City Council], under the idle Pretence,

that an additional Chamber to the *Pump-Room* would draw the Company from his Son's House, and spoil its Trade.
*Wood, Essay, 1742-3, vol.2 pp.78-9*

### 105. 1744 A Hospital surgeon under criticism
When the Physicians and Surgeons were going round the House [i.e.Hospital] together, Mr.*Cleland* not being present... one *Pugsley*, a Patient of Mr.*Cleland*'s, complained that his Foot grew worse; and all the Gentlemen stopping, he removed his Dressings, and showed his sore. Mr.*Pierce* [the chief surgeon] observing a large Fungus, and that the Dressing was Basilicon, said, *It would never be cured by such Dressings*; and so went about his Business, without further interfering with Mr.*Cleland*'s Patient: But tho' Mr.*Cleland* asserts, *That this Man was cured in ten or twelve Days, by the same Dressing*; it is well known, that his Foot was not well when he went out of the Hospital, (he being discharg'd for fear of falling into a Hectic Fever) and the Apothecary supplied him, at his Departure, with some Dressings for his Foot.
*Bath General Hospital, A Vindication, 2nd paged sequence p.28*

### 106. 1745 Improved complexions and parboiled guides
Those yellow-faces you complain of at the Pump-Room, tho' they are disagreeable to look at, are worth watching, for you will find most of them in a few weeks brighten up to a healthy red, so as hardly to be known again; and look as happy as they did dejected and miserable before... The nastiest sight, I think, that can be seen there, is the guides in the Bath; they look sodden and par-boil'd, and I have often wonder'd at seeing the nicest Ladies embracing 'em as if they had neither sight nor smell.
*Cowper, Letters, p.43, S.Cowper to his brother, 2nd Earl Cowper, 10 Apr 1745*

### 107. c.1748 Lady Bolingbroke finds spa facilities wanting
My health is in a very weak state and my comrade's [Lord Bolingbroke's] is scarcely any better in spite of his drinking the waters. The pain from his sciatica is constant. I put more trust in pumping which he started this morning, but the only place it can be undertaken is so disagreeable and unsuitable that while he seeks relief from one complaint he is almost certain to catch a chill. Everything here is organised for the benefit of assemblies and balls, and nothing for the convenience of invalids. On that score you English are more uncivilised than the Germans, because at Aachen, you know, everything to do with health is very well managed.
*HMC 8 part 1, p.567, Lady Bolingbroke to Lady Denbigh, Bath 12 Sep c.1748 (original in French)*

## 108. 1749 In justification of the Hospital

... we have few Persons sent to us but such as labour under Leprosies, Palsies, old inveterate Rheumatisms or Lamnesses, many of them contracted long ago, by some fatal Hurt of the Part, scarce ever to be remedied. Physicians well know how difficult of Cure these Distempers are in their most recent State; but when they consider how few of them ever fall under our Care, in this *Hospital*, 'till all Methods have been tried upon them, in their own Country, and the Disease has, by Length of Time, been riveted in their Constitutions, they will be so far from wondering that we cure no more, that they will return Thanks to GOD, that... so many of them have... been quite restored, or greatly relieved.
*Bayly, Sermon, p.25*

## 109. 1751 Life-saving measures

Last Sunday Morning... one Grist, a Youth about fourteen Years of Age, presumptiously went into the River, for the Water was then Brink high; as he did about 12 Months ago, when he was almost drown'd; but this Time his Life was despair'd of, being under Water for near ten Minutes: When taken up, there was not any Appearance of Life, but luckily Mr. Dodd, a Surgeon and Apothecary of this City, being near when the Affair happen'd, (and thro' him, under GOD, the Boy owes his Life) he bled him; and, by holding him up by the Legs, well rubbing his Body, and blowing a Pair of Bellows up his Fundament, after some Time, Life was perceiv'd in him: He was carried home, put into a warm Bed, and next Morning was perfectly recover'd.
*Bath Journal 5 Aug 1751*

## 110. 1756 The drug culture

... the poor patient, who is made to believe, and tells you, he is actually under a proper course of this or other water, swallows implicitly, almost insensibly, a greater number than ever of pills and boluses, draughts and potions... Had not this often been the case, how could so many physicians and such numbers of apothecaries make fortunes at Bath and other water-drinking places? Or, how should the pump room be rendered loathsom, as the ward of an hospital, by the dispensation of the medicines of numberless patients, as we find it at Bath and other places? What is more preposterous, than to see people cloyed with incongruous shop compositions, where they come a long journey to drink onely of a certain water? What is more nauseous and offensive, than to see each patient come loaded with his drench of drugs; to be taken at the pump, to the great annoyance of his neighbour, if not of himself! - Nothing can surely be, but seeing the fair dispenser of the salutary waters employed in mixing and giving of medicines with them! I have often reflected on the disasters, that may well happen at Bath upon the removal or changing of this cool and clear-headed maid, that now attends the great pump at Bath. If we should see a less attentive and discreet servant in the room [i.e.place] of this, who after the first visit, knows every body, and, at entrance, presents each with, Your Grace's pills, Your Lordship's bolus, Your Ladyship's

drops, Your Honor's draught, potion, powder, &c. &c. &c. What confusion may not be induced in this important branch of Bath-practice?
*Lucas, Essay on Waters, pp.247-8*

### 111. 1757 Lord Chesterfield's deafness

I have tried these waters in every possible way [seeking a cure]: I have bathed my head; pumped it; introduced the stream, and sometimes drops of water, into my ears; but all in vain.
*Stanhope, Letters, vol.5 letter 2028, 8 Nov 1757*

### 112. 1762 Nature's kindliest medicine

These two Mountains [Lansdown and Claverton Down], thus tinged by Rain Water falling from the proper Heights, meet in some Caverns in the Valley, and there fermenting, produce that hot, milky, soft Liquid, called BATH WATER, far beyond any other hot Mineral Water, for its Delicacy, and is thought to be superior to any other hot Water, for its comfortable Heat, hitherto discovered on the habitable Globe, as it possesses that Milkiness, Detergency, and middling Heat, so friendly adapted to weakened Constitutions, which all other hot Waters want in due Degree; either being too hot, or too cold... These Waters are beneficial in almost all Chronicle Distempers, and can hurt in none, except in Hemorrhages, Inflammations, or bad Lungs... they are very grateful to the Stomach, have a fine sulphureous steely Taste, like that of the German Spaw [Aachen], or Pyrmont, and procure a great Appetite, and good Spirits, if cautiously managed; but if high Meats and strong Liquor be indulged, they create inflammatory Disorders. - However, in weak Stomachs, decayed Appetites, Cholicks, low Spirits, in the Intervals of the Fits of the Gout and Stone, in Rheumatisms, Palsies, Nervous Disorders, and finally, in the Cure of all those Infirmities of Body which go under the Denomination of the Cold Diseases, they are more kindly and beneficial than any medicine known in Nature; they introduce a natural Warmth and a new internal Heat into decayed worn-out Constitutions; and if a light Regimen, due Exercise, and good Hours, be joined with them, they will truly work Wonders: But, by the Neglect of these, their Efficacy is often lost, and their Credit brought into Question.
*New Bath Guide, 1762, pp.9-10*

### 113. 1762 Smollett experiences the benefit of the pump

I believe my breathing so easily is owing to the warmth and moisture of the air at Bath, which seems peculiarly adapted to my Lungs. Yet I can feel a very sensible Effect from the waters. I have no sooner drank a large Glass of them hot from the Pump than my Face, my Hands, and Feet begin to glow; and this Sensation is succeeded by an itching and tingling all over the Surface of my Body, resembling what is called the prickly Heat in the west indies. I think I can plainly percieve these mineral waters opening up the obstructed Capillaries, and restoring the Perspiration which in the Extremities had been

in great measure lost. I intend in a few days to bathe with a View to open still
more effectually the Strainer of the skin.
*Smollett, Letters, pp.109-10, T.Smollett to Dr W. Hunter, Bath 2 Oct 1762*

### 114. 1771 Perseverance
I have been in the Kettle this morning, with a Lady that told me She had been
in above ninety times, & is very far from being cur'd, tho' better than She was.
*BCL, AL 1874/1, Mrs M. Sneyd to Mrs Stears, Bath 8 Apr 1771*

### 115. 1774 The Pumper tries to protect his profits
WHEREAS great quantities of Bath water are daily carried off from the
lower pumps belonging to the Master of the Bath Waters, (by higlers, carriers,
and others, to several neighbouring towns, &c.) and as the rent of the several
pumps amounts to a very considerable sum: This is to inform the public in
general, that no Water will be permitted to be carried from the said pumps
without a proper acknowledgment for the same. // And whereas great
quantities of common Spring-Water are sold in different parts of this kingdom,
and the neighbouring ones, for genuine Bath Water from the Hot springs:
This is further to acquaint the public, that none are genuine but what are
sealed with the Bath Arms and my Name. B.HAYWARD, Pumper.
*Bath Chronicle 18 Aug 1774*

### 116. 1786 Getting all wound up
... my health... has been perfectly reestablished by the Bath waters. I was
carried there from Oxford, at the age of twenty-one... and by those admirable
waters was wound up again for twenty years: at the expiration of which time
I was obliged to return to them again: but then, alas! the winding up, though
equally effectual at the time, would last only six years. How long the third
will last, God only knows; but I am deeply impressed with gratitude for his
goodness in restoring me.
*Roberts, Memoirs of H. More, vol.2 p.45, Mr Pepys to H. More, 31 Dec 1786*

### 117. 1789 But the doctor knows best
Well: a *third* miserable object arrives; - a debauched - debilitated Nobleman!
- no, a well-fed rich Citizen... the Doctor is sent for - 'the Doctor is very
busy; he is engaged at present (*at Cards*) but will wait on you as soon as
possible'. He arrives. 'I am very bad, Doctor, very ill indeed! extreme
weakness - and excruciating pain; - but here is a letter from my good friend
Dr.—, of London. - It will inform you better than I can tell you - of my - my
deplorable, my wretched situation'. - // Now this happens to be really a case
in which bathing in and drinking these powerful waters, *properly*, without
any medical help, would immediately give the happiest relief... and while
the greedy pores drank in for hours the milky antidotal balsam - he should
quaff in full cups... the specific fluid. But, alas! the miserable man must first
be prepared: - he must not touch, nor even think of the water, till he has taken

several dozens of saline draughts, nervous alexipharmic bolusses, anodyne draughts (to settle the commotions raised by the nervous alexipharmic bolusses) - febrifuge powders; quart bottles of pectoral aperient apozem - and three doses of cooling physic - to unload and undo, what the saline draughts, the hot irritating bolusses - the pectoral alozem - the febrifuge powders - the anodyne draughts, and the hot room with double doors, sand bags and double listing, have done. He may now venture to drink the water; and, by and by, to bathe. - Well; he goes out and feels refreshed with the pure cool air; - he drinks a glass of the water at the Cross Bath. - It is the most grateful, and the most comfortable liquor he ever tasted. - *Nature* is delighted with its simple, friendly, and very genial influences. - *She* calls aloud for more: but not one drop more for the whole world. The Doctor has ordered a gill glass twice a day: *in a few weeks* he may indulge him, and at the King's Bath, with even double that quantity... // Next morning the patient is carried into the Bath - Nature is glad - *she* chuckles and exults in its soothing and most comfortable influences. - But, 'Mr. Norris,' shouts the chairman, 'Master's time's up.' - Sir, says the guide, 'you must rise... your time is up; you have been in ten minutes: - The Doctor orders you *not* to stay in *no* longer' - Pray, stop a few minutes, says the Patient, - it's *so* comfortable - I feel *so* easy. - 'Come, come, Sir, you must rise... it's two minutes more than your time;' - Well, to be sure, the Doctor knows best what's proper...

*Graham, New Treatise on the Bath Waters, pp. 5-7*

### 118.  1799  Jane Austen doubts the electrical treatment

What must I tell you of Edward?... He drinks at the Hetling Pump, is to bathe tomorrow, & try Electricity on Tuesday; - he proposed the latter himself to Dr. Fellowes, who made no objection to it, but I fancy we are all unanimous in expecting no advantage from it.

*Austen, Letters, vol.1 p.20, J.Austen to her sister Cassandra, Bath 2 Jun 1799*

# VISITORS

*Summer, not winter, was the prime season at other watering places and at the up-and-coming seaside resorts. At Bath this held true only up to c.1730 when visitors began arriving both later and earlier in the year, so that a principal autumn season (September-December) evolved, followed by a lesser one in spring (late April-early June). As it became fashionable to overwinter at Bath, or to retire there permanently, the eventual outcome was an almost unbroken season stretching from September round to May. Summer then became the quietest, emptiest time of the year, when lodging-house keepers took their own break, shops did their stocktaking, and Bath's masters-of ceremonies went off to preside elsewhere - as Nash and Derrick, for example, did at Tunbridge Wells. Why the season evolved in this way, differentiating Bath from its competitors, has various explanations, among them the timing of Parliamentary sessions, the improvement of roads (so permitting winter travel), the fact that Bath alone offered the luxury of hot-water bathing, its relatively benign climate, and its large investment in comfortable lodgings and indoor entertainment. It is true that current events - a smallpox scare, an outbreak of war, the presence of royalty at the spa - might affect the statistics of visitors in any one year, but in spite of annual fluctuations the trend was rapidly, unstoppably upwards. Early in the century people might complain of the thin attendance and the absence of congenial company, but soon it was the excessive numbers, the crowded public rooms, the dilution of the quality by the quantity, that aroused most comment. By the 1790s as many as 30,000 persons a year may have been making the pilgrimage to Bath, an endlessly varied parade of humanity. Sophisticated courtiers and metropolitans had once looked exotic in a homely country town, but in the end it was the visitors who often appeared homespun among the sophistications of Bath.*

*119. 1706 Aristocrats and gamesters*
The Bath has not been known at any time to be fuller than it now is, the Duke of Norfolk, the Duke of Beaufort, the Duchess of Shrewsbury (the Duke being gone hence and left her behind), the Lord Hyde, who is just gone, Lord Grantham, Lord Gore, Lord Granville, are the principal quality with abundance of Ladies. The Duke of Norfolk is said to have designs upon Sir Nich. Sherborne's, of the North, daughter and heir, who is here also, who has upwards of 3,000l. [£3000] per annum and red lettered. The Duke lives great both in table and equipage. // ... There are about fifty known gamesters and sharpers come here from London; they want cullies [dupes] and are forced to devour each other.
*HMC 29 Portland, vol.4 p.329, Baron R. Price to R. Harley, Bath 13 Sep 1706*

*120. 1716 Provincial sophistication*
When I came into my inn I got myself shaved and put on a clean shirt and better wig and made the best figure I could in a riding dress and went to my sister, not finding her at home. Her maid conducted me into Harrison's Walks... very pleasant and filled with company. I was surprised when I came into Bath to see in a country town as I passed through it so many fine ladies walking in the streets and appearing at the windows.
*Ryder, Diary, p.239, entry for 22 May 1716*

*121. 1716 The Duchess of Marlborough endures Bath*
Her Grace of *Shrewsbury* is here, and of a much happier Temper. She plays at Ombre upon the Walks [i.e. at Harrison's Rooms], that she may be sure to have Company enough, and is as well pleased in a great Crowd of Strangers as the common People are with a Bull-baiting or a Mountebank. I have been upon the Walks but twice, and I never saw any Place Abroad that had more Stinks and Dirt in it than *Bath*; with this Difference only, that we are not starved, for here is great Plenty of Meat, and very good, and as to the Noise, that keeps One almost always awake. I can bear it with Patience, and all other Misfortunes, as long as I think the Waters do the Duke of *Marlborough* any Good.
*Cowper (Countess), Diary, p.197, Duchess of Marlborough to Lady Cowper, Bath 3 Sep 1716*

*122. 1722 Where they meet*
... the small pox is pratty well over in thes parts... wee have a good dell of company in town and they met every night ither at hayis [Hayes'] linsees [Linsey's] or cornishis [Cornish's] for harrison has shut up this long time [at the Assembly Rooms] he not thinking it worth his while...
*BCL, AL 987, Mrs Francis Vaughan to J.Somerset, Bath 23 Nov 1722*

### 123.  1729  An influx of unknowns

The company increases daily, but everybody complains they are people that
nobody knows; for my own part I think it is of no great difference whether 'tis
a crowd of quality or plebeians. Harrison's rooms are so full every night 'tis to
me very disagreeable; if one had an inclination 'tis next to impossible to get a
table to play, which I have only done once since I came. My sister Mary seems
to relish the place as little as I do...

*HMC 42 Carlisle, p.61, Lady A.Irwin to Lord Carlisle, Bath 24 Sep 1729*

### 124.  1732  More criticism

... To the great joy of all the people here Mr. Nash is come, and I think if
possible this place grows more disagreeable every hour. There is now such a
crowed that it is with difficulty that we can get to the Pump to drink our
watters. But I think they have no great reason to brag of thare company.
There was a grand ball last night, which in my way of thinking was very
stupid...

*HMC 78 Hastings, vol.3 p.14, Countess of Huntingdon to her husband, Bath 12 Apr
1732*

### 125.  1736  The art of fleecing by numbers

(*Clear-Bottom*)  Now let you and I reckon in what manner they run the
Gauntlet. The first Attack that's made, before they come into Town, is by a
Set of Touting Inn-Keepers, Ostlers, and Trades-People: The Second, is the
Ringers: The Third, the Stair-Case Musick: The Fourth, for a Subscription at
the Pump-House: The Fifth, at *Thrifty's* [Harrison's] Great-Room: The Sixth,
at the Book-sellers: The Seventh, for the Walks: The Eighth, the Coffee-
Houses, for Pen, Ink, and Paper: The Ninth, for the Curates: The Tenth, for
the Charity-School: The Eleventh, for decay'd Gentlemen: The Twelfth, for
the Poor Strangers: The Thirteenth, for the wretched Lepers: The Fourteenth,
for the Players: The Fifteenth, for Puppet-Shows: The Sixteenth, for Dissenting
Parsons: The Seventeenth, for Horse-Racing: The Eighteenth, for Cudgel-
Playing.
(*Guthall*)  All this is very true: Besides, they have no Rest in their Lodgings
for the Lace-Women, Milliners, and Clear-Starchers: No sooner have they
fereted them out of their Burrows, but the Toy-shops, China-shops, Milliner-
shops, and other Shops, are ready to pull them in Pieces for Raffles: Then
there's the Doctors, Apothecaries, and Surgeons... that make Work for one
another... Then there's the Sexton... that they have no Rest on a Sunday: So
that the Place of Sanctuary is turn'd into a Theatre; for without a Silver Key,
there is no Passage-Way to the Heavenly Ray...// Now... take Notice how the
Gentry runs the Gauntlet the Second Time, when they leave the Town. First
of all, there's a Guinea to the Pumper: Second, a Crown to the Boy at the
Pump-handle: Third, Half-a-Guinea to the Serjeant: Fourth, a Crown to the
Cloth-Woman: Fifth, a Crown to the Bath-Guide: Sixth, a Crown to the Chair-
Men: Seventh, a Guinea to the Cook-Maid, where you lodge: Eighth, two
Guineas to the Chamber-Maids: Ninth, Half-a-Guinea to the Scullion: Tenth, a

Crown to each Porter at the Long-Room [Assembly Room] Doors: Eleventh, to the Ostlers and Boot-Catchers one Guinea: The last of all, is a Present to the Stripmy-Coach-Beggars.
*(Clear-Bottom)* If all this is strictly perform'd, the Road in their Passage home, will be crowded with kind Wishes, Prayers, and Blessings. If there is any Abatement, the first Days Journey will be attended with ill Wishes and Curses enough, to unravel all the Virtue they have gain'd by drinking the Waters.
*Golding, Fortune-Hunter, pp.23-4*

### 126.  1742  The lengthening high season
[Whitsuntide] falls in with our spring season pretty much, so that you will see a great deal of good company here. The autumn season is just over, but we still have many invalids as well as a considerable number of gentlemen's families who make this their winter residence. I like this place upon the whole better than London.
*Trigg, Correspondence, pp.264-5, D. Hartley to J.Lister, 2 Dec 1742*

### 127.  1754  Easy retreat and honourable marriage market
... Bath... every year becomes more frequented, and is a most easy retreat for people of all conditions, especially for those whose estates lye at a distance from the Capital, and who can dispose of themselves during the hot months of summer in some other places; not to mention that there is no place in the world so fit for the necessary and honourable business of making alliances, which causes a great increase of buildings here, and many people are building houses for themselves...
*Pococke, Travels, vol.2 p.32*

### 128.  1757  *Visitors* versus *citizens*
Bath, a gay, sauntering good-for-nothing Place for a young Woman to live in. The Town's People, tho' ever so genteel, even the wives of the *Physicians*, despised by the Guests of ye Place.
*Eaves and Kimpel, Richardson, p.477*

### 129.  1761  The cosmopolitan Irish
The usual times for taking the water are spring and autumn; but it is principally taken during the autumn, as the company is more numerous and of a better class before the opening of Parliament, and before the winter gaieties of London, both of which last far into the summer, and prevent many people from visiting Bath during that time. But as the baths can be taken at all seasons, I am told Bath is never without society, more especially as the cheap living attracts people, who come for four or five months or more in the winter to economize... // The quantity of Irishmen here, of whom the greater part are Roman Catholics, who have been educated out of their own country, in France and the Netherlands, without doubt contributes very much to make

this place especially pleasant to foreigners. They are easy of access, and take pleasure in showing civility to strangers; in this they are aided by their French, which they speak more frequently and better than most Englishmen.
*Kielmansegge, Diary, pp.120, 126-7*

### 130.  1766  The Elder Pitt, Earl of Chatham, formerly M.P. for Bath

Lord Chatham is here, with more equipage, household, and retinue than most of the old patriarchs used to travel with in ancient days. He comes nowhere but to the Pump Room; then he makes a short essay and retires.
*Jesse, Selwyn, vol.2 pp.60-1, Gilly Williams to George Selwyn, Bath 1 Nov 1766*

### 131.  1770?  Glad to be in the crush

Bath is by no means full yet; but there are however on some nights, enough to make it tolerably disagreeable; but the people luckily are all agreed in calling it pleasant, otherwise one might be apt to mistake. But the Ladies are still in great hopes of being so crowded as not to be able to walk. Tho' I must confess 'tis but policy in the present set to wish to be jumbled in a crowd, for most of those I have seen as yet, are as ugly as Lions.
*Sheridan, Letters, vol.1 p.20, R. B. Sheridan to Mrs Angelo, 13 Oct 1770?*

### 132.  1778  A showplace for young ladies

The Men of Reading will find Libraries always open to them; the Men of Conversation, a Variety of Company to form an agreeable Party with. To the Gay and Youthful of both Sexes, it is a Paradise; to Men in Years, a most comfortable Retreat. To young ladies it is, in a particular Degree, the Place where they have the best Opportunity to improve, and shew their Persons to best advantage, as well as to have their prudent Conduct observed; there being no Place in *England*, where they have more Liberty allowed them; and we are happy to observe, that there is not any public Place where that Liberty has been attended with fewer bad Consequences.
*New Prose Bath Guide, pp.vi-vii*

### 133.  1780  The youth of today!

To judge by their dress their manners must have a strong accent; the misses have the air mien and habit militaire... [They]strutt about in a morning in Riding dresses and uniforms and the Maccaronies [dandies]... trip in pumps and with Parasols over their heads... If the sun is so powerfull as to be dangerous to Misses beauty she does not retire to her chamber till the fervour of the noon is over, but takes her Umbrella; if dripping rains, snow, or hail threatens to impair the gloss of her apparel, and spoil her shoes, she adds a pair of pattens to her equipment, and if the North East wind rages she takes refuge in a Mans surtout coat... I never saw such a set of people as appear in the publick rooms, their dress is most elaborately ugly. A frisseur is employ'd three hours in a morning to make a young Lady look like a Virgin Hottentot or Squaw, all art ends in giving them the ferocious air of uncomb'd savages. I

met a young man who I took for one of the Cherokeee Kings lately arrived but
was assured he was an Irish beau who was to begin the ball.
*Montagu, Queen of the Blues, vol.2 pp.81-2*

### 134. 1781 Portrait of a fop
Next let the MACARONI come,
All paste, all powder, and perfume,
With conscious air, and saunt'ring gait,
With club of most prodigious weight:
A cambrick bandage round his throat,
With demi-pockets to his coat;
Where, as he idly stares about,
His handkerchief hangs dangling out;
With his seals or rattan playing,
Or, what is worse, himself surveying;
With antick tricks, and plum'd conceit,
With purse as empty as his pate;
Yet every bauble still pursuing,
And each flirting female wooing...
*Madden, Bath Macaroni, p.14*

### 135. 1787 French courtiers at Bath
(24 May) The Duke de Polignac, Master of the Horse to the Queen of France;
the Duchess of Polignac, Governess of the French King's children; his
Excellency Count d'Adhémar, Ambassador from the Court of France; the Count
Vaudrieul [Vaudreuil], Grand Falconer of France; the Viscount and Viscountess
Vaudrieul; Duke of Guiche, and his Duchess, daughter of the Duchess of
Polignac; Madame la Comtesse Diane de Polignac; with three other Foreigners
of distinction, attended by a grand retinue, visited Stowe and Blenheim, previous
to their arrival in this city for the benefit of the waters. Two large houses on the
North-Parade are occupied by the above illustrious foreigners. - They all
yesterday paid a visit to the Marquis of Lansdown at Bow-wood.
(21 Jun) The French Ambassador, the Duke and Duchess of Polignac, and
the other noble foreigners in their suite, took leave of the city on Saturday last.
// *Bath* is probably indebted to the late Commercial Treaty for the honour of
having entertained a whole month so splendid a group of French Noblesse.
They seemed all perfectly pleased with this place, and they have passed their
time agreeably, as well as spent their Louis d'ors liberally.
*Bath Chronicle 24 May and 21 Jun 1787*

### 136. 1788 A nine-year-old visitor is entranced
Bath was a new world to me... The Pump Room, with its statue of Beau
Nash, the waters sending up their columns of steam, the band of music... and
the vast ever-shifting throng of gaily dressed company, was to me a scene of
constant enchantment. The beautiful green-house plants or artificial flowers
at all the doors of approach to the Pump Room, and the silver balls to attract

the flies, completely dazzled my view. // ... [The ladies] wore huge balloon
bonnets with magnificent ostrich feathers... ample muffs and long tippets, and
fur linings, of the silken Angora goats' hair... The music, too, I felt most heart-
stirring; and then the beauty of the shops, which I was never tired of looking
at... I particularly remember those in the Abbey Yard.
*Hankin, SchimmelPenninck, pp.79-81*

### 137. 1794 Wartime troop movements
(12 Jul) Yesterday a regiment of Royal Irish Rangers, consisting of 646,
exclusive of Officers, arrived here from Bristol - their further route is not
known... // Two hundred of the Cornish Cavalry, commanded by Lord Falmouth,
likewise came here, this week, in order to learn the Horse Discipline from Mr.
Dash and his sons [at the Riding School]... // The Military billetted last night
at the different Public-houses in this City amounted to upwards of twelve
hundred.
(19 Jul) Colonel Cameron's regiment of Volunteers, consisting of 1000 men,
dressed in the Highland uniform, arrived in this city on Tuesday, and proceeded
the next morning on their route to the Camp near Southampton. // This morning
the 34th regt. of foot marched into this city from Bristol, on their rout to
Chippenham. // Thr regiment of Royal Irish Rangers have received orders to
march from this city towards Salisbury.
*Bath Herald 12 and 19 Jul 1794*

### 138. 1794 Haydn remarks on the tourist industry
The city is not thickly [densely] populated, and in Summer one sees very few
people; for the people taking the baths don't come till the beginning of October,
and stay through half of February. But then a great many people come, so that
in the year 1791, 25,000 people were there. All the inhabitants live off this
influx, without which the city would be very poor...
*Landon, Haydn in England, p.266*

### 139. 1797 Royalty in town
Grave as the times are, Bath never was so gay; princes and kings that will be,
and princes and kings that have been, pop upon you at every corner; the
Stadtholder [the exiled William V of Orange] and Prince of Wales only on a
flying visit; but their Highnesses of York are become almost inhabitants, and
very sober and proper their behaviour is. The Duchess contributes, by her
residence in it, to make our street alive [i.e. Great Pulteney Street].
*More, Letters, p.133, H.More to Mrs Boscawen, Bath .....1797*

### 140. 1799 The Irish contingent again
You and I agree perfectly about our ideas of Bath, for I never was in a place I
disliked more, though it always did me so much good. You need not tell me
how full of Irish the town is at present: I am told there are two thousand families,
and I believe I know forty at least.
*Frampton, Journal, p.104, Mrs C. Grumbleton to Lady H. Strangways, 29 Jan 1799*

# LODGINGS

*Visitors displayed a natural anxiety about securing suitable rooms, especially if they envisaged a lengthy stay (and for those undertaking the cure six weeks was the norm). Habitués of Bath, having once found congenial quarters, would return to them whenever they had the chance. Newcomers might arrange with friends and relatives already on the spot to book them rooms in advance, or maybe come armed with recommendations on where to put up. For others the first port of call would be the inn where the coach had deposited both them and their luggage on arrival: probably at the White Hart, the White Lion, the Bear, the Christopher, or the York House. All these were large, bustling establishments with much coming and going, serving meals at most hours of the day, and with plenty of sleeping accommodation, public meeting rooms, and extensive stabling. Comfortable and centrally located as they usually were, inns were too expensive to put up at for long, but served as a temporary base while lodgings were sought out - if necessary by enquiring in person at the various addresses listed in the Bath guidebooks. The majority of lodgings comprised no more than decently furnished suites of rooms (including servants' garrets) in houses where the lodgings keeper also lived; guests had to eat out or cater simply for themselves. Boarding houses on the other hand offered 'pension' terms, the guests dining together at the common table at set times. The cost of a room varied between high and low season, but not, surprisingly, between the different lodgings themselves despite inevitable disparities in quality: the general effect of this custom was probably to raise standards as a whole. Only when whole houses were let for a period was there some flexibility over charging. The best lodgings in the earlier decades were to be found in Westgate and around Orange Grove, and then from the 1740s in the Parades. After the middle of the century*

*many visitors, unless they were invalids, preferred the glamorous*
*upper town.*

### 141. 1723 Lady Bristol makes do with her accommodation
(14 Sep) ... my lodgings... are really extream inconvenient, but I must submit
to necessity till I can better my self, for at present there is not a room to be got
if I woud give £5 for it, so that it was lucky Jack did not come with me, for he
must either have lain in an inn or a garret, & ye room kept for Betty, which is
within mine, is impossible to make shift with, but ye town is so full as was
never known...

(23 Sep) Our company increases daily, so that people of fashion is forcd to
be content with garrets, and I shall remain where I am, for the people of the
house are so unwilling to part with me... tis very airy, quiet and free from
stinks, but there are some inconveniences, which tho' they are very well for
me alone, cannot be made sheift with when you are here; but as a remedy for
that those that are in the upper part of the house are so very obligingly civil to
offer to change with me at an hour's warning.
*Hervey (J.), Letter-Books, vol.2 letters 773 and 782, the Countess to the Earl of
Bristol, Bath 1723*

### 142. c.1725? Advice to a poorer visitor
... when you come to ye Bath Inquire for Mr John Row at ye Sine of ye Ship
near ye Cross Bath... you may Insist with John Row or any other for 4 shillings
a week for your Lodging but that you may bargen as well as you can and tell
them you well be willing to shift your Room if better Lodgers come and as for
your Diat you may have a cut of any thing you like at any time of ye day for
John Rows keeps a Cooks Shop and if you Like not there wayers [their wares]
there and there prices you may goe to another and not obliged to call for any
Ale but smale bear [small beer] or any thing you please...
*BRO, 28/822, Anonymous MS letter, c.1725?*

### 143. 1746 Fire at Princess Caroline's lodgings
Last Wednesday Morning, about Ten O'Clock, a Fire broke out in the Lodgings
belonging to her Royal Highness Princess Caroline, (tho' not in her Highnesses's
Apartment) which damag'd three or four of the upper Rooms, where it began,
and destroy'd the Roof; the whole to the Amount of 150 Pounds, or upwards.
How it began, is not known, but most People attribute it to the Airing of Linnen
by the Fire. Her Royal Highness was gone out in her Coach, when it was first
discover'd, but returning soon after she was inform'd of the Affair; upon which
she immediately order'd all her Servants to be as assiduous as possible, in
endeavouring to secure her Effects, and extinguishing the Flames. In the mean
Time her Royal Highness was carried in her Chair to a neighbouring House.
As it was near the Baths, there was a sufficient Supply of Water; tho' too much
cannot be said in Commendation of the Inhabitants of Bath, and of the Soldiers
quarter'd here; nor were our Magistrates less vigilant on this Occasion; every
Body being ready to give their Assistance, either by supplying the Engines
with Water, or whatever else was necessary; nay some Men got upon the Roof,
and pull'd off the Tiles, in the midst of the Confusion, that the Water thrown up
by the Engine, or otherwise, might have its Effect; which was happily

accomplish'd by One o'Clock; no Person receiving any great Hurt, nor were
hardly any of the Effects in the House destroy'd. // When the Danger was
over, Mrs Umphreys, who keeps the Lodgings, waited upon her Royal Highness,
and express'd her great Concern at the Event. Her Royal Highness considering
the dreadful Consequence of the Fire, and the Prejudice it was to those Persons
who suffer'd by it, assur'd her, that she wou'd still continue at her Lodgings;
and wou'd do all the Service that lay within her Power. Accordingly her Royal
Highness return'd Thursday Evening; lying Wednesday Night at the House of
Richard Nash, Esq.
*Bath Journal 14 Apr 1746*

### 144. 1747 Dining in company

Time now drawing on for Dinner, I betook myself to my Lodgings; where,
having dressed myself, I attended some of the Company, that were in the House,
to a Boarding-Table, where, I think, every Thing was elegantly provided; for
they have, at this Place, as good Provisions in general, as in any Part of *Europe*.
We were about fifteen of us in Company; and I think that single Persons, who
frequent this City, cannot do better, than by boarding with the People of the
House. Here you generally meet with Company; and the Ladies make no Scruple
to dine with the Gentlemen, if they are ever so great Strangers: For Conversation
soon renders each other acquainted, and these make each other agreeable, by
their Familiarity during their Stay.
*Draper, Brief Description, p.7*

### 145. 1747 Lord Cowper's brother commiserates

It vexes me that you have lost your Lodgings at Leakes [the bookseller on
Terrace Walk], and more as you have got such sad ones. My Landlady was an
Atwood, but her house stood pleasantly on the Bank of the river in Orange
Grove, I suppose this is a son of hers. I know Leake too will be miserable
about it, for I beleive you was the best Tenant he ever had.
*Cowper (Spencer), Letters, p.96, Spencer Cowper to his brother, 2nd Earl Cowper, 8
Nov 1747*

### 146. 1763 The Elder Pitt lets 7 Circus

... we have taken Mr.Pitt's house in the Circus, for five years certain, to give
£120 a year and pay the Taxes wch will amount to ten more. An Extravagant
Price for an unfurnish'd House at Bath! But however a House was quite
necessary, and my Sister is much better pleas'd wth this house than she was
wth that in the Square [Queen Square], on account of the Prospect, wch is still
more delightful than in the House we are now in. // The Eating Room, and the
Room over it are thirty feet by nineteen, wth a large Bow Window in each
Room. There are three Rooms on the two first Floors, and four very good
Bedchambers on the third Floor... We are to go into [it] by the first of March,
and we have agreed wth Hill, of Marlborough, [upholsterer and furniture maker]
about furnishing it... Mr.Bury is to make the third Room on the first Floor, next

the Garden, his Library, which I fancy will amuse him to fit up.
*Proc. Bath Branch SANHS, 1914-18, p.278, P.Bury to Lady Tynte, Bath 29 Dec 1763*

*147. 1764 Suspension of the January-February price reductions*
The Inhabitants of Bath... acquaint the Public that they shall not lower the Price of Lodgings the two Winter Months as usual, on Account of their Rents being greatly advanc'd, Provisions much dearer, and Taxes greatly increas'd.
*Bath Chronicle 13 Dec 1764*

*148. 1766 A Cornish parson feels well accommodated*
Our apartments consist of three Rooms, a Parlour and Two Bed-chambers, the Parlour and our Bed-chamber handsomely cieled, and Fanny's papered.- The Parlour hath in it a Beaufet, 6 Mahogany Chairs with Hair-Bottoms, an Easy-Chair, a Dining Table, and Pillar and Claw Table both of Mahogany, Chimney Looking glass, and Looking-Glass against a broad Mullion between the Window Frames. Handsome Chimney-Furniture with Marble Hearth... Our Lodging Room has a blew and white flowered Linen Bed, Window Curtains the same, Walnut Chairs with blew Bottoms, Chest of Drawers, Dressing Table, Looking-Glass: Inside, a closet with hanging Press and Shelves. Fanny's Bed white, with all conveniences, and a closet. The House we live in, is on the west side of Abby Green, fronting East and West: but Fanny's Room has a window, which looks up a long Lane towards the Church-yard.
*Penrose, Letters, pp.28-9, letter of 11-12 Apr 1766*

*149. 1771 The other guests*
... our Family is deminishing very fast; Mrs.Rohder's apartments are taken by Justice Shallow, & his Man Davy, a Sister of his Worships, & her Son, a Gawkee Young Fellow, that either is, or is to be, a Parson... Miss Knox's sett off for London this Afternoon - Mrs Iredell has only 2 boarders, no Servants with them, & the queerest Fellows you ever saw in your life, one of them is in a bad state of health, & oblig'd to keep good hours, which is happy for me, as he lies over my head, but then he getts up very early in the Morning, & trotts about as heavy as a Coach-Horse; & the other goes whistling up & down stairs, like a Ploughfellow. - There are nothing but a few sick People coming to Bath this Season; & the old Stagers are going off every day, that you see but little Company on the Parade; when it's a fine day, all go to Spring Gardens, which are now open'd.
*BCL, AL 2086, Mrs M. Sneyd to Mrs Stears, Bath 4 May 1771*

*150. 1773 The Duchess of Kingston finally makes amends*
The last time the Duke and Duchess [of Kingston] came to Bath, she took lodgings of Mrs.Hodgkinson, in the Orange-Grove, for one month: but not finding them agreeable, she removed before the expiration of the time agreed on to the Abbey Bath-house, from whence she again removed his Grace to the centre house on the South Parade, where he died. During his illness she sat by

his bed-side, when any of the [medical] faculty or others entered, with a prayer-
book in her hand... // Some time after his Grace's death, Mrs.Hodgkinson,
expecting to be paid for the full time the lodgings were engaged, was informed
by the Duchess she never would agree to it. As she was ever positive in every
thing she said, not bearing to have her will disputed, therefore, rather than pay
this just demand, she made her a present, a short time afterwards, of a piece of
plate ten times the value of the debt.
*Whitehead, Original Anecdotes, pp.185-6*

### 151.  1774  A thankful removal to somewhere quieter
We left Tetbury about 10, & had a pleasant ride to Bath, the day being very
fine & the road good. I was *very hot* coming down the Hill, but the airings will
use [accustom] me to *that*. The Bear [Inn] was so very noisy & dismal & so
*very indifferent* that I cd not forbear crying... Mr.Wake procured us this Lodging
[in Milsom Street] & we came here in Chairs after Tea, wch was much better
than staying at the Bear. Our Street is airy & quiet, 2 rooms on a floor, not very
large but comfortable. Papa & James sleep on the Parlour floor [i.e. street
level], I & Sally in a two pr. of stairs room [i.e. two floors higher], with
convenient closets &c. Next week we are to have the Dining Room (& adjoining
Bedchamber) to receive *my* company but it is now occupied... We could not
unlock the Tea chest which was a sad *misfortune;* fancy the Lock is shot with
jumbling but *he* says I have *lost* the right Key... The *Music* has been to serenade
us, but I was not drest...
*Elwin, Noels and Milbankes, pp.34-5, Elizabeth Noel to her sister Judith, Bath 27 Jan
1774*

### 152.  1776  The tariff for lodgings
The general custom for letting Lodgings at Bath, is at Ten Shillings per week
per room, during the months of March, April, May, September, October,
November, and December; the other five months at Seven Shillings per week.
// N.B. Garrets 5s. per week throughout the year. // ... The people who let
Lodgings are not *compellable* to let them at a lower price in the usual months;
but custom has made it so general, that if attempted (unless in some very eligible
situation, and elegant accommodation) it would be deemed exorbitant. - This,
however, extends only to single rooms and apartments, which are lett by the
week, no abatement being usual when a whole house is taken for a month or
longer time, unless previously agreed by the Landlord and Lodger. // ... I
know of no internal police in Bath for settling disputes concerning lodgings;
the magistrates are ever ready to receive complaints from any person, who
think themselves aggrieved, and give redress as far as lies in their power, but
no magistrate can fix a price at what any person shall be *compellable* to let, or
sell their property.
*Bath Chronicle 15 Feb 1776*

*153. 1777-8 John Wilkes's plump landlady*
(22 Dec 1777) ... I lodge at Miss Temple's, a perfect *Huncamunca* [fat character in Fielding's *Tom Thumb*], in Gallway's Buildings, there being no room on either Parade, or in the Grove. Colonel Whitmore, Mr.Diggs, and three ladies, occupy the rest of the house, with Miss Temple.
(12 Apr 1778) Constancy! thy name is Wilkes: and constancy to Huncamunca is a prodigy... I am here again, in Miss Temple's lodgings in Gallway's Buildings, and my fair landlady has been just dropping me such a broad-wheel curtesey, that I trembled for the floor, and the floor trembled likewise.
*Wilkes, Letters, vol.2 pp.48 and 80, John Wilkes to his daughter, Bath 1777-8*

*154. 1778 An accolade for Bath's newest inn*
YORK HOUSE. // An excellent Hotel, the only House of Reception, which is situated in an open airy Part of the City [i.e. George Street]; and, to the Advantage of its excellent Situation, the Stranger will find what can be found scarce any where else in *England*, a sensible honest Host [Robert St John Lucas], who is not only a Man of good Family, but one who has had a liberal Education: From such a Man, every Person who comes to his House is sure of meeting with Politeness, Diffidence, and a proper Reception... When *York House* is full, the *Bear* is the next best Inn, and, for People of inferior Rank, the *Greyhound*, or the *White Lyon*, in *the Market Place*.
*Thicknesse, New Prose Bath Guide, p.62*

*155. 1780 The Countess of Pembroke gives her son instructions*
At present Miss [Georgiana] Herbert and I intend being at Bath on Tuesday by three o'clock, and shall drive to the York House, where we hope to find a note from you to tell us if you shou'd have got any where a lodging, a room for me, another for Miss Herbert, and *one* for our two maids, which we hope you will be able to do, as it will be much quieter and better oeconomy than in the hotel. It must be in the Upper Town, that is, not lower than Bond Street, as much higher as you please... We mean to stay at Bath till Sunday the 7th... You must order some mutton chops to be ready for us, wherever we are to remain the first two hours; shou'd it be in the middle of the street, you must be so good as to take care they are kept cover'd, as the weather is now cold. If there be any rooms for us pray order fires from early... // Shou'd any misfortune hinder our coming we will let you know the soonest possible, and then we will pay you for the lodging, and you may eat the Chops, but I hope we shall certainly come.
*Pembroke Papers, pp.79-80, Lady Elizabeth to George, Lord Herbert, 29 Dec 1780*

*156. 1783 A complaint to the Mayor about street noise*
... the loud crying of the hours and half hours by some of the watchmen, particularly by one of the most stentorian lungs, is a grievance complained of by many persons of weak nerves and vigilant [wakeful] habits. I know one gentleman who has twice changed his lodgings to get out of this man's beat... // Another annoyance... is the custom of the drivers of carriages, who come to

take up travellers early in the mornings, to keep their horses in exercise while
they are waiting, by a continual driving up and down the streets. The annoyance
is particularly grievous to the lodgers and inhabitants in the Circus and Square
[i.e. Queen Square], and it is carried even to the length of livery stable keepers
training their horses by driving them in perpetual round in empty carriages
before the inhabitants are up.
*Bath Chronicle 10 Apr 1783, letter fom 'A Lodger'*

### 157.  1783  Inflation brings an extra cost
*To the Publick frequenting Bath.* // CANDOUR must acknowledge, it has
been a Custom of long standing... for the house-keeper to find the Lodger in
LINEN without charge. But an Alteration of Times directs an Alteration of
Measures: And it is humbly presumed that a recollection of the late enormous
Increase of Taxes and Rents, and of course the advanced Price of the Necessaries
of Life, will abundantly justify the House-keepers' moderate Charge for the
Use of the Linen. All who please may use their own: But it is expected from
this time, that such as are supplied with this article by the House-keeper must
pay for it in proportion to the quantity used. // [N.B.] Boarders to be charged
only for the Chamber Linen.
*Bath Chronicle 4 Sep 1783*

### 158.  1793-5  Parson Woodforde's verdict on two Bath inns
(11 Oct 1793) We got to Bath... about six o'clock this Evening, to the White
Hart Inn in Stall Street, kept by one Pickwick, where we drank Tea, supped
and slept, a very good, very capital Inn, everything in stile.
(15 Oct 1793) We then packed up our things and removed from the White
Hart to the White Lion, as we set off [by stage-coach] from thence to Morrow
Morn' at 6. o'clock for Oxford. Then paid my bill at the W.Hart, 2.6.5... As we
go early to Morrow Morn' paid my Bill at the White Lion this Evening for
Dinner &c. 0.17.6 money enough I think. To Servants gave 0.3.6. The White
Lion is a very good Inn but very dear.
(29 Jun 1795) ... this Evening between 9. and 10. o'clock, we were put down
at the White Hart in Stall Street kept by Pickwick & Wife and there we supped
and slept, and a very excellent House it is, everything so good and neat &c.
*Woodforde, Diary, vol.4 pp.64, 67 and 210*

### 159.  1794  The desirability of servants
Having come to Bath without a servant it is necessary that we shou'd board,
from the Bath guide we learn that though lodging houses are numerous there
are but few that take in boarders. Noon - We are return'd... after an unsuccessful
search. My brother wish'd my Father to take a servant & we find a want of one
more than I expected, for the boarding houses we have yet met will take nobody
without one.  Night - Miss C. Isted [a distant relative] had the goodness to
accompany us... & by her assistance we are settled in very handsome apartments
No.5 Oxford Row. We left the White Hart after dinner, it is an excellent Inn,

the business very great but everything managed with regularity & comfort. We are to pay 18 shilling a week each for board, half a guinea a week for each room & 3s 6d a week for each fire. Although we have no servant we are obliged to pay for servants rooms & servants hall 3 shilling a week each as it is a rule not to set [let?] the good rooms without the suit[e] & 5 shilling a week each to the master of the house for the use of the servants, but as we were one family this is to be lower'd to half a guinea a week among us...

*Wilson, Shropshire Lady, p.96, entry from Katherine Plymley's diary for 8 Oct 1794*

### *160. 1795 Billeting troops during the war years*

The burthen sustained by the Innkeepers of Bath, in consequence of the numerous Soldiers and Horses quartered upon them, is immense. - So astonished were a number of respectable Tradesmen a few days since at seeing the particulars of the expences incurred within this twelvemonth, by one of our Innkeepers, that they immediately resolved on a voluntary subscription for the general benefit of One Shilling a week, in order to alleviate those burthens, and which they intend to continue during the war. An example which we hope will be followed throughout the city.

*Bath Herald 25 Apr 1795*

### *161. 1799 The Austens settle in at 13 Queen Square*

We are exceedingly pleased with the house; the rooms are quite as large as we expected. Mrs.Bromley is a fat woman in mourning, and a little black kitten runs about the staircase. Elizabeth has the apartment within the drawing-room; she wanted my mother to have it, but as there was no bed in the inner one, and the stairs are so much easier of ascent, or my mother so much stronger than in Paragon as not to regard the double flight, it is settled for us to be above, where we have two very nice-sized rooms, with dimity quilts and everything comfortable. I have the outward and larger apartment, as I ought to have... the beds are both as large as any at Steventon, and I have a very nice chest of drawers and a closet full of shelves - so full indeed that there is nothing else in it... I like our situation very much; it is far more cheerful than Paragon, and the prospect from the drawing-room window, at which I now write, is rather picturesque, as it commands a prospective view of the left side of Brock street, broken by three Lombardy poplars in the garden of the last house in Queen's Parade.

*Austen, Letters, vol.1 pp.60-2, Jane Austen to her sister Cassandra, Bath 17 May 1799*

Continued . . .

*162. 1800 Joseph Farington R.A. records the dining arrangements*
... at 4 I dined at Mrs.Esdailes [i.e. at his lodgings]

                    Mrs.Esdaile
Mrs.Jeffries                        Mrs.Brown
Miss Holden                         Mrs.Salisbury, a visitor
Miss Brown                          Miss Lambert
H.Hamond                            Mr.Brown
Miss Lethbridge                     Mr.Curling
J.F.                                Mr.Tickell
Captn.Thomas                        Mr.Luxmore
                Miss Fenton Woollery

... The custom at Mrs. Esdaile's is // To dine at four oClock. // The Ladies retire about $^1/_2$ past 5. // The gentlemen quit the room at $^1/_2$ past Six that it may be prepared for Tea at 7. // After Tea Card parties are made. // Supper at Ten. // Retire about Eleven, - or the rule is to quit the *dining parlour* at $^1/_2$ past 11.
*Farington, Diary, vol.4 pp.1455-6, entry for 22 Nov 1800*

# FOOD AND DRINK

'... the provisions better than ever I tasted', admitted the fastidious Horace Walpole in 1766, echoing the general sentiment all through the period. Bath's gastronomic distinction owed much to its fortunate setting. Its suburbs were patchworked with small plots, market gardens, and orchards, even a productive vineyard until the mid-century. The surrounding countryside grew grain and raised beef and dairy herds, while flocks of sheep fattened on Lansdown. Further east lay the arable country of Wiltshire, further west the Severn fisheries and the entrepôt of Bristol - the source of important staple foodstuffs as well as luxuries, from rice and sugar to Mediterranean fruits, Caribbean turtles, wines, rum, chocolate, and many other imports. The wholesale and retail provisions market, much admired after its enlargement and re-siting in the 1760/1770s, came under the Corporation, which annually appointed two of its number to the profitable sinecure of market Bailiffs. Periodically the Corporation undertook campaigns against fraud and profiteering, and it was also responsible for the 'assize of bread' (setting the weight of standard-priced loaves), the licensing of dealers in alcohol, and the appointing of porters and 'basketwomen' to carry items purchased at market back to peoples' houses. Greenstuffs, fish, and milk were all commonly hawked door to door, and almost every sort of foodstuff was retailed at permanent shops by butchers, poulterers, cheesemongers (who also sold hams and preserved meats), fishmongers, grocers (dealers in non-perishable and imported products), greengrocers, fruiterers, confectioners, and bakers. The pastrycooks, above all Gill in Wade's Passage and later Molland of Milsom Street, were almost civic institutions, purveyors of savoury and sweet take-aways but equipped too with eating rooms on the premises, and hence favourite haunts of visitors not boarding at their lodgings. Alternatively, meals and refreshments could be had at inns, *taverns, coffee-houses and, in summer, the pleasure gardens. But while the most recherché delicacies reached some Bath tables (and graced the menu at certain lavish Corporation banquets), the worst-off citizens still lived perilously near the breadline. Bad harvests quickly inflated prices and encouraged rigging of the market, so that food riots were averted in hard years only by emergency soup kitchens and the distribution of cheap rice and potatoes.*

### 163. 1724 Local vintages

I shall begin with taking Notice of some Particulars relating to the celebrated Vineyard near *Bath*, which has made so much Noise in the World: ... it lies upon the Side of a steep Hill, facing the South, the Ground very rocky or stony: In this Place, the Vines are planted in Lines about six Foot asunder, and are treated much after the Manner that Vines are manag'd about *Germany*. The Sorts of Grapes here planted, are the White Muscadine, and the Black Cluster-Grape, which, however... are not of proper Wine-making Grapes, and are not the most early in ripening, yet there was made sixty-six Hogsheads of Wine four Years ago, from this Vineyard, which contains six Acres of Ground: But in the Year 1721 there was made... not above 3 Hogsheads, and the last Year, 1722, when I was there, *July* the 26th, the Vines were then hardly in Blossom, so that little could be expected of them that Year; but as there was then upon them a great deal of good bearing Wood, I suppose this Year they may produce a good Crop, especially considering the extraordinary Summer we have had... //... the wine made in *England*, may not always be worth 10l. [£10] *per* Hogshead, though that at *Bath* has been sold for that Price...

*Bradley, General Treatise, vol.3 pp.116-17 and 125*

### 164. 1726 The standard form of announcing bread prices

We the s[ai]d Mayor and Justices do set Ascertain and appoint.................. per Bushell on the Assize of bread on the several Bakers in this City including the allowance for baking And.................. per bushell on the Assize of bread on the Several Country Bakers frequenting the Market in this City with bread including the allowance for baking, And we do direct and appoint that on such bread be marked and imprinted the Sort price and weight thereof, And also the first Letter of the Christian and Surname of the Maker.

*BRO, Bath Quarter Sessions Book 1724-43, 9 May 1726*

### 165. 1738 A cook advertises his services

... HENRY TRINDER, Cook, from the Three-Tuns in Stall-street, BATH, now keeps the *Christopher-Inn* in the Market-Place... where is kept a good Ordinary [fixed-price meal] every Day at Two o'Clock; and where Gentlemen may depend upon the civillest Usage, and good Entertainment - Board and Lodging - and all Sorts of Neat Wines sold at the cheapest Rates. // He likewise dresses Dinners at Gentlemen's or Ladies Houses or Lodgings; and all Sorts of Soups, and Made [prepared] Dishes drest...

*Gloucester Journal 17 Jan 1738*

### 166. 1738 Table lay-out at the banquet for Frederick, Prince of Wales

Last Thursday the Mayor and Corporation waited on his Royal Highness, and Presented him with his freedom of this City, in a fine Gold Snuff Box... after which the Prince honoured them with his Company in the Town Hall at Dinner - of which the following is the Bill of Fare -

| First Course | Second Course |
|---|---|
| | Pheasant Guinea Hen |
| | Partridges Cocks and |
| | Quails |
| Soupe a la Reine - Remove Salmon | Asparagus |
| Chickens with Noodles and Crayfish | Rhenish Wine Cream |
| Fillers of Beef and Mango | Ragoo Meller, and Roasted |
| | Sweetbreads |
| Partridge Pye | Croquant and Tartlets |
| Haunch of Venison | Oysters in Lemon broiled |
| Soupe Sante - Remove Fish | Two Capons with Cresses |
| Tuckies with Sallery [celery] Branch | Puptoon [baked ragout] of |
| | Lobsters |
| Veal Cutlets glace | Cold Meats in Plates |
| Ducks corbonaded and Salmi [game ragout] | Calves Ears and Ducks |
| | Tongues forced |
| Chine of Mutton a la St Menhaut | Grape Tart and Puffs |
| Grand Sallad | Grand Sallad |
| Hind Quarters of Veal larded Sauce Picant | Rasbery Tarts and |
| | Cheesecakes |
| Ducks corbonaded & Salmi | Calves Ears and Ducks |
| | Tongues Forced |
| Veal Cutlets glace | Cold Meats in Plates |
| Tuckies with Sallery Branch | Puptoon of Lobsters |
| Soupe Sante - Remove Fish | Two Capons with Cresses |
| Haunch of Venison | Oysters in Lemon broiled |
| Pasty | Croquant and Tartlets |
| Fillers of Beef with Mango | Ragoo Meller and |
| | Sweetbreads Roasted |
| Chickens with Noodles and Crayfish | Rhenish Wine Cream |
| Soupe a la Reine - Remove Salmon | Artichoaks |
| | Pheasant Guinea Hen |
| | Partridges Cocks and |
| | Quails |

After which came the most elegant Desert that could Possibly be Procured, the Dinner was conducted under the Directions of the Earl of Chesterfields Servants, without any manner of hurry or Confusion.

*BCL, MS 1517, Anonymous letter, Bath 4 Nov 1738*

### 167. 1749 Superlative provisions, incomparable cooks

... People... are sure to find their Tables covered with the best of Provisions of all Kinds: Our Mutton is celebrated; and that which is really fed upon our own Downs, has a Flavour beyond Comparison: Our Butter cannot be exceeded; the Herbage in the Neighbourhood being sweet; the Housewifry neat and clean: And we have Fish in great Plenty, as fresh and as good as even the greatest Epicure can desire. So that if good Provisions can be called an Addition to the

Pleasures of the Place, BATH will yield to none in this Point, especially since no City in the World can be furnished with better and cleaner Cook Maids to Dress them; and the extraordinary Abilities of those Maids have long rendered the Town a Nursery for supplying not only the neighbouring Country with such Kind of Servants; but Families in the most distant Quarters of the Kingdom; Gentlemen, every Season, Hiring the *Bath* Cooks, and, on their leaving the City, taking them to their respective Places of Abode, even in *London* itself.
*Wood, Essay, 1749, vol.2 p.442*

### 168. 1749 The work-shy turnspit dogs
The extraordinary Love which the *Bathonians* have for Dogs, induced our Ancestors to... [use] a Species of Lazy Dogs [to turn their cooking spits]. // The Animals thus employed have not only exceeding long Backs but short bandy Legs; and some of them are naturally so Idle, that, to avoid their Work, they will sneak into the most obscure Holes and Corners; where they will lie perdue for Hours... // OF these ugly, deformed, lazy Animals, the City is now Blessed with about three thousand in Number by some Computations; but by other Reckonings with many more.
*Wood, Essay, 1749, vol.2 p.416*

### 169. 1753 A wine merchant's list
BATH. // Sold WHOLESALE by the IMPORTER, // *Isaac de Vic*, Wine-Merchant, // *At his* VAULTS *in this* CITY, SOUTHAMPTON, and GUERNSEY, // All Sorts of FINE NEAT OLD WINES, *By the* PIPE, HOGSHEAD, *or* DOZEN, *viz.*

| | |
|---|---|
| FRENCH CLARET, of the First Growth, | Excellent OLD RED PORT, |
| CHATEAU MARGAUX, | MOUNTAIN ten Years Old, |
| LAFFITE, | LISBON, |
| BURGUNDY, | SHERRY, |
| CHAMPAGNE, | WHITE PORT, |
| OLD HOCK, | RHENISH, |
| MADEIRA, from the West-Indies, | CANARY, |
| | TENT... |

The above WINES may be sent from his sundry VAULTS, to most Parts of *Great-Britain* and *Ireland...*
*Bath Journal 26 Mar 1753*

### 170. 1764 Re-siting of the vegetable market
The Corporation has lately made a new Green Market, with convenient Sheds for the Gardeners; and no place in England is better supply'd with garden Stuff of all Kinds than Bath.
*New Bath Guide, 1764, p.35*

### 171. 1765 Against profiteering butchers and poulterers
... the Purpose for which the present Subscription was set on Foot, is, that both the Inhabitants and *Strangers* who reside in, and resort to this City, may

enjoy the *equal* Benefit of a *free and open* Market; a Benefit, from which...
they have hitherto been most injuriously excluded, principally by the illegal
Practices of the Town-Butchers and Poulterers. These Persons, by Forestalling
the Market, and by other fraudulent Methods, get into their Possession the
Prime of those Commodities in which they respectively deal; and leaving the
*Refuse* to be vended in the Market, enhance the Price of these Provisions, by
retailing them to their Customers at an unreasonable Profit... [And], conscious...
that those Families who wou'd supply themselves with the *best* Provisions of
these Kinds, must necessarily have Recourse to their Shops, they add *Insult* to
Injustice, and treat those Persons who presume to question the Equity of their
Demands, with the utmost Indignity, and even *Abuse*.
*Bath Chronicle 2 May 1765*

### 172. 1766 A Bath institution, Gill's of Wade's Passage

...Of all the Cooks the World can boast,
    However great their skill,
To bake, or fry, to boil, or roast,
    There's none like Master GILL...

O taste this Soup, for which the Fair,
    When hungry, cold, and chill,
Forsake the Circus and the Square
    To eat with Master GILL...

He who would fortify his Mind,
    His Belly first should fill;
Roast Beef 'gainst Terrors best you'll find;
    *'The Greeks knew this,'* says GILL.

Your Spirits and your Blood to stir
    Old GALEN gives a Pill,
But I the forc'd meat Ball prefer,
    Prepar'd by Master GILL...

*Anstey, New Bath Guide, 1766, pp.65-6,68, 'A Charge to the Poets' [excerpts]*

### 173. 1766 The Cornish take breakfast at the pleasure gardens

We this morning were most elegantly regaled with a Breakfast at Spring
Gardens, with all the other Cornish Gentlemen and Ladies now in Town... In
these Gardens is a large handsome Building, wherein is a Breakfast Room
capacious enough to hold many Sets of Company... When we entered the Room,
the Tables were spread with singular Neatness. Upon a Cloth white as Snow
were ranged Coffee Cups, Tea Dishes of different sizes, Chocolate Cups, Tea
Pots, and every Thing belonging to the Equipage of the Tea Table, with French
Rolls, Pots of Butter, all in decent order, and interspersed with sweet Briar,

which had a pretty Effect both on the Sight and Smell. At the Word of Command were set on the Table Chocolate, Coffee, Tea, Hot Rolls buttered, buttered hot cakes. What should hinder one from making a good Breakfast? Yet I was so moderate, and had such a philosophical command of my appetite, that in the midst of all this Plenty, I eat but one Roll and one Cake, and drank but one cup of Chocolate, two of Coffee, and two of Tea.

*Penrose, Letters, p.96, letter of 9 May 1766*

### 174. 1774 An ice-cream parlour on Pulteney Bridge
AT BENJAMIN FORD's NEW ICE CREAM SHOP, No.13, on the New [i.e. Pulteney] Bridge, leading to Spring-Gardens, may be had all kinds of different flavour'd ICES, made from the best sweetmeats, essences, and fruits, for plates, compote bowls, and all large glasses, from curious shap'd moulds, of pints, quarts, or upwards, on a very short notice. // The true Orgeat, Lemonade, and Jellies, at 3s.6d. per dozen, made new every day, as will be Almond, Lemon, and Diet Bread Cakes, of a pound each. - Thick plumb, saffron, and royal Queen Cake, to cut out in small quantities. // Italian and all sorts of fine Biscuits, Sweetmeats, and Confectionary. - Ice Creams of all kinds in small glasses at 4d. each, kept constantly, having new Ice Wells on the spot. / / [N.B.] Deserts served of all sizes, ornamented in a new and elegant taste.
*Bath Chronicle 6 Jan 1774*

### 175. 1778 Bath objects to the Bill to conserve fish stocks
That large Quantities of Plaise Flounders Soles Whitings Herrings Sprats Eels Tumblin and Shrimps are taken in the River Severn below a certain Weir... called Hock Cribb... in the parish of Trethern... and from time immemorial have been so taken of a proper size (and without destroying the Spawn) by Putts [basket traps], and from the nature of the River such Fisheries cannot be carried on so as to afford an ample supply to the markets in any other manner, nor can Salmon be taken in large Quantities below the said Weir... but by Netts of a peculiar construction and of different Dimensions from those intended by the said Bill, And therefore should the same pass into Law in its present Form the usual Supply of Fish would be much lessened to the great and manifest Injury of the Inhabitants of this City and the Nobility and Gentry who resort thereto.
*BRO, Bath Council Minutes, 7 Mar 1778, part of petition to Parliament*

### 176. 1778-9 Food parcels for John Wilkes' daughter
(22 Dec 1778) I beg the favour of you, my dear Polly, to accept a pair of very fine soles, and a beautiful *piper* [gurnard] - I must *pay the piper* too, but I do it with pleasure for you - I remember your jokes on my marked partiality for Bath mutton, but I hope to convert you...

(24 Dec 1778) I... would advise you, my dearest Polly, to commend exceedingly the Bath mutton and cheese, which you will receive to-morrow; because, if you hesitate even, you may be embroiled with the good people of Bath... Instead of soles, I find Hancock ['the great fishmonger here'] sent you

several whitings; but the profane wretch *swears* they were that day better than
Bath soles.
(7 Jan 1779) I send you a country loaf of brown bread, as I think exquisite,
made by a baker three miles from hence... you will find in the same basket a
brace of woodcocks, and some fish from Hancock. Woodcocks are here very
scarce and dear, half a guinea a couple. These were given me by Colonel
Whitmore...
*Wilkes, Letters, vol.2 pp.117-21, 143, John Wilkes to his daughter, Bath 1778-1779*

### 177. 1780 The latest table delicacy

A *New* Species of Luxury has taken place this winter here, *chickens* are fatted
with *chopd almonds & Raisins*, & sold at 2 Guineas a Couple. The Pastry
Cooks who have introducd this will get fortunes, as many are sold daily at that
price... Well may Raisins be dear - where will extravagance end?
*BCL, MS B920 Edmund Rack, A Disultory Journal of Events... at Bath, entry for 22
Jan 1780*

### 178. 1785 Quality teas, guaranteed pure and unsmuggled

The Cheapest Tea Ware-House in Bath. // ... JOHN COLES... will sell all
sorts of FINE TEAS fresh from the East-India Company's Warehouses, (which
he clears himself) at as low a price, and as good in quality, as any person in the
kingdom. // He has his whole life-time been employed in the Trade, and needs
not the *Direction or Patronage* of any one. His present prices are as follows. /
/ Good Bohea Tea 1s.10d. per pound. The best ditto 2s. Congous and Souchongs,
from 3s.6d. to 8s. Good Green Tea at 3s.4d. Fine speck'd Leaf Singlos 4s. to
6s. Hysons 7s. up to the best superfine 10s. // N.B. An allowance to wholesale
dealers. // As Souchong Teas are expected cheaper in about a fortnight, J.Coles
advises his friends and customers to purchase no more than will serve them till
that time. // Notwithstanding John Coles thinks the *word* of every tradesman...
should be sacred as his Oath, yet in compliance to the present fashion, with
every parcel of Tea sold by him of a Quartern and upwards, will be delivered a
copy of the following Affidavit. // *I JOHN COLES... do make Oath, that I
never bought, or ever will buy... any Smuggled Tea. - Also that I never did or
ever will adulterate... any Teas, but will sell them genuine, as I clear them from
the India Warehouses. // Sworn before me // March 29, 1785, Wm. STREET,
Mayor. // Witness, J. Morgan, Officer of the Excise.*
*Bath Chronicle 31 Mar 1785*

### 179. 1788 Crack-down on gin shops

... the Magistrates of this city, at the last licensing day, signified their
determination to the retailers of spirits, that after the present year no licence
would be granted, allowing the retail of spirits in SMALL quantities; - so that
the worst of all nuisances (the petty gin-shops) will, by this resolution, be
abolished.
*Bath Chronicle 17 Jan 1788*

## 180.  c.1790  The fare at a private girls' school

There was no want of good living at Belvedere House, generally roast beef on Mondays; on Tuesdays and Fridays, roast shoulders of Mutton; a round of beef on Wednesdays; Thursdays boiled legs of mutton, and stewed beef with pickled walnuts on Saturdays, which was much liked. Then two days in the week, we had 'choke dogs' dumplings with currants in them, other days rice or other puddings, but after the meat not before, as was the case in some Schools. A few of the girls remained a few minutes after the others had gone up to the School room, and had a glass of port wine each (for which an extra charge was made).

*Sibbald, Memoirs, p.38*

## 181.  1794  Earl Camden celebrates becoming Recorder of Bath

On this occasion his Lordship gave a sumptuous dinner at the Town-Hall...[when about] 70 sat down to table. The dinner was at once profuse, elegant, and splendid; never were three *lively* turtles, and a brace and a half of fat bucks, done more justice to; the table was three times covered with every possible dainty of the season. The desert of pines [pineapples], grapes, &c.&c. was particularly elegant and plentiful. // The entertainment was conducted by Mr.Pickwick of the White-Hart, who, being unlimited in the point of expence, gave one of the best dinners ever witnessed at Bath. His wines (particularly the burgundy and claret) merit equal praise. // An excellent band of vocal and instrumental players attended, who sang and played alternately all the evening. - Loyal and popular toasts were very numerous, and drunk with most animated bursts of applause. The fervency, however, of the noisy acclamations of *hip! hip! hip!* and the *three times three* loud huzzas, rather interfered with social harmony and pleasure.

*Bath Chronicle 14 Aug 1794*

## 182.  1794  Good eating at a lodging house

Having been a fortnight in our lodgings to day we discharged them... We have been most comfortably situated... we were supplied with excellent eatables at breakfast, even an elegant dinner, never less than two good dishes & a pudding or tart, generally a remove besides. Bread & butter with our tea in an evening & some cold meat at supper. Wine, tea, & sugar we provided for ourselves. Our candles were charged to us...

*Wilson, Shropshire Lady, p.100, entry from Katherine Plymley's Diary for 2 Oct 1794*

## 183.  1795  How to bring down prices at the market

The late rains (says a correspondent) will undoubtedly increase the crop of Pulse beyond example - and would the Public refrain from purchasing peas for a few days only, their price in our markets must inevitably be considerably under what will otherwise be demanded of them. Genteel Families giving orders to their servants to purchase such and such articles without limiting them to any sum, serve greatly to enhance the price of provisions here. - We again repeat that this city does not owe its prosperity more to the salubrious effects

of its waters than to the excellence and cheapness of its markets.
*Bath Herald 20 Jun 1795*

*184.  1795  No more baking on Sunday afternoons*
   THIS is to give Notice, That we the Master Bakers of this City, have
unanimously agreed... to discontinue the practice of Baking Meat, Pies, and
Puddings, in the Afternoon on the Sabbath Day - after Sunday, May 24, 1795.
// Therefore, those that are desirous to have such things baked on that day, are
particularly requested... to get it ready for the Oven between the hours of Ten
and Eleven in the Morning, that it may be done by One o'Clock.
*Bath Chronicle 28 May 1795*

*185.  1799  Sans Pareil bread and Sally Lunns*
   W.DALMER,  //  LARGE BREAD AND BISCUIT BAKER.  //  *Nearly
opposite Walcot Church, Bath,*  //  BEGS leave to offer to the Publick his
SANS PAREIL BREAD, which... is light and easy of digestion, keeps
remarkably moist, and he flatters himself will be found to exceed in quality
and quantity any Bread in the city. - For the better accommodating his
Customers, and to prevent the trouble and inconvenience of sending [customers'
servants to his shop], he purposes delivering it in any part of Bath.  //  N.B.
SALLY-LUNS, and other *Breakfast Cakes,* sent out warm every morning in a
portable oven, constructed for the purpose, which means the public will have
them in the greatest perfection.  //  SYDNEY TEA ROLLS, and different kinds
of BISCUITS, every afternoon.  //  *The Sally-Luns and Breakfast Cakes should
be cut with a sharp knife, and the butter either melted or cut in thin slices...*
Various kinds of BISCUITS, at the following prices: Oliver's, 3d. per dozen. -
Prince of Wales's, 3d. per dozen, made by no other person in Bath. - Nelson's
and Warren's, 4d. per dozen each.  //  WHEREAS a Baker's Boy, who was
seen to run towards Brock-street, made an Attempt last Night in the Circus, to
set on fire a Barrow constructed for the purpose of carrying the above Goods.
- A reward of *One Guinea* will be given, on conviction of the offender, by me
//  W.DALMER.
*Bath Chronicle 19 Dec 1799*

*186.  1800  Emergency food relief*
   After an unwearied attention of upwards of nine months to the relief of the
poor of this city, the PROVISION COMMITTEE closed their laudable efforts,
for the present, on Wednesday last. The liberality of the affluent has enabled
them to render essential service, during a most trying period, to hundreds of
distressed families, who have generally expressed their gratitude in the most
fervent terms; whilst a few others, we are sorry to say, daily received the bounty,
without being conscious of the benevolence extended to them. The provisions
which have been disposed of, soup, potatoes, and rice, were of the very best
quality that could be made or purchased -

Above sixty thousand Quarts of Soup,
Upwards of two hundred Barrels of Rice,
An equal number of Sacks of Potatoes,
And full 317 Tons weight of Coal.
Have been distributed at a price much under what those articles could be bought at, even in times of the greatest plenty.

*Bath Herald 27 Sep 1800*

## ASSEMBLIES, GAMBLING AND POPULAR DIVERSIONS

What made Bath a 'vortex of amusement' was not its sedater
pleasures - visiting one's acquaintance at the spa, sauntering
about town, doing the rounds of the shops, taking the country air
- but the public diversions. Most of the company frequenting the
spa in the earlier decades had an obsession with the gaming
tables - to the material profit of the assembly rooms where play
was chiefly but not exclusively centred. Acts of Parliament against
dice and the more notorious card games, and subsequently
against the type of roulette which superseded them, never
succeeded in banishing high-stake gambling from Bath even
though it was forced mostly out of public sight. Furthermore,
betting had endless other outlets in bowling matches, billiards,
cockfights, cudgel- and sword-bouts, bare-knuckle prize fights,
and of course horse-racing (timed for September to launch the
autumn season and held at the Claverton figure-of-eight course
until its transfer to Lansdown in 1784). Another popular event,
for working-class and farming people in particular, was the
Lansdown Fair on 10 August when the sale of cheese and
livestock was accompanied by sideshows, roundabouts, boxing
matches, and hearty drinking. Other customary but little-known
celebrations also punctuated the Bath calendar, including the
annual flower-growers' competition. For the fashionable world
on the other hand, the evening full-dress ball, with its special
rules of precedence and protocol, signalled the prestigious peak
in a hierarchy of public gatherings that also embraced theatre
visits and concerts (see next section), breakfastings, gala
occasions at the pleasure gardens, card assemblies, and the
excess of private parties and routs later in the century that
threatened to undermine 'official' entertainments. Blasé
observers might sometimes denigrate the balls, but at their best
they matched anything the metropolis and Court could offer and
set the standard of conduct for assemblies across the country. To

*youthful participants they conjured up images of sheer enchantment.*

## 187. 1700 Gambling fever

About five in the Evening we went to see a great match at Bowling; there was *Quality*, and Reverend *Doctors* of both Professions, Topping *Merchants*, Broken *Bankers*, Noted *Mercers*, Inns-of-Court *Rakes*, City *Beaus*, Stray'd *Prentices*, and *Dancing-Masters* in abundance. *Fly, fly, fly, fly;* said one: *Rub, rub, rub, rub*, cry'd another. *Ten Guineas to five, I uncover the* Jack, says a third. *Damn these Nice Fingers of mine*, cry'd my Lord, *I slipt my Bowl, and mistook the Bias*. Another swearing he knew the ground to an Inch, and would hold five Pound his Bowl came in. But in short the Citizens won the Courtiers Money, and the Courtiers Swore to be Reveng'd on their Wives and Daughters. // From hence we went to the *Groom-Porters*, where they were a Labouring like so many *Anchor-Smiths*, at the *Oak, Back-Gammon, Tick Tack, Irish, Basset*, and throwing of *Mains*. There was *Palming, Lodging, Loaded Dice, Levant*, and *Gammoning*, with all the speed imaginable; but the *Cornish Rook* was too hard for them all. The *Bristol Fair Sparks* had but a very bad bargain of it; and little occasion for Returns. *Bank-Bills* and *Exchequer-Notes*, were as Plenty as *Fops* at the *Chocolate Houses*, or *Pater-noster-Row*.
*Ward, Step to the Bath, pp.163-4*

## 188. 1709 A spectator to the diversions

This town is extream full of company, and highly entertained with Singing and Musick, by the famous Nicoleno & Valentinio, besides plays, baths, puppet-shows, ladder Danceing, &c., and some gameing, but I don't see much of that, high amongst the Ladies, being but few of Quality at this place now. I sometimes take the air on horseback, and other's[wise] am a gazeing Spectator to their diversions...
*Verney Letters, vol.1 pp.187-8, Lady Cave to Lord F[ermanagh?], Bath 3 Sep 1709*

## 189. 1711 Rich conduct

At the Bath there was a perticular set of company six men and six wemen that mett two or three times a week to dance, and won night all the candles was blown out, and the men was very rude, upon which Mr.Gore desired her to goe no more into that company, but she told him she would and if citizens pretend'd to marry Quality they must take it for their pains.
*Wentworth Papers, p.219, letter from Lady Strafford, 4 Dec 1711*

## 190. 1721 Lady Bristol watches the stakes rising

(30 Aug) ... company and diversions increase daily. I have playd four or five times at ombre, but now Mr.Herbert is gone to fetch his wife that entertainment is spoyld, and I have taken to hazard, which is very low, for most of the ladys play silver. Mr.Nash talks of several gamesters that are coming this week; fine ladys come in apace... but if they dont bring some fine men, they will pass their time sadly, for here is such a scarcity in this place they are ready to be devourd.

(13 Sep) ... for play there has not been temptation enough to make me transgress... which has made it very bad for Harrison [at the Assembly Rooms], for till last week... he has had very little to do, tho' he has the Groom Porter

[the Court gambling master] and several of the deep gamesters arrived. Banester
I hear lost £300 t'other night at Pharon [Pharaoh/Faro]...
   (20 Sep)   ... I threw fifteen mains [playing hazard] yesterday morning, and I
got but fivety pound by it... here is very deep play; Mr Stanup [Stanhope] has
improvd it since he came; Nash lost fivety pound a Saturday at Harrisons, and
as they say broke all the windows [kicked up a fuss?] according to custom.
*Hervey (J.), Letter-books, vol.2, letters 630, 643, 649, the Countess to the Earl of
Bristol, Bath 1721*

### 191. 1721 The busy round
   Now I must tell you the devertion of this place. Last Thursday we came here,
that night a play bespoke by Lady Harold, so we did not see anybody, next day
a ball where we was, and saw all ye great Ladys. My Brother Byng dansed
french danses with Mrs.Key, who has seven thousand a year settled on her, and
Country Danses with Lady Jemima Grey, Duke Kent's daughter, we left them
dansing and went with some Ladys to Lindseys where I sate down to G[u]inea
Comerce [a card game]... the pooll seven gineas and I very near wining of it. /
/ Saturday was a play bespoak by Lady Bristol. She asked us to go, as we
accordingly did, but first went to make a visit with my father to Lady ffranklin,
in the meantime came to see me the Dutches of Wharton, Lady Bristol, Lady
Lucy and more of our Ladys, which was a perticuler favour, they not being of
my acquaintance before, and what is very seldom done in these places. Sunday
to Church and to return all my Visits, then in to Harison's room, where was a
varst number of people... Gray ye poet lodges in our house so he has supt with
us.
*Osborn, Letters, pp.21-2, Sarah Osborn to her brother Robin Byng, Bath 30 Aug 1721*

### 192. 1725 Lady Lechmere's rashness
   The discreet and sober Lady Lechmere has lost such Furious summs at the
Bath that 'tis question'd whether all the sweetness that the Waters can put into
my Lord's blood can make him endure it, particularly £700 at one sitting, which
is aggravated with many astonishing Circumstances. This is... another
Demonstration of the latent Fire that lyes under cold Countenances. We wild
Girls allways make your prudent Wives and mothers.
*Montagu (Lady M.W.), Letters, vol.2 p.57, Lady Mary Wortley Montagu to her sister,
Sep 1725*

### 193. 1732 Not a place for peace and quiet
   There is nothing at Bath but gaiety and ludicrous diversions, so that even at
London there is much more privacy and retirement than at Bath, especially
since at Bath all people will be acquainted with one whether one will or no.
*Hearne, Reliquiae, vol.3 p.83, 31 Mar 1732*

### 194.  1737  Lord Chesterfield is almost bored to death
For my own part, were it not for the comfort of returning health, I believe I should hang myself. I am so weary of sauntering about without knowing what to do, or of playing at low play, which I hate, for the sake of avoiding deep play, which I love, that I look upon the remaining five weeks which I am to pass here as a sort of eternity...
*Stanhope, Letters, vol.2 letter 609, Lord Chesterfield to the Countess of Suffolk, Bath 14 Nov 1737*

### 195.  1744  Annual gathering of the carnation fanciers
On Friday last the FLORISTS FEAST was held at Mr.Edward Trueman's, the Sign of the George in Walcot-street: There were a great many fine Blossoms of Carnations produc'd; the Silver Spurs were won by Mr.William Harding, and the Gold Ring by Mr.George Allen, both of this City; the Ordinaries and Extraordinaries by Mr.Holdstock, of Walcot. - There was a very elegant Entertainment [meal] provided; and the whole was conducted with good Order and Decorum.
*Bath Journal 30 Jul 1744*

### 196.  1750  Teaching them young
A fine Boy of about nine Years of Age, whom every Body carressed and admired for his Sprightiness and Vivacity, had this Morning half a Crown given him by a Gentleman in the Rooms; the little Rogue, as soon as he received it, with a Bow, ran to the EO Table [a game like roulette], and staked Sixpence, and won; and immediately afterwards another one with the same good Fortune. This so transported him, that he called for a Chair, and sat down, with Hopes of getting a great deal of Money: While this was doing, his Mamma came up, and seeing the pretty Infant so innocently engaged, she asked him what Luck he had. O dear Mama, says he, I have won two Sixpences, and I sit here quite comfortably... Ay, my Dear, says she, you are better in a Room, you don't wear your Breeches out so fast, and you can't get so much Cold: you have better Luck than I; be sure you mind how you play, for I must go to my Party at the other End of the Room; and when it is Dinner Time, I will call on you to go home.
*Narrative of What Passed, pp.3-4*

### 197.  1760  Manly exercises
The Backsword-Playing on Monday and Tuesday last afforded tolerable good Diversion to the Spectators; some of the Militia-Men for this County were Sharers in the Prizes each Day, and their Skill and Dexterity in that noble Science and manly Exercise were applauded by all present. The Heroes of the Fist, likewise, made no small Part of each Day's Diversion, there being several Boxing Matches.
*Bath Journal 28 Jul 1760*

### 198. 1763 An out-of-town cockfight
THERE will be a Cock Match fought at Widcombe near Bath, known by the Name of Mount Pleasant. To shew Thirty one Cocks on each Side in the Main, for four Guineas a Battle, and forty Guineas the odd Battle. The Gentlemen of Wiltshire, and Gloucestershire, against the Gentlemen of Somersetshire. To weigh on Saturday the second Day of April, and fight the Monday and Tuesday following. FEEDERS [i.e. gamecock rearers] TIDLY and BUTT against RUSS.
*Bath Chronicle 31 Mar 1763*

### 199. 1771 Affairs at the new Upper Assembly Rooms
Standing under one of the chandeliers with Gainsborough, admiring the figures which the ingenious Committee [have] had drawn [on the window blinds?] by Garoy, the *landscape* painter, we narrowly escaped having our crowns cracked by a branch falling out of one of the chandeliers: it was taken little notice of by the company; but the Committee met upon it the next morning, and that the public might not be alarmed by it... [put an] advertisement in the paper, which had so good an effect, that the next night they had not two hundred people in the room... The Committee go on pretty amicably, considering there are seven or eight of them; - a little of 'you lie,' and 'you lie;' and 'damme, I'm a gentleman;' and 'damme, I'll tell guineas with you;' - 'take care of your nose;' 'don't come within reach of my fist;' and such trifles as that; but not a word of gunpowder [duelling?] since their first meeting. The subscription yesterday was - to the Balls 220 - Concerts 261 - for walking in the rooms, 290 ladies at 5s. each, and 237 gentleman at 10s.6d. each; so as yet, you see, they go on well... though after their novelty is over, I cannot think they will succeed any way equal to their expectations. They have made an odd regulation, for every person to pay sixpence for their tea at the door, which, I think, must appear strange and mean to a man of fashion at his entering so elegant a room...They have, however, got themselves the title of the Sixpenny Committee from it... The lower rooms [Gyde's] have only 70 to the balls, but about 400 for walking.
*Garrick, Private Correspondence, vol.1 pp.455-6, John Palmer to David Garrick, Bath [Oct 1771]*

### 200. 1776 Dressing up for the minuets
The Master of the Ceremonies begs leave to remind the Ladies who chuse to dance Minuets at the Dress-Balls, that a suit of cloaths, or a full-trimmed negligès with lappets and hoops, are the only dresses proper for the occasion; that all other fancy dresses, such as polonèse, French night-gown, &c. however elegant, are not sufficient dresses, and are highly improper to be worn with lappets. // He likewise begs leave to request the parents of young ladies, who are in robe coats, that their cloaths be full trimmed, and to be worn with a hoop; all other fancy dresses are not proper for a minuet at the dress balls at Bath. // He further begs leave to remind those Gentlemen who chuse to dance minuets, that a suit of full-trimmed cloaths, with their hair or wig dressed with

a bag, is the only dress proper for a minuet, except the military gentlemen of
the navy and army, who are desired to wear their hair or wig en queue with
their uniforms; that all other fancy dresses, with a flash sleeve or pocket, turn-
down cape, &c. are not proper dresses for the occasion. - And as it is highly
necessary to keep up a propriety of dress, and not to introduce any new fashion
that may in the smallest degree lower the elegance of the Assembly, to the
great disadvantage of the Ladies in particular, Mr.Wade flatters himself that no
person can, or ought to be displeased, at not dancing a minuet who do not
comply with the established Rules of the Assembly.
*Bath Chronicle 28 Nov 1776*

### 201.  1777  Racegoers flock to Claverton Down

We have the pleasure to assure our polite readers and the Lovers of the Turf,
that our Races have not been honoured (since their first institution) with such
a numerous and brilliant appearance of Company as at this time. - It is computed
that about 800 carriages, and not less than 20,000 persons on horseback and a-
foot, were on the Down yesterday, when, it was generally allowed, the sport
was equal to any ever seen on a race-course in one day.
*Bath Chronicle 18 Sep 1777*

### 202.  1778  A young curate in raptures at the Upper Rooms

... Miss Grenville, Miss Woodley, Miss Singleton, Miss Moore, Miss Balch,
Mrs Weld, Mrs Powis, exhibited such a profusion of charms that had the Idoean
Sheppard [the mythological Paris] been dispatch'd here to decide the Palm of
Beauty betwixt them he wd have been far more puzzel'd, I think, which to
present the Apple to than when he had the great honour as well as satisfaction
of unpetticoating the Celestials. Upon the exactest Calculation that cd be got
there were present upwards of a Thousand; I need not describe... the agreeable
feelings excited in a juvenile Mind by seeing such a Number of beautiful,
well-drest Females in a Spacious Apartment superbly and elegantly lighted up
with the addition of Musick, &c; Every Nerve I had seem'd to be fresh strung
on the Occasion, and I was so elated with joy that I cd hardly persuade myself
that I mov'd in no higher character than that of a poor Country Curate. It brought
to my mind some of the Visionary Scenes in the Arabian Nights Entertainments...
*WRO, 1915/252, Charles Wade to Henry William Fitch, Bath 15 Feb 1778*

### 203.  1779  An encounter with one's great aunt

Really Mrs.Rowney seemed so glad to see me... I was playing Commerce in
the Rooms last week & she came to the Table & accosted me, with - What-e
now I suppose you are playing very high? & upon being told it was only half
Guinea's - Well to be sure! that is very low indeed! beant it very dull to you to
play so low? Well to be sure Who would have thought of your playing half
Guineas, why we little people play that sometimes!
*Elwin, Noels and Milbankes, p.132, Judith Milbanke to her aunt Mary Noel, Bath 13
Jan 1779*

### 204. 1780 The poetic contests at Batheaston Villa

Sir John [Miller] came to request I would write an Elegy on the Death of Capt Cook, that being the Subject for the next Vase day at Batheaston... He tells me they had 70 carriages there last 5th day. It must cost him no small matter to entertain such a Company once a fortnight for 9 months with Chocolate & Sweetmeats. He says however that write or not I must go, and as there will doubtless be some excellent peices on the death of that great Circumnavigator, I intend to make one of the Company on the Occasion.

*BCL, MS B920, Edmund Rack, A Disultory Journal of Events... at Bath, entry for 29 Jan 1780*

### 205. 1784 The racing moves to Lansdown

... we find, that a very excellent Course is marked out on Lansdown for our Races, and that good sport is expected. This alteration has long been wished for by the gentlemen who generally send their horses here, as they allow there is not a finer turf in the kingdom for running in all seasons, than that on Lansdown - whilst the Claverton course in dry weather, from being so near the rock, was very prejudicial to the horses; it is likewise much nearer and more convenient to the gentlemen of Bristol, Gloucestershire, &c. The continuance of the races is certainly of great consequence to the city, as it in some measure marks a commencement to our season and part of it's amusements, which for some years past have gradually been later and later, and [it] occasions the Theatre being opened a month sooner than otherwise it could possibly be.

*Bath Chronicle 2 Sep 1784*

### 206. 1790 Gala night at the pleasure gardens

Friday being the anniversary of his Majesty's birth-day... in the evening there was an excellent Concert of Musick, and a superb display of Fire-Works at Spring-Gardens, which were brilliantly illuminated on the occasion, and were honoured with the presence of above 2000 persons, among whom were most of the principal Gentry of the city and neighbourhood. // During the interval of the performance... some valuable musical instruments [flutes and oboes], and the whole of the music to the *Banish'd Muse...* were stolen from the orchestra. The dilemma of the performers, the mark'd disapprobation and the doubts expressed by the company on account of this odd theft, occasioned a scene of laughable confusion, from which the inimitable fire-works of Sig.Invetto afforded a pleasing relief.

*Bath Chronicle 10 Jun 1790*

### 207. 1791 Sharpers' paradise

There is perhaps no part of the world, setting aside the infernal purlieus of St James's, where gaming is carried to so high a pitch as at Bath. This is owing, in great measure, to that swarm of daemons, who under the general name of *black-legs*, or *sharpers*, infest all places of public amusement. In Bath one is never secure from the insidious designs of these indefatigable harpies. They infest the rooms, the promenades, nay, inconsistent as it may seem, the very churches

are not free from the profanation of these vermin... What is our police? Where
are our magistrates?... why sleeps the rod of justice? when scoundrels with
white hairs, I had almost said venerable villains, are suffered to patrole our
streets, arm in arm with the flower of our nobility, whom they pillage at their
leisure, under the assumed and specious mask of gentlemen.
*Clarke, Tour in 1791, p.147*

### 208.  1792  Manoeuvres at the ball

... by dinner time Yesterday, your humble Servant as likewise... the other
Ladies, were equipped, not to say, made as smart as possible, for the Ball; I
was dressed the same as for the Concert, except that I wore the Lawn, which
was much admired, instead of my Muslin Jacket, & petticoat. - at length a little
past Seven arrived, we *set Sail*, were soon safe landed, at the upper Rooms. by
that time I felt all impatience to be in the Ball Room, & was picturing to myself
all the charms I could concieve... such a Place to have; when we entered it, I
was fully gratified, for to be sure I never [saw] so brilliant an assembly. it was
amazingly crouded although the minuets had not begun; so much so, that we
found some difficulty to get seats - I was very much entertained with the bad
minuet-dancers, especially with a Mr.*Badcock* who was obliged to stand up
with seven, or eight Ladies successively, to the great diversion of the Spectators.
I believe there were twenty minuets which was rather tiresome, but at last the
Country dances began, there was great humming, & hawing whether or no I
should dance... & I declared... that I should like to dance if I could get some
mighty *smart* partner, but that at any rate I should like to wait till after Tea;
when we went into the Tea room, we could not get a Table, so they agreed to go
to cards, till some of the People returned into the Ball Room... while at Cards
Mrs Leigh... sent some good Man, to look for some dapper little personage for
me, & indeed he succeeded very well, for he soon brought us, a Young *Gem'mon*
of about *fifteen*... [However] the pride of the Old Aunts was up at the Idea of
my making my first Essay with a... Boy...[and in the end] your poor little picksy
was obliged to content herself without cutting cappers... but the next time I go
to a Ball now that I know the Manoeuvres of it, I shall get them to look out for
a partner earlier in the Evening, & then I shall have a better chance.
*BCL, AL 2388, Elizabeth Canning to her mother, Bath 18-21 Dec 1792*

### 209.  1793  The battles of Lansdown

On Monday the annual return of the mart of business and pleasure,
LANSDOWN FAIR, was held at the usual place, about three miles from this
city. The day proving uncommonly fine, the crouds that attended from the
neighbouring country were immense... The usual diversions of bowling, fidling,
raree shews, wild *beastesses*, with Punch and all his motley train, which the
proprietor swore he was cursedly hurt to exhibit for a penny, were as conspicuous
and as troublesome as on any former occasion. To keep up the charter of the
place there were a great number 'of battles bravely, hardly fought.' The spirit
of the great Sir beville Grenville [Royalist officer mortally wounded here, 1643],
annually arising on this spot, inspires the surrounding youths with ferocious

courage. Amongst these, scarcely any were worthy of particular notice but
one, betwixt a long celebrated Hero of the fist, and a hardy Vintner of this city
[his victor]...
*Bath Herald 17 Aug 1793*

### 210. *1797 Professional gamblers blight the assembly rooms*
In the Reign of the IMMORTAL NASH, it was looked on as a sort of Heresy
to have Routs or Parties which clashed with the Public Amusements. Such
things are now become frequent, and fashionable. The Rooms which used to
be open every Evening for Cards and Conversation are shut up; and the
Gentlemen who frequented them, have formed themselves into private Clubs.
// ... The Ostensible Reason given for quitting the Public Rooms is, that improper
Company attended there. - In all *Public Places* it is difficult to draw a line of
Exclusion. The Company complained of are *Gentlemen* who labour incessantly
in their *Vocation of Betting*, and who, by a marked assiduity, can calculate the
chances to a Fraction, when they see how the simple Students in Whist and
*Masters of Arts* are combined as Partners. // As the objectionable Company
does not attend on *Public Nights*, suppose the Card-Room was open to the
Public on those Nights only; and that the Club had the exclusive use of it at all
other times. Such a Regulation would satisfy every Gentleman who plays for
*Amusement*. In the Coffee-Room there is no need of being guarded against any
notorious practices. It is not in such places that the *Chevalier d' Industrie* attends
to reap his Harvest.
*Bath Herald 6 May 1797, letter from 'A Well-Wisher to Bath'*

### 211. *1799 Fate of the billiards champion*
The Dutch Gentleman, whose play success in this city has been the subject of
much comment, was, a few days since, taken into custody under the Alien Bill,
to be sent out of the country. He was not, as has been stated, the marker at a
billiard-table at Hamburgh, but an Officer in the Dutch army previous to the
Revolution; he is said to be the best billiard-player in Europe.
*Bath Chronicle 9 May 1799*

### 212. *1800 Giddy times*
We are getting fast into such Follies *here* and the Fancy of the Winter has
been to stop the Musick when the Public Balls are over, and they dare not Play
another moment at the Rooms - to take the whole Orchestra away from the
Door, and carrying them off, make them Subservient to a private Company at
some fine House till Breakfast Time next morning - When at sober Bath - The
Town for Invalides, for Green Misses just coming into the World, and Grey
Veterans just going out of it - such Tricks are played - What does your Ladyship
think is doing at the Metropolis?
*Piozzi, Letters, vol.3 p.168, Hester Lynch Piozzi to Lady Williams, Bath 24 Feb 1800*

# THEATRE AND MUSIC

*Support for the Bath stage came initially from wealthy patrons staying at Bath who commanded special performances for themselves and their friends. But while regular seasons of plays eventually became the norm, the actual theatres - first on the Hospital site, then in Kingsmead Street and the basement of one of the assembly rooms - were too small as yet to generate enough income from takings to maintain an adequate company of players. It is true they staged The Beggars' Opera in 1728 with the author's own assistance, and in 1733 received lavish new costumes in the form of royal cast-offs, yet live drama at Bath still made little more noise than 'puppet' (i.e. marionette) shows. In 1750, however, the Orchard Street Theatre opened and, after battling seven years against its rebuilt rival at Simpson's Assembly Rooms, finally bought the latter out. Under the Palmers' control and more capable management it now went from strength to strength. It secured the vital royal patent in 1768, remodelled its premises, and then in 1779 widened its operation to play alternately at Bristol, thus extending the season and perhaps doubling audiences. Already the foremost theatre outside London, it nurtured not only acting talent but dramatists too, with a repertory that ranged from Shakespeare to the sensational melodrama of the 1790s. Music meanwhile followed a similar trajectory of improvement, only financed for the most part through subscription rather than the box office. The resident musicians were at first divided between the city band (or 'waits'), who serenaded the visitors for tips, and Nash's band, paid out of subscriptions, who played at the Pump Room and balls. Higher flights of music were mostly left to guest performers, often Italian virtuosi like Geminiani (at Bath in 1721) and singers from the London opera. The second half of the century brought a transformation in musical standards and far more vigorous concert promotion, especially in the 1760s and 1770s, under the direction of Thomas Linley, and again in the last two decades when the matchless Rauzzini was able to call on some of the best singers and instrumentalists in Europe. Bath produced some notable musical figures of its own, including the keyboard composer and Abbey Church organist Thomas Chilcot, who helped initiate the great charity oratorios, and the younger Linleys - the stunning soprano Elizabeth and the violinist Thomas, friend of Mozart. If the city's record in church music was generally indifferent (with better singing to be heard at the Huntingdon Chapel than at the Abbey Church), there was more to boast of in the remarkable, but socially exclusive, male-voiced catch- and glee-clubs of the 1780s and 1790s.*

*213. 1709 The marionette master*
... a Person who keeps a Puppet-Show in the Town of *Bath*... Mr. *Powell*...
but... I can look beyond his Wires, and know very well the whole Trick of his
Art, and that it is only by these Wires that the Eye of the Spectator is cheated,
and hinder'd from seeing that there is a Thread on one of *Punch*'s Chops,
which draws it up, and lets it fall at the Discretion of the said *Powell*, who
stands behind and plays him, and makes him speak sawcily of his Betters.
*The Tatler no.44, 21 Jul 1709*

*214. 1716 Whigs at the theatre*
Went to the play, where Mrs.Marshall and sister were gone before in chairs. It
was a play called *Love Makes a Man* [by Colley Cibber]. The plot and dialogue
of the play put me into a very grave humour and I found myself more in love
with Mrs.Marshall than ever. There were one or two of the low comic parts
acted pretty tolerably well but the rest were acted very ill. But besides this
there was acted the *Cobbler of Preston* [by Christopher Bullock], which was
diverting enough but the whole diversion lasted so long that it tired us. The
play was bespoke by Mrs.Walpole and was very much crowded and the Whig
parts of the first [play were] clapped very much.
*Ryder, Diary, p.241, entry for 23 May 1716*

*215. 1718-21 Private music making: Francesco Geminiani and others*
(26 Sep 1718) I was called in to Mr Harington at Kelston. I got Mr.Du Burg
[Matthew Dubourg, Geminiani's pupil], Mr Shojan, Mr Walter, and Mr David
Baswiwaldt, to go with me. We returned to Bath in the Evening; and I entertained
them with 3 Fowles and Wine in the great new Dining-Room at the 3 Tuns
where I had a Performance of Musick by these extraordinary Hands.
   (7 Oct 1721) Mr Ash went with us to Bath, & introduc'd us into the Company
of Geminiani, (at Mr.Stagg's House) [a dancing master], & he [i.e. Geminiani]
entertain'd us with the utmost Civility as well as his wonderful Hand on the
Violin.
*Morris, Diary, pp.64 and 88*

*216. 1728 John Gay directs* **The Beggar's Opera** *in person*
We hear from the *Bath*, That last Week all the Quality were at the Play-House,
to hear the Rehearsal of the *Beggars-Opera*, collected a handsome Sum and
presented the Actors with [it]: And that on *Monday* and *Wednesday* last,
notwithstanding the Pit and Boxes were laid together, they were so full, that
they turn'd away as many as they took in: 'Tis evident, they were pleas'd with
the Performance, because there was a Purse of Gold made up at the *Pump-
house*, and presented to *Lucy Locket*, and *Polly Peachum*, to buy each of them
a new Dress in which they are each to perform their Part this Evening. We hear
also, that they are to come to Act the said *Opera* in the Long-Room near the
*Hot-Well* [at Bristol], on Tuesday next. // We don't indeed much wonder at
their performing of it well, when we hear that Mr.GAY hath taken so much
Pains to instruct them... [he being] the Author of that Humourous Piece.
*Farley's Bristol Newspaper 11 May 1728*

## 217.  1733  Costumed from royal cast-offs

Our Comedians have receiv'd from Mrs.Mooring in London, Dress-maker to the Court and Theatres, (with which they intend to open this Season at Mrs.Hayes's) four Suits of Men's rich Cloaths, and three of Women's, let off by the Royal Family, with a new Sett of Roman Shapes, and a *Falstaff*'s Dress made by her; so that they may be justly said to have Stock far superior to any in England out of London, and for Quantity to equal any of the Houses.
*Gloucester Journal 23 Jan 1733*

## 218.  1733  The civic musicians re-established

Agreed that the City Waits, now established by this Corporation, whose business is to attend the Corporation on all occasions shall have four Guineas p.ann. for their trouble.
*BRO, Bath Council Minutes, 26 Mar 1733*

## 219.  1740  Organ prelude

Yesterday [19 Feb] the new Organ, made by Mr.Jordan, for the Abbey Church, (which is a very fine Instrument) was open'd with great Solemnity. An excellent Sermon was preach'd on the Occasion by the Rev.Dr.Coney, Rector: There was a great Number of Instruments to accompany the Organ, and two Anthems were sung; the Musick was compos'd by Mr.Chilcot, Organist of the Abbey...
*Gloucester Journal 26 Feb 1740*

## 220.  1747  Proposal for a theatre worthy of Bath

*Theatrical Performances*, when conducted with Decency and Regularity, have been always esteem'd the most rational Amusement, by the Polite and Thinking Part of Mankind: - Strangers, therefore, must be greatly surpriz'd, to find at BATH Entertainments of this Sort in no better Perfection than they are; as it is a Place... where might reasonably be expected (next to *London*) the best Theatre in *England*. // The present *Play-House*, or rather *Play-Room*, is so small and incommodious, that 'tis almost impossible to have Things better done in it than they are. The Profits arising from the Performance, as now conducted, will not support a larger, or better, Company of Actors: And nothing can be more disagreeable, than for Persons of the *first Quality*, and those of the *lowest Rank*, to be seated on the same Bench together... // To remedy this, and for the better Entertainment of the Quality, it is humbly proposed to erect a Regular, Commodious THEATRE, on the most convenient Spot of Ground that can be got; to be managed by Mr.HIPPISLEY, (who for many Years has been a Performer in *London*) and Others; and to add such a sufficient Number of good Performers to the present Company, as will (it is hoped) never fail of giving Pleasure and Satisfaction to the most judicious Audience, and greatly contribute to rendering BATH the most *agreeable Place* in the *Kingdom*.
*Bath Journal 30 Nov 1747*

### 221. 1757 The trials of an actor-manager: Henry Brown complains

It is now near six Years that I have, through Variety of (exceeding bad) Fortune, through the Struggles of a most cancorous Opposition, and *unparalleled*, as well as *unprecedented* Series of cruel Treatment, made my utmost Efforts to administer to your Pleasures as an Actor, to gain a (very precarious) Subsistence as a Man, and to live an inoffensive Member of Society, in this City of Bath... Has any Man, I mean any Actor... more studiously *endeavoured* to please? Has anyone more intensely laboured to give Satisfaction in that Variety of Characters I have been forced to attempt; a Variety, I may averr, that no other Man ever was reduced to, and required to *top* them all? - As a manager what have I done? Have I not regularly built upon the Plan I had long drawn of rescuing my Stage from Ribaldry, Profaneness, and Obscenity? Has there in the whole Course of my Management, or while I had Influence before I managed, a single Scene been admitted where a modest Woman has Occasion to hold up her Fan, or the gravest of Divines to have sat uneasy upon his Seat? These, I presume, are not Reasons that any Gentleman, and much less a Lady, will care to give for persecuting and exploding me: And as to the Catalogue of Plays, I would gladly submit it to public Examination, both in Choice and Number, though I must confess the *Chances*, the *Double Dealer* or the *Relapse* will not be found in it. - This, however, I will venture to affirm, that no Stage before has seen two new Plays brought on, in one Week, both admitted to be *tolerably well* performed, and I hope no Stage hereafter will see them performed to empty Boxes, and half Charges of the House.

*Bath Advertiser 23 Apr 1757, letter from Henry Brown*

### 222. 1759 How Robert Dodsley's Cleone was received

I need not tell you that it was represented to a *crowded* audience - & I think the principal parts were well perform'd... I fixed myself ... in the Centre of the Pitt - in the midst of young Milliners & Abigails [servants] - where [I] had the pleasure of observing the Effect of your Genius upon undisguis'd humanity - Neither indeed was there a young or handsome face in the Boxes but what... [being] conceal'd with an handkerchief - Shew'd that the... [fair] Lady either *was* deeply affected - or was conscious that she *ought* to be so - I had the satisfaction of silencing (with a single Hiss) one or two fellows who... were clamorously rallying Mrs Br—ias & two or three more very pretty women upon their amiable Sensibility...

*Dodsley, Correspondence, Richard Graves to Robert Dodsley, Bath 27 Mar 1759*

### 223. 1767 Audience power

Last Monday night a most remarkable contest happen'd at our theatre, between the audience and the manager [John Arthur]; the former of whom unanimously insisted on Mr.Reddish's performing the character of Richard [in *Richard III*], in the room of Mr.Sherriffe, whose name was in the bills. As soon as the curtain drew up, the manager was call'd for; who, refusing to comply with their demand, was at last oblig'd to make an hasty retreat; and after repeated efforts made not

to consent, (which kept the house an hour in suspence) the point was carried in favour of the town, and the play received, by a numerous audience, with universal applause.
*Bath Chronicle 19 Feb 1767*

### 224. 1770? Sheridan discovers the musical Linleys
... there is a Mr.Linley here, a music master, who has a daughter that sings like an angel; perhaps you may have heard of her: the Father too sings in a particular natural stile, likewise a little daughter who has been at London. The public concerts do not begin 'till after Xtmas; but we heard them at a priv[a]te one in Mr.L[in]ley's hous[e].
*Sheridan (R.B.), Letters, vol.1 pp.19-20, R.B.Sheridan to Elizabeth Angelo, Bath 13 Oct 1770?*

### 225. 1773 The wrong Rishton attends the concert
I have been vastly disappointed in not going to Fischer's concert to-night. I suppose all Bath will be there, for it is the last time the eldest Linley [Elizabeth] sings at Bath, she is engaged for the oratorios [at Covent Garden] - but Rishton who is rather more exact about dress than I am, can't think of my appearing... [He] wanted me to buy a suit of mignionet linnen fringed for the second mourning - but my economy prevaild over that, and as he was unwilling I should appear else, I gave up the dear Fischer... [but] Rishton is gone... [though] fischer's hautboy [oboe] has the same merit with him the Bagpipes or Jews' trump might.
*Burney (F.), Early Diary, vol.1 p.193, Mary Rishton to Fanny Burney, Bath [April?] 1773*

### 226. 1774 The former city musicians in disgrace
ORDERS have been sent by authority to the Musicians, or City Waits to desist from playing at Lodging-houses, to the great disturbance of the sick and others who resort to this place. - And these orders having been disobey'd, *Notice is hereby given*, that information against them, either as vagrants or extortioners, will be received by the Magistrates at the Town-Hall any Monday morning at eleven o'clock.
*Bath Chronicle 15 Dec 1774*

### 227. 1775 First-night nerves
Well the great day at Bath is over, you guess I allude to the Captive [Hannah More's play *The Inflexible Captive*], we went to see it a party of fifteen and met H[annah] there, who spent the three preceding days with our very, very great friend and favourite David Garrick. She refused going with them to the play and author-like had a place behind the scenes. Never were mortals in such trepidation as the performers. Poor Regulus *alias* Henderson was near fainting to play so great a part, being the original in it, before one of the most Brilliant Audiences that were ever assembled there, but that was nothing to Garrick and the author. She forgot her anxiety for the piece in the pains she took to exhilerate

the spirits of the actors. The whole piece was performed beyond what we could have expected, for our expectation was very mediocre indeed... Mrs.Macaulay [the historian] graced it with her presence, all the world of Dukes, Lords, and Barons were there. I sat next a Duke and a Lord and they all expressed their highest approbation... A shout continued for some minutes after the curtain dropt which is the highest mark of distinction that can be paid to an author.

*Bath Herald 6 Mar 1909, Sarah More to Mrs Gwatkin, Bath 18 Apr 1775, quoted by A.M.Broadley*

### 228.  1775  The Orchard Street Theatre remodelled

The House is in every repect highly improved both in convenience and beauty. The considerable enlargement of it backwards has enabled it to accommodate more Company... The heat formerly so much complained of will be... prevented... by a new Ventilator erected at the top of the building: this will supply a quantity of fresh air equally diffus'd over the whole house... In cold weather it will I suppose be kept close shut... // The House is likewise now furnished with a large lobby or waiting room, and proper retiring rooms; the Pit is rose higher, and the space betwixt the seats enlarg'd and made more convenient; the Dome that was so injurious in many parts of the Theatre both to the sight and hearing, and its furniture of Apollo and the Muses, so preposterously mix'd with the Gothic architecture, is remov'd. The Grecian Orders are now introduc'd, so much more proper to a Theatre than the Gothic. The Stage itself appears much enlarg'd, and the whole building improv'd in such a manner that not only the Performers, but the Audience appear to much greater advantage.

*Bath Journal 25 Sep 1775, letter from 'An Old Inhabitant'*

### 229.  1776  Another talented Linley: the violinist Thomas

If you take a Master for the Violin, during your Residence at Bath, I wd recommend to you Mr Linley Junior, who is a Charming Performer, and of a Good School, having been under Nardini, Tartini's best Scholar, in Italy, a considerable Time. I therefore Enclose a Letter to him upon a supposition that he is by this Time returned to Bath, after leading at the oratorio in Drury Lane & at 2 or three Hospitals...

*Burney (C.), Letters, vol.1 p.207, Charles Burney to Brigg Fountaine, 5 Apr 1776*

### 230.  1779  The impact of Siddons and Sheridan

... I will venture to add a paragraph relative to our stage matters; and it is only to do justice to an excellent actress which has appeared here this season, (a Mrs. Siddons,) who I really think is as much mistress of her business as any female I ever saw... and I declare my opinion of her to be all that my ideas can reach... Her Portia, Belvidera, and other pathetic parts in tragedy, are, I think, exquisitely fine... // Palmer [the theatre manager] goes on bravely. I wish, however, Sheridan would write no more, for nothing now will go down [i.e. succeed] but 'School for Scandal' and 'Duenna'.

*Garrick, Private Correspondence, vol.2 p.331, John Taylor to David Garrick, Bath 14 Jan 1779*

### 231. 1779 A scintillating musical occasion

Had a Ticket sent me for the Concert this Evening at the New Rooms... went thither, and found the most brilliant Assembly my Eyes ever beheld. The Elegance of the room, illuminated with 480 wax Candles, the prismatic Colours of the Lustres [chandeliers], the blaze of Jewels, and the inconceivable Harmony of near 40 Musicians some of whom are the finest hands in Europe, added to the rich attire of about 800 Gentlemen and Ladies, was, altogether, a scene of which no person who never saw it can form any adequate Idea. - It began at half past 6 & ended at 10. The highest decorum was observd throughout the whole. The Concertos by [Franz] La Motte, & [J.C.] Fischer surpass all discription. On the violin and obeo [oboe] they are not equalld by any performer in Europe... Rauzina [Venanzio Rauzzini] is a *Eunich* & has a fine shrill Pipe... Nearly 60 of the Nobility were present & several foreigners of Distinction.

*BCL , MS B920, Edmund Rack, A Disultory Journal of Events at Bath, entry for 29 Dec 1779*

### 232. 1789 Betsy Sheridan opts for the 'green boxes'

I have taken two places in the Green Boxes for tonight to see Miss Wallace [i.e. Wallis, a new actress]... I hear her performance well spoken of. I prefer this mode of going as by avoiding the expence of dress and chair Hire it makes our freedom of the Theatre [free admittance] a real convenience... // *Wednesday Morng* - I was too late for the post yesterday, so can tell you about Miss Wallace. Upon the whole we liked her very well. Her face does not appear handsome on the Stage, but her figure is very good and her deportment really Ellegant... The Play was the *Conscious Lovers* [by Richard Steele] which you know is dull enough but the Performers appear'd to me as good as we see any where. The Theatre is very pretty and the green Boxes particularly convenient, as there are backs to the Seats which rise almost as high as your head so that the people behind are not leaning on your Shoulders, and the seats are sufficiently raised to allow every one to see.

*Sheridan (E.), Journal, pp.187-8, entry for 1-2 Dec 1789*

### 233. 1789 A young black musician makes a hit

The amateurs of music in this city received on Saturday last at the New Rooms the highest treat imaginable from the exquisite performance of Master Bridgtower, whose taste and execution on the violin is equal, perhaps superior to the best professor of the present or any former day. The Concert Room, Recesses and Gallery were thronged with the very best of company, and scores went away without being able to procure a hearing. Those who had that happiness were enraptured with the astonishing abilities of this wonderful Child - for he is but ten years old. He is a Mulatto, the Grandson, it is said, of an African Prince. - The greatest attention and respect was paid by the Nobility and Gentry present to his elegant Father, who is one of the most accomplished men in Europe, conversing with fluency & charming address in its several languages.

*Bath Journal 7 Dec 1789*

*234. c.1790? For three male voices: a Catch Club favourite*

I Cannot sing this Catch, I shall laugh,
  O Lord, I shall laugh, ha! ha! ha!
For shame, you silly calf,
  Don't ye laugh, ha! ha! ha!
You will not sing it half,
  But make us all to laugh, ha! ha! ha!
Look at his face, ha! ha! ha!
  When he sings the bass, ha! ha! ha!

*Selection of Catches, Glees, etc., Dr Henry Harington, 'Laughing catch' [complete text], c.1790?*

**235. 1796 Poor singing at the Abbey Church**
PERMIT me... to express my regret that more attention is not paid to the Musical Part of Divine Service in the Abbey Church... where, instead of those elevated Strains which inspire Devotion, the mind is fatigued by a dull Monotony disgusting to the musical ear... I cannot conceive from whence such neglect... arises in an Edifice so well calculated for the effect of Sound, especially as the Parish possesses an EXCELLENT INSTRUMENT, A GOOD ORGANIST, and a CAPITAL BASS VOICE IN THEIR CLERK - a *few* Choristers only are wanting... instead of the present unmeaning Strains of squalling Boys, who are no sooner brought to a little knowledge of singing than they are necessarily put out of the School [i.e. the Bluecoat Charity School, traditional source of the choir] as Apprentices - let it be remembered that such a Choir... will aid the GREAT CAUSE of the CHRISTIAN RELIGION.
*Bath Herald 3 Sep 1796, letter from 'Z'*

**236. c.1796 The tenor Michael Kelly remembers Rauzzini**
On our way to Plymouth, we passed a few very agreeable days at Bath, with my old friend and master Rauzzini... Every thing at Pyramid (the name of his residence) [i.e. Perrymead] breathed content and happiness; professional people, of all descriptions, were welcome to his hospitable table, which was always supplied with the best viands, and choicest wines. // While we were staying with him, Madame Mara and Signora Storace [singers] were also his inmates, and every evening we had music of the best sort; Rauzzini himself presiding at the piano-forte, and singing occasionally. He had lost the soprano part of his voice, but his lower contra altro tones were very fine, and his taste was exquisite; he was also a delightful composer... // [At Bath he was] beloved and respected by the inhabitants and visitors... He had a great deal of teaching, which, added to the profits of his performances, enabled him to entertain his friends in the hospitable manner he did. The expences of those performances were to him comparatively small, as it was almost an article of faith among the profession to give their services free. I have known Mrs.Billington [singer] renounce many

profitable engagements in London, when Rauzzini has required the aid of her
talents, and at her own expense, travel to Bath, and back to London, as fast as
four horses could carry her, without accepting the most trifling remuneration.
The singers at the King's Theatre [Haymarket], were always allowed by the
proprietors to give him their gratuitous assistance.
*Kelly, Reminiscences, vol.2 pp.118-20*

*237. 1798 Melodramatics:* **The Castle Spectre** *staged at Bath*
To the prodigious applause with which this piece was received, if we add its
*hysterical effects* on several ladies, it must be considered as a *chef d' oeuvre* in
its way. Nothing, at one period of the play, was to be heard but hysterical
affections in the boxes, nothing to be seen but delicate ladies crying and fainting,
and nothing to be smelt but *hartshorn* and *thieves vinegar* [restorants]; with
which articles it would not be amiss if the orange women were to provide
themselves, and dispense them to the ladies on reasonable terms with their
fruit and play-bills at all future representations of *The Castle Spectre*.
*Bath Chronicle 26 Apr 1798*

*238. 1799 A triumphal return visit*
It was not till Saturday night last, that Mrs.SIDDONS was announced to appear
a few nights at our Theatre - and at an early hour on Monday, there was not a
seat unlet in the boxes for any of her performances. Her first character was the
GRECIAN DAUGHTER: the avenues to the Theatre were crowded at an early
hour... to procure a sight of this unequalled Actress, in a part which she had so
often played on the same boards with, what was then thought, the summit of
excellence and admiration. Mrs.Siddons has, we find, in many situations of
this interesting play, adopted a new manner; her attitudes are improved in grace
and dignity; and by playing less in some inferior passages, the effects of her
sublime efforts are considerably heightened. In short her whole performance
was the emanation of genius and inspiration, guided by correct taste, and
matured by professional knowledge - it was honoured by the best applause -
rivetted attention whilst on the stage, and the loudest plaudits at every exit...
Those who have seen her play that character in London, say that she produced
far greater effect here to what they ever witnessed on that larger stage - her
tenderness came nearer to the bosom, and her distresses were more poignant.
*Bath Herald 2 Feb 1799*

*239. 1799 Two patronesses: Miss Wroughton and Lady Nelson*
The once celebrated beauty, Miss Wroughton, still keeps up her consequence
by her large parties, and fine concerts every Sunday evening, where Ranzini
[Rauzzini], and many amateurs sing and play. The Prince [of Wales] always
attended to hear Miss Mayo (Mrs.Lutwyche's niece), sing and play, and indeed
I never heard any one so charming... // The amiable Lady Nelson, who as usual
was at Bath with her father-in-law, had some music sent her from Russia

endeavouring to be expressive of her lord's victories. She sent it to Ranzini, and some of the opera musicians came from London to perform it. The great ballroom was the place fixed upon, and there were about one thousand three hundred people, but the amateurs were disappointed, as the 'Battle of the Nile', as one might suppose, was only a monstrous continued noise.

*Powys, Diaries, pp.327-8, entry for April-May 1799*

### 240. *1799 Attraction of the Pump Room music*

The Pump-Room Band is one of the oldest and best establishments of this place; it draws the visitor and inhabitant from the most distant parts of the city to one general place of morning rendezvous; there long-parted friends indulge in unexpected meetings, whilst the inspiring melody of the Orchestra spreads a general glow of happiness around; as these are but a few amongst the many benefits arising from this long-established pastime, we hope the Subscription-book, now open, will so fill as to warrant its early commencement and long continuance. // Perhaps none are more interested in the Pump-Room Band, than the Tradesmen in the lower parts of the city; and as it undoubtedly draws the Company down to their shops, it particularly behoves them to give it every assistance and support by their subscriptions and recommendation.

*Bath Herald 2 Nov 1799*

## EXCURSIONS AND HEALTHY EXERCISE

*The general recommendation to take exercise seemed almost superfluous at Bath where smooth pavements, public walks and agreeable architectural spaces were an open invitation to promenading. Beyond the built-up area a web of highways and footpaths led to hidden valleys and open downs, to picturesque villages, high viewpoints, and landscapes that Gainsborough loved to paint. Having as early as 1699 laid out a circuit on the Common for riders and coaches, the Corporation in 1722 leased Claverton Down specifically for airings and horse-racing, and ensured in its turnpike legislation that people on simple outings had their toll charges reimbursed. In fine weather the ways about Bath were thronged with excursionists on horseback, in carriages, and on foot. Nearby hamlets and villages, local beauty spots, rural tea gardens, country houses (Prior Park the closest), and places of interest such as Twerton lock, 'Wicksteed's machine' (a water-powered seal-engraving device), or the Grenville monument on Lansdown, all made convenient destinations. Even a trip to Bristol and Clifton might be accomplished in a long day, and horses, vehicles and coach-drivers were readily available on hire for this or any other excursion. In 1768, moreover, the first riding school opened. Well-positioned on the northern fringe of Bath near the ascent of Lansdown, the establishment taught the basics as well as the finer points of horsemanship. In due course the addition of an open-air ride on the site, and in 1777 a real tennis court, well-equipped and professionally staffed, left no excuse for the healthier spa visitor not to keep fit.*

## 241. 1724 Airings encouraged

Of all the *Exercises* that are, or may be used for Health, (such as *Walking*, *Riding* a Horseback, or in a Coach, *Fencing*, *Dancing*, playing at *Billiards*, *Bowls*, or *Tennis*, *Digging*, working at a *Pump*, *Ringing* a dumb Bell, &c.) *Walking* is the most *natural*, as it would be also the most *useful*, if it did not spend too much of the *Spirits* of the *Weakly*. *Riding* is certainly the most manly, the most healthy, and the least laborious and expensive of the Spirits, of any; shaking the whole Machine, prompting an universal Respiration and Secretion of all the Fluids... and thereby, variously twitching the nervous Fibres, to brace and contract them, as the new Scenes amuse the Mind. Those who cannot ride, must be carried in a Coach or Litter, which is the best Exercise for the Lame and Crazy, and the only one proper for old and decrepid Persons... The Home Exercises... ought to be follow'd only when the Season forbids being Abroad; for being in the Air, contributes much towards the Benefit of Exercise.
*Cheyne, Essay, pp.94-5*

## 242. 1743 A rambler's diary

(5 Sep)  Walk upon the Hill which is very delightfull to the village of Walcot from whence we had a fine prospect of the City the River & Country about. in the afternoon cross'd the River & went to Bathwick, the mannor of ye Earl of Bath - a pleasant walk  Saw Mr Allen's Brewhouse & the Key for the Landing of the Stones, as also Mr Morrisson's [i.e. Harrison's] walks it Lays near the Grand Parrade but being very Low is but Little frequented tho they Run by the Side of the River & is well Planted with Tree's.

(6 Sep)  walk by the River to Twiverton [Twerton] a mile from ye City, partly planted with Tree's & fine meddows on Each side the River, past by [?]ause Hall a house of Entertainment & Small Garden it has a water for Drinking Good for Sundry Disorders, called Limewater, at the town, is a Brass mill for wyer [wire] & Plate w[h]ere they make all sorts of things in ye Brass way - & is a Large manufactory - saw Mr Cawleys Vine Yard a fine plantation on ye side of ye hill & has a Good Veu [view] of the Bath.

(7 Sep)  Rambled about the City & then walk upon the Hills to the Ring, half a mile out of the City it is the place where the Sick are Caryed for Air & others Air in Coaches, it Lays behind Queen Square & Say'd to be the Sweetest part of Bath, Near this place is a few house's Called Belvider, a fine Situation w[h]ere some of ye people of Bath have Gardens & Houses, in the afternoon went to Lincomb about a mille out. it has a very steep hill to Assend to it, there is one Large House to Lodge in & a few near it, it is famous for a well of Water in high Repute hear Say'd to be as good as the German Spaw water but will not keep. I think it tastes as the water of Islington wells, the House is Incloses [inclosed] by other High Hills which makes it very Rural and there is abondance of Springs of water Esewing [issuing] out of these & allmost all the Hills round about Bath - from thence went to Wincomb [Widcombe] ° a Mile from it a delighfull Situation for Summer it lays on the Side of the Hill & has a Butefull valley under it we say [saw] the House & Gardens of Mr Bush of Bath & also:

of Mr Bennet the Member [M.P.], which is a fine Building and Small Gardens
of some others went to see Sr: Phillip Parker's house it is in a Bottom an
Indifferent place.

    (8 Sep) took a walk to Mr Allen's house & his Quary of Stone it is a Large &
Butifull Building... & Stands upon the Brink of a hill Next ye Garden's which
look's into a Deep Bottom... the Quarry is a Surpriseing place w[h]ere he diggs
the Stone's, which is done with Great Ease... they drive in Iron wedges & then
Losen it with Iron Crow's, which often Brakes of[f] p[iece]s of a prodigious
Sise, then they fix a Large Chain round it & Crane it up - it goes by a horse,
when at ye top of ye pit it is placed upon a Carrage of wood which has Iron
weales about it 18 Inches High, - this goes on a Grouve fixt in the Earth &
when it comes to the desent of the Hill, it is mannaged by One Man... [Mr
Allen] has also Built a Long Row of Houses Near the Quary w[h]ere many of
his work men live, he has also all his Iron work for the makeing his Instruments
of all Kinds for the use of the Quary - & also Carpenters &: - there is a Large
Space of Ground Not got dugg up & tho the pitts are very deep & is free from
water yet he has a pump near one of them over a well which Supplys them with
water.

    (13 Sep) walkt to Bathwick... it is a place for the people of Bath to walk to
[and] many of them has Garden's with pleasure house's to which they Resort.
it has also a small number of Inhabbitants who are Gardeners which Supply
the Bath with Greens & Roots. thro the whole town they have the Springs Run
in a Troffe & at Each house they have a hollow Stone which contains water,
which they laid out with a bole [bowl] for there use, the water is very Cleair &
Comes from the fine Rilles which descend from the Hills Round them.
*BrRL, Pb.A.S.R.38, Diary of an Unknown Traveller, 1743*

### 243. 1745 Viewpoints in the neighbourhood

    Amongst your amusements you have not mentioned riding out, I suppose
you are yet too lame; but when you do, you will find most beautiful and romantic
Prospects for your Entertainment, and the riding to some of 'em pretty good.
Tho' they were other Peoples rides, they were all within my walks, for there
are none above a mile distance from the Town, and I own I took great Pleasure
in them. Every way the views are fine, and the Town, considering what a hole
it is in, is seen from many to great advantage, particularly one, wch shews the
New Square [Queen Square]... but my favorite one is from the road to Clerken
[Claverton] Down... The River is generaly intolerably foul and yellow, but is a
great addition to the prospect.
*Cowper (Spencer), Letters, pp.43-4, Spencer Cowper to his brother, 2nd Earl Cowper,
10 Apr 1745*

### 244. 1754 Another keen excursionist

    When I was at Bath I made some excursions. On the 18th [June] I went a
mile to Lyncombe, a sweet retirement, where there is a Chalybeat water, and a
very good house for lodgings, &c., on the same terms as at Bath. A mile and a
half farther is South Stone [Stoke], and as much farther Combe Hay, on a

rivlet... Here Mr Smith [John Smith, M.P. for Bath 1766-75] has a very good house, and has made a fine serpentine river by stopping the water. From this place we cross'd the hill a mile and a half to Wellow, on another stream... the high ground on each side of the rivlets is very beautifull, and there are many pleasant villages on them. On the [19th] I took a very pleasant walk to Triverton [Twerton], where there is a furnace for making brass, and mills for beating it into plates. On the 20th I rid out, went to Batheaston, visited Mrs Ravoe, who, with Mrs Riggs, a widow, has built a very good house, highly finish'd, improved the side of a hill to the road in beautiful lawn, walks, garden, cascades, a piece of water and a stream running thro' the garden, and live here in very agreeable retirement. I turned up the hill by the rivlet, called here Boxbrook... came to the famous Fossway... and, missing the way to Castlecomb, we went to Nettleton, a small town of about 100 houses... they are chiefly farmers and clothiers, and here, as in most parts, they kill meat twice a week and carry it to Bath...

*Pococke, Travels, vol.2 pp.32-3*

### 245.  1765  The elder Pitt braves Claverton heights

Thank Heaven that I am able to hold a pen, and tell my love the feats that I have this day performed. I have visited the fair down of Claverton, with all its piny forests, and have drunk one glass of water as I returned, sitting in my coach of state, in Stall-street.

*Pitt, Correspondence, vol.2 pp.331-2,  William Pitt to his wife, Bath 18 Nov 1765*

### 246.  1769  But why do the men shun the riding school?

I have been... observing the amazing inattention of the inhabitants of this city and *Bristol*, to what abroad would be reckoned the chief ornament of their cities; the excellent *Riding-houses* lately built in both places; at a very great expence, I fear, to very little purpose: At *Bristol* indeed I was not so much surprized, on being informed that few scholars rode at the manège; a mercantile town... is by no means a place, where the polite accomplishments can expect to meet with many votaries; but at *Bath*, the elegant seat of ease and pleasures, ... to find so healthful an exercise and elegant accomplishment so totally neglected, I confess, amazed me: I could scarcely believe that there are hardly any scholars of the sex we should soonest expect to find at a Riding-house; and that but for the ladies, the manège would be quite deserted. - Is it that we want taste for so noble an accomplishment, so highly honoured by our manly ancestors? or that the young gentlemen of the present age, are of such a delicate texture of nerves, that the exercise is too violent for *them*, tho' found agreeable to... the more delicate frame of the *fair sex*?

*Bath Chronicle 16 Nov 1769, letter from 'A Traveller'*

### 247. 1774 Humouring papa

*My* prime Boar [bore] is our airings, wch are very frequent (*tho'* they cost
7s.6d.) nor *can* I *wish* them less so, as they are of infinite service to *him*. The
roads to be sure are very fine, & the adjacent Country the finest I ever saw; our
views consisting of hills, dales, rivers, bridges, hamlets, *houses*, & fine verdure
are beautifully romantic & *often* have I made that *pretty* observation when
conversation fails...
*Elwin, Noels and Milbankes, p.38, Elizabeth Noel to her sister Judith, Bath 24 Feb
1774*

### 248. 1777 Away from the throng

During a month's residence at Bath I pursued my own inclination so entirely
and joined so little in the follies of the place (well knowing that one ball or
assembly is as like another, as a fig is like a fig) that I was unable to answer
fifty questions which were put to me to-day about Mr.Wade [the Master of
Ceremonies] and his ball, and the concerts, and the breakfasts, and the Duke of
Cumberland, and the gambling, and the dresses... but I could pass a strict
examination about the walks and rides, the hills and valleys, and Landsdown,
and Granville's Monument, and the [Wick] Rocks, and a number of pleasant
scenes unknown to those who amuse themselves with walking backwards and
forwards on the parades.
*Jones, Letters, vol.1 pp.229-30, William Jones to Viscount Althorp, 8 Jan 1777*

### 249. 1778 Up the valley to Claverton parsonage

... some of the Bridle-Roads being known to but few, should be pointed out...
The pleasantest of which is, from BATH to *Claverton*, the lower Way; passing...
from *Bath Wick* to *Bath Hampton*... After entering that Village, a broad,
handsome Road offers itself on the right Hand, which leads up to the Race-
Ground, on *Claverton*; but instead of ascending the Hill, take the first left-
hand Lane, which leads through a Variety of beautiful Meadows, not far from
the Margin of the River, and afford[s] also many picturesque Objects. This
Road leads into the Village of *Claverton*, where stands a goodly-looking
Mansion-House, and one of the prettiest Parsonage-Houses in *England*, now
inhabited by the Ingenious and Reverend Mr.GRAVES, the well-known poetic
Friend of SHENSTONE... And if you are not tempted by the retired, and
beautiful Scenes, which this Ride has afforded, to return the same Way, you
may pass over *Claverton Down*, and enter BATH by the *Old Bridge*. Just below
the Church at *Bath Hampton*, there is a Ferry-Boat, which conveys Horses and
Carriages... and lands you near *Bath Easton*: but it is not always passable; and
indeed it is necessary to smooth the Brow of the *Jezabel* who is the *Bateliere*,
as well as the Face of the Waters, to pass over it *calmly*.
*Thicknesse, New Prose Bath Guide, pp.57-8*

### 250. *1778 Winter sports: riding and real tennis*

I ... take the dust in the *manège*, and play at tennis when there is no snow to prevent me...

*Jesse, Selwyn, vol.3 p.266, Anthony Morris Storer to George Selwyn, Bath 4 Jan 1778*

### 251. *1779-80 Robert Southey's childhood ambitions*

... at this time [aged five or six] my greatest pleasure was a walk in the fields; and the pleasure was heightened beyond measure if we crossed the river in the ferry boat at Walcot, or at the South Parade; short as the passage was, I have not forgotten the delight which it used to give me. There were three points beyond all others which I was desirous of reaching, the sham castle on Claverton Hill, a summer-house on Beechen Cliffs, and the grave of a young man [the Viscount du Barré], whom a practised gambler, by name (I think) Count Rice, had killed in a duel [in 1778]. The two former objects were neither of them two miles distant; but they were uphill, and my aunt regarded it as an impossibility to walk so far. I did not reach them, therefore, till I was old enough to be in some degree master of my own movements. The tomb of the unfortunate duellist was at... [Bathampton], and we got there once, which was an extraordinary exertion; but the usual extent of our walks into the country... was to a cottage in an orchard about half way to that village.

*Southey, Life, vol.1 pp.43-44*

### 252. *1780 Inquiries from a tennis fan*

To whom does the Tennis Court belong now? J'y suis intéressé [I have an interest in it], being a £50 subscriber. Is the Marker a tolerable player, & how are the racquets, & balls, etc.?

*Pembroke Papers, p.78, 10th Earl of Pembroke to his son George, Lord Herbert, 27 Dec 1780*

### 253. *1786 Betsy Sheridan gets out and about*

(1 June) ... went to the Crescent fields [just below Royal Crescent] which is the present Mall of Bath and I think the pleasantest I ever was in as one is litterally walking in the fields with a most beautiful prospect all around at the same time that you meet all the company that is now here. There is something whimsical yet pleasing in seeing a number of well-dressed people walking in the same fields where Cows and Horses are grazing as quietly as if no such intruders came among them... [And] in the Evening I walk'd with Mrs Paterson to a new Walk which has been made by Belvidere, Shelter'd to the North by an immense Hill where they purpose building the New Crescent [Camden Crescent], and on the other side commands the most beautiful prospect immaginable, we then adjourn'd to the Crescent Fields to see the World and I again tir'd myself.

(10 July) ... we set out to a House [and pleasure garden] call'd St James's Palace beyond where the Bagatelle was formerly; that House is now quite forsaken and the garden overrun with weeds. When we arrived a little Girl

inform'd us thro' the gate that we could not be admitted as it was Witcombe
*revel* [Widcombe Fair] - on those occasions they shut up all public places here
so fearful are they of anything that might promote mirth. She would let us in
but no tea was to be had. Mrs F. is neither young nor very light so even a seat
was acceptable and we stroll'd round the gardens which are really very pretty.
*Sheridan (E.), Journal, p.93, June-July 1786*

### 254.  1788  A favourite outing now denied
... Prior Park, the beautiful seat of the late worthy Mr.Allen... and afterwards
of Bishop Warburton... The external beauties of the grounds, formed into
winding walks, gardens, terrace, &c. are esteemed highly finished, and
command... the most delightful prospect to Bath. It is much to be lamented,
that the traveller cannot be indulged with a more minute inspection of this
delightful place, which, since the death of the late possessor, (truly styled from
his amiable and liberal qualities, the Genius of Bath) is seldom or [n]ever shewn.
*Shaw, Tour, pp.299-300*

### 255.  1797  A further threat to public access
Wherever the beauties of Bath have been celebrated, the delightful Ride on
the fine Turf of Lansdown has usually been celebrated also. The steep hills
about Bath, and the badness of the materials for repairing the Roads made that
Ride doubly valuable. The Western Breeze inhaled on the verge of the hill, and
the delightful Prospect over a beautiful and extensive Country, have exhilerated
the mind, and contributed to restore health and spirits to Thousands... But alas!
some busy meddling person has persuaded the Owner into an Act [a
Parliamentary Enclosure Act], expensive to himself, and injurious to the Public...
but had the public injury been foreseen, and properly considered of... had the
least application been made to prevent it... Lansdown never would have been
inclosed: And... even now, by a proper application, the valuable Convenience
may be reclaimed.
*Bath Herald 22 Apr 1797, letter from 'A Well-Wisher to Bath'*

### 256.  1799  Jane Austen's evening stroll to Charlcombe
We took a charming walk from 6 to 8 up Beacon Hill, & across some fields to
the Village of Charlcombe, which is sweetly situated in a little green Valley, as
a Village with such a name ought to be... We had a Miss North & a Mr.Gould
of our party; - the latter walked home with me after Tea; - he is a very young
Man, just entered of Oxford, wears Spectacles, & has heard that Evelina was
written by Dr.Johnson.
*Austen, Letters, Jane Austen to her sister Cassandra, Bath 2 Jun 1799*

*257. 1800  Real tennis turns out profitable*
[For sale] THE TENNIS-COURT adjoining the Riding-House, which is allowed to be one of the completest Tennis-Courts in Europe, not only by its improvements on all other Courts, but to its adjoining the Riding-House, and the conveniences of different exercises for health and amusement. After it was opened about 20 years ago, it was taken by Mr.Hathway, who occupied the Court 19 years, till he accumulated a fortune. The present occupier is by no means a good player, but a good marker; very assiduous to his business and civil.
*Bath Chronicle 5 Jun 1800*

## SERIOUS INTERESTS

*To tread the streets of Bath, for anyone with a Classical education, was to feel the spell of Rome. Few may have subscribed to John Wood's wilder imaginings on the prehistory of the spa, but of its Roman past there could be no doubt. Roman fragments were forever turning up. Ancient inscriptions could be seen embedded in the town wall. A bronze head of Minerva, unearthed in 1727, stood on display at the Guildhall. In 1755 a section of the Roman* thermae, *hypocausts and all, came to light; in 1773 a trove of coins; in 1790 many thrilling finds from the pagan temple. Nor were antiquities the only diversion for the serious-minded. Bath's renowned bookshops-cum-circulating libraries were as well stocked with scholarly reading as with novels and plays. Meeting places for the literati and sometimes equipped with reading rooms, they supplemented the coffee houses which likewise acted as news centres, providing their subscribers with newspapers, writing materials, and endless opportunities for debate. Courses of lectures offered another source of rational entertainment. The science populariser Desaguliers may have been the first itinerant lecturer to include Bath on his tours, but many others followed in his footsteps. It was the stimulus of such lectures that led to a 'philosophical' or science society being founded in late 1779, opportunely as it turned out for one of its members, the musician William Herschel, then on the verge of momentous astronomical discoveries. (Indeed his sighting of what proved to be a new planet, Uranus, was first announced to this gathering of amateur enthusiasts). Finally Bath was, by the later eighteenth century, an art connoisseur's delight. Resident and visiting artists, portraitists above all, abounded - from society painters like Gainsborough and Hoare to everyday miniaturists and silhouettists. One of the earliest provincial art exhibitions took place at Bath, but in any case the constant displays in artists' own studios, at printshops and at auction rooms, gave art lovers and collectors ample scope to indulge their fancies.*

258. *1724 Careless regard for Roman inscriptions*
The walls round the city are for the most part intire, and perhaps [comprise] the old Roman work, except the upper part, which seems repaired with the ruins of Roman buildings; for the lewis holes are still left in many of the stones, and, to the shame of the repairers, many Roman inscriptions: some sawn across, to fit the size of the place, are still to be seen, some with the letters towards the city, others on the outside... Here they suppose (with probability) stood the Roman temple of Minerva, patroness of the Baths. Before it was a handsome square *area*, but lately deformed with houses encroaching... Since Mr.Camden's time [William Camden the antiquary, d.1623] two inscriptions have been set in the eastern wall of the cathedral, fronting the walks: but this is as imprudently done as those in the city walls; for besides the rain and the weather, they are exposed to the boys, who throw stones at them: one is that of Julius Vitalis... the other... seems to have been the top of a monumental stone over some common horseman. Harrison's house [i.e. the Assembly Rooms], they say, is built against some basso's [bas-reliefs] and inscriptions... At Walcot has been a camp, and many Roman antiquities are frequently found. Lord Winchelsea has an urn, a *patera*, and other things, found in a stone coffin, wherein was a child's body, half a mile off the Bath.
*Stukeley, Itinerarium, vol.1 pp.146 and 148*

259. *1730 Coffee house debaters*
I spend every day two hours in the evening at the Coffee House, with pleasure and improvement, especially in such public places as the Bath and Tunbridge, because of the great resort of gentlemen thither for their health or amusement, out of whom a few who are of the same turn of conversation... naturally select one another out and form a sort of society... The set I met constantly with since this last arrival at Bath were the Speaker of the House of Commons, Dr.Gilbert, Dean of Exeter, Dr.Carleton, a physician, Mr.Glanvil, member of the House of Commons, and Mr.John Temple. The three former are gone, and their room is supplied by Mr.Joy, son to a late director of the South Sea [Company], but one who reads much and had University education; Mr.Peregrine Bartue, a gentleman of estate in Suffolk or Sussex, Mr.La Mot, chaplain to the Duke of Montague, who was my schoolfellow... and is now beneficed in Northamptonshire, and Sir Justinian Isham, knight of the shire for that county.
*HMC 63, Egmont, Diary, vol.1 pp.117-18, entry for 19 Nov 1730*

260. *1731 James Leake of the circulating library*
... flying from the Centre of all polite Conversation [the Pump Room] to the Asylum of all polite Literature, I entered the Palatinate of Mr.Leake, the Bookseller. // This Leake is a most extraordinary Person. He is the Prince of all the Coxcomical Fraternity of Booksellers: and, not having any Learning himself, He seems resolved to sell it as dearly as posssible to Others. He looks upon every Man, distinguished by any Title, not only as his Friend, but his companion, and he treats him accordingly: but he disposes of his Favours and

Regards as methodically as Nash takes out the Ladies to dance, and therefore speaks not to a Marquiss whilst a Duke is in the Room. As yet he is ignorant that my Earldom lies in Ireland, and to keep him so, I have borrowed the only Book of Heraldry He had... // His Shop is a spatious Room, filled from the Cornice to the Skirting. But I could not help observing to him that, 'The Binding of his Books did not make so glittering a Figure as might be expected from the Library of a Person as illustrious as himself'. He owned my observation was right, and added that, 'Some Fellows whose Ancestors, he belived, were Snails, had been daily expected from London, to illuminate and glorify his Musaeum.
*Orrery Papers, vol.1 pp.99-100, John, Earl of Orrery to Counsellor Kempe, Bath 16 Oct 1731*

### 261.  1737  A notable science lecturer visits the spa
*This is to give Notice,* THAT Dr.DESAGULIERS intends to begin, next Week, a Course of Experimental Philosophy at BATH: In which (besides the usual Experiments to demonstrate the Principles of Mechanicks, Hydrostaticks and Opticks) will be shewn the PLANETARIUM, which he has contriv'd to explain and expose to View, the Motions, Magnitudes, and Distances of the Heavenly Bodies, and all the Phenomena of Astronomy, in a better and truer Manner than has ever yet been shewn by any Machine. // N.B. He has just made a new Instrument to shew the Phenomena of the Tides by Clock-Work (never yet shewn to any Body) which he designs to make use of in his Course...
*Gloucester Journal 6 Sep 1737*

### 262.  1742  The Arch-Druid's capital: some imaginative prehistory
The Antiquity of BATH being thus fixed to about the Year 480 before CHRIST; I shall now proceed to my *Description* of the Place, as well as of the [*Ancient*] *British Works* in its *Neighbourhood*: In which I hope to be able to prove, almost to a Demonstration, that BLADUD not only introduced those antient Priests, call'd the *Druids*, into *Britain*, [but] that he himself was the first *Arch-Druid*, and fixed his chief Seat at BATH; which, on that Account, became the *Forum* of the Western Part of the Island; and a Place was set apart, in that City, for Chapmen and Traffickers to meet in to transact their Business...
*Wood, Essay, 1742-3. vol.1 pp.12-13*

### 263.  1742  Imaginative prehistory exposed
During my confinement... I have read over J.Wood, Architect's Essay, towards a description of Bath, & I think I seldome have so much mispent my time... in short it is a silly pack of stuff, collected together from our fabulous historians, & where their fictions or traditions are not sufficient to support his fancys, he never wants falsitys of his own invention to supply their defect.
*Stukeley Family Memoirs, vol.1 p.337, Roger Gale to William Stukeley, 19 Oct 1742*

### 264. 1746 A serious man among whist players

I should be [miserable] here, but for the coffee-house and a good bookseller's shop. The public rooms I go to - but he that does not play, is a very insignificant person here; and, therefore, I look over the best whist-players, in order to learn the game, that I may, at least, be able now and then to make one with the ladies...

*Garrick, Private Correspondence, vol.1 p.44, Gilbert Walmesley to David Garrick, Bath 3 Nov 1746*

### 265. 1755 More of the Roman baths revealed

(18 August) A most valuable antiquity was discovered here. Under the foundation of the abbey house, now taking down, in order to be rebuilt by the duke of *Kingston*, the workmen discovered the foundations of more ancient buildings, and fell upon some cavities, which gradually led to further discoveries. There are now fairly laid open... the foundations and remains of very august *Roman* baths and sudatories... with floors suspended upon square brick pillars, and surrounded with tabulated bricks, for the equal conveyance of heat and vapour. Their dimensions are very large, but not yet fully laid open, and some curious parts of their structure are not yet explained.

*Gentleman's Magazine vol.25, 1755, p.376*

### 266. 1760 At Gainsborough's studio

This morning went with Lady Westmoreland to see Mr.Gainsborough's pictures, (the man that painted Mr.Wise and Mr.Lucy,) and they may well be called what Mr.Webb *unjustly* says of Rubens - they are '*splendid impositions*'. There I saw Miss Ford's picture - a whole length with her guitar, a most extraordinary figure, handsome and bold; but I should be sorry to have any one I loved set forth in such a manner.

*Delany, Autobiography, ser.1, vol.3 p.605, Mrs Delany to her sister Mrs Dawes, Bath 23 Oct 1760*

### 267. 1761 Romans and Saxons

It is proved that the Romans settled here... and that they built several hot baths, a part of which has been found lately under the surface, close to the present ones. They cannot be called good specimens of the famous and splendid Roman architecture, but it is obvious that they were built of bricks, without any great art or science, and probably by the Roman soldiers themselves, and it was not worth our while to go and see them. // Round one part of the town there still remain portions of an old wall, which to this day is called the Saxon wall, and was without doubt built by the Saxons. In many places bricks [i.e. stones?] with Roman inscriptions are to be found, which were employed in the masonry, and in several, which have been used to fill up the gaps, inscriptions have been cut through - a proof that the old Saxons were not as curious as we are nowadays about such things.

*Kielmansegge, Diary, pp.127-8, entry for Oct/Nov 1761*

### 268. *1762  The painter William Hoare expected back in town*
Hoare ... will have an opportunity to repair his neglect... of his family, who have expected him home every day for some time. He has been all this summer at Lord Lincoln's, and suffers Gainsborough here to run away with his business.
*Warburton, Letters, William Warburton to Charles Yorke, Bath 18 Oct 1762*

### 269. *1764  Further commissions for Gainsborough*
Sir Onesiphorus Paul and his Lady are the finest couple that has been seen here since Bath was built. By the by, her ladyship drinks most d—bly. They have bespoke two whole-length pictures, which some time or other will divert us. His dress and manner are beyond my painting; however, they may come within Mr.Gainsborough's: that is the painter by whom, if you remember, we once saw the caricature of old Winchelsea.
*Jesse, Selwyn, vol.1 pp.312-13, Gilly Williams to George Selwyn, Bath 1 Nov 1764*

### 270. *1773  Reaping the numismatic harvest*
A great number of Roman copper and brass coins have been dug out in clearing the hot-bath, the impressions of many of which are fair and perfect; among others are, those of the Emperors Nero, Adrian, Trajan, Antonine, &c.&c. - The workmen had for a few days a fine harvest; as they sold those whose impressions were the most perfect from 1s. to 2s.6d. each. - The Inscription on the stone [also dug up at the site] is sent to some members of the Antiquarian society; and as soon as the coins can be all collected, those which are the most curious will also, we hear, be sent to the same Society.
*Bath Chronicle 29 Jul 1773*

### 271. *1774  Hoare draws the line at bones*
I went with Br[other] and Bow[ater] to see Hoare and Gainsbro's Pictures... I saw nothing capital at the two Painters, excepting a portrait of the D[uche]ss of Kingston in her weeds [mourning dress], looking at a picture of the Duke, her Robes carelessly behind her on a Chair, & an Hour glass & Scull on the Table, all her own device - she wd have had some bones at her feet, but Hoare wd not comply with *that*.
*Elwin, Noels and Milbankes, p.37, Elizabeth Noel to her sister Judith, Bath 24 Feb 1774*

### 272. *1776  Another artist tries his luck at Bath: Wright of Derby*
(9 Feb) I have now past one season, the biggest of the two, without any advantage. The Duchess of Cumberland is the only sitter I have had and her order for a full length dwindled to a head only, which has cost me so much anxiety, that I had rather have been without it; the great people are so fantastical and whining, they create a world of trouble, tho' I have but the same fate as Sr Jos. Reynolds, who has painted two pictures of her Highness, and neither please. I am confident I have some enemies in this place, who propagate a report that I paint fire-pieces admirably, but they never heard of my painting portraits... There is a scheme of some artists here ... to work me out, and certainly it

proves at present very injurious to me, and I know not whether it will be worth my while (considering how little business is done here these four or five years past) to stay to confute 'em. I have heard from London, and by several gentlemen here, that the want of business was the reason of Gainsborough's leaving Bath. Wou'd I had but known this sooner, for I much repent coming here... I wish I had tried London first... What I have seen since I have been here has so wounded my feelings, so disturbed my peace, as to injure my health, but I will endeavour to shake it off.

(5 Apr) I have sent my two pictures [Italian 'fire-pieces'] to the Exhibition [at the Royal Academy], where I hope they will meet with as much approbation as they have here, and better success with regard to the sale of them, or I shall run aground with this year's expenses. I have only painted 4 heads yet; the prejudice still runs high against me. I am now painting a half-length of Dr.[Thomas] Wilson & his adopted daughter, Miss Macauley [the historian]; this is for reputation only, but you must not say so. The Doctor is a very popular man, and is fighting my case stoutly... indeed, if I stay I shall need of all the friends I can make.

*Bemrose, Life of Wright, pp.44-5, Joseph Wright [both letters to his brother?], Bath 1776*

### 273. 1778 Bath artists risk a joint exhibition
A London Artist, who hath seen the Bath Exhibition of Paintings, remarks, that (as it is only in its infancy) it reflects no small honour on the genius of the Bath artists in general. He observes, that several pieces by Messrs.Beach and Pine in particular, would be an ornament to a Royal [Academy] Exhibition: He further remarks, that a landscape painting, by Mr.Ackland, of this country, is a master-piece of its kind.

*Bath Chronicle 30 Apr 1778*

### 274. 1779 Herschel joins the new scientific society
(Dec 1779) I moved to a house in River[s] Street, and having no room for my 20 feet telescope I hired a convenient garden for it on the rising ground at the back of the Crescent. // About the latter end of this month I happened to be engaged in a series of observations on the lunar mountains, and the moon being in front of my house late in the evening, I brought my 7 feet reflector into the street and directed it to the object of my observations. While I was looking into the telescope a gentleman coming by the place... stopped to look at the instrument. When I took my eye off the telescope he very politely asked if he might be permitted to look in, and this being immediately conceded, he expressed great satisfaction at the view. Next morning the gentleman, who proved to be Dr Watson jun.(now Sir William), called at my house to thank me for my civility in showing him the moon, and told me there was a Literary Society [of mainly scientific interests] then forming at Bath, and invited me to become a member of it, to which I readily consented... [and] during the time I attended the Society, 31 papers of mine were read...

*Herschel, Scientific Papers, vol.1 p.xxiii*

## 275.  1779-80  Entertaining, rational and instructive

(22 Dec 1779) This day I began to attend a Course of Phylosophical Lectures on Electricity - the Air, Chemistry, Astronomy, Hydrostatics, & the Globes - these Lectures are given by Wm Arden of this City, a very Ingenious Man, & who has a Noble Apparatus of the best Instruments. Entertainments of this kind are the most truly Rational & instructive of any that can Employ the Human mind. And a few Lectures explaind by experiments convey more lasting instruction than many volumes of theory. We have them read here all winter. At these Lectures were many Men of great Scientific Knowledge...

(8 Jan 1780) ... at 12 O'Clock went to a publick Lecture on Optics, in which several Eyes were dissected, and the wonderful Structure and Use of the Several parts explaind in a clear manner. It was very curious and instructive as well as entertaining. Here is also a Course of Lectures on Oratory - and an Exhibition of Bees, Several Auctions of Books; and a Company of wire Dancers, and wild Beasts with dexterity of Hand. Of these however I know nothing but by Theory as displayd in the hand Bills.

(14 Jan 1780) ... to J Bryants Esq to see some curious electrical Experiments made on his new machine by Himself, Arden, & Herschel. some of them were quite new & astonishing, such as firing Pistols, Cartridges, &c & lighting candles by the Electrical sparks.

*BCL, MS B920, Edmund Rack, A Disultory Journal of Events, 1779-80*

## 276.  1782  At the cutting edge of astronomy

After the play I went with Mr.Hershel, who plays at the playhouse on the harpsichord, to his house in New King street, where thro' his telescope, which magnifies 460 times, [I saw] the double star Castor, the treble one in Zeta Cancer, the new planet [Uranus] in Gemini. In his papers on Saturn I saw there were two belts on the body [of the planet].

*Hervey (W.), Journals, p.327, entry for 12 March 1782*

## 277.  1784  A cosy public reading room

Circulating Library, Cheap-street, Bath,  //  10s.6d. a Year, 4s. a Quarter,  // *S.HAZARD most respectfully acquaints his Subscribers and the Company resorting to this City, that, in order to render his Library as agreeable as possible, he has opened a large Room up one Pair of Stairs (fronting the Church-Yard) where they may amuse themselves with the NEWS PAPERS and NEW PUBLICATIONS during the Intervals of drinking the Bath Waters, being very near the Pump Room, and a way to it from the Church-Yard... - He flatters himself it will be found a very comfortable Retreat, as it is covered with a Carpet, and a good Fire will be kept.*  //  Besides a select Collection of near SEVEN THOUSAND VOLUMES, including the most approved modern Publications, NEW BOOKS, Reviews, Votes of the House of Commons, and the following NEWS-PAPERS, are procured for the use of Subscribers,

                      Three London Daily Papers,
Two Bath,        Chester,       Liverpool,      Reading,
Three Bristol,   Dublin,        Leicester,      Salisbury,
Birmingham,      Exeter,        Manchester,     Sherborne,
Belfast,         Gloucester,    Northampton,    Worcester,
Bury,            Hereford,      Norwich,        York, &c.
Cambridge,       Leeds,         Oxford,
*Bath Chronicle 1 Jan 1784*


### 278.  1788  Hopeful attributions

BATH.  //  EXHIBITION-ROOM, BOND STREET,  //  TO be SOLD by
AUCTION,  //  By WILLIAM CROSS,  //  On Thursday the 10th of January
next, and the following day,  //  Part of the Capital Collection of PAINTINGS,
belonging to Dr. [Rice] CHARLTON, (retired from Bath;) amongst which are
the Works of the following Masters:

Titian            Carlo Maratti      Ferg
Guido             Correggio          Brughel
Julio Romano      Claud Lorraine     Ostade
Guercino          Rubens             Wovermans
Paul Veronese     Rembrandt          Worledge
Michael Angelo    Vinckenbooms       Gainsborough, &c.

With the above will be sold a few Busts and Figures, belonging to the said
Dr.Charlton.
*Bath Chronicle 3 Jan 1788*


### 279.  1792  Highly respectable Aquae Sulis

We went this morning to see some Antiques. They have been found within
this year or two as they were digging the foundations of some houses, and are
collected together; they are thought to belong to a Temple of Minerva from an
Owl's Head being on one of the stones. There are a great many stones very
well carved, a Medusa's Head in excellent preservation, a Jupiter and Juno,
Diana's Head with her Crescent, parts of pillars etc etc; skulls of Greyhounds,
heifers, etc. that were sacrificed to the Deities. The Circus and the Crescent are
very handsome, but I cannot but be of opinion, that Bath 1800 years ago made
a still more respectable appearance than it does now...
*Holroyd, Girlhood, p.128, Louisa Holroyd to her sister Maria Josepha, Bath 9 Mar
1792*


### 280.  1799  An awkward customer at Bull's library

You say very comically what a valuable Subscriber I am to Bull. And the
Compliment is kind as well as flattering - but Bull hates the very Sight of me
the while, because I come to his shop at 8 or 9 o'Clock in the Morning always
- the only Leisure hour the Man has from Readers who sit round his Table all

Noon and Footmen who ferret after him for Novels all Night -: and I make him clamber for me and reach Books which do not answer [her needs], and then he has to mount the Steps again, and so we go on: I have not routed after Spanheim [Friedrich Spanheim, Calvinist historian] yet, but I will see if he has got the Ecclesiastical History...

*Piozzi, Letters, vol.3 p.62, Hester Lynch Piozzi to her daughter Hester Maria, Bath 12 Feb 1799*

### 281.  1800  Bath's first public museum

The very curious remains of Roman splendour which from time to time have been dug up in various parts of this city, are now collected... up in a building erected for the purpose by the Corporation near the Cross-Bath; in the front of which are placed the two antique statues of *King Coel* and *King Edgar*, which we remember formerly adorned the north side of the old Guildhall. Many antiquarians visit these relicks with enthusiastic veneration; and we hear that Lord Powis has employed Mr.Lancashire, the statuary, to copy several of the most curious of these mutilated altars and mouldering ornaments to be placed among the choice antiquities of Powis Castle.

*Bath Herald 15 Nov 1800*

༺ ༻ ༺ ༻ ༺ ༻ ༺ ༻ ༺ ༻ ༺ ༻ ༺ ༻ ༺ ༻ ༺ ༻ ༺ ༻ ༺ ༻ ༺ ༻ ༺ ༻ ༺ ༻

# EDUCATION

*Two schools enjoyed official status. The fee-paying Grammar School delivered an orthodox Latin-dominated curriculum to boys from better-off Bath families, reaching particularly high standards later in the century under Morgan's headmastership. For years, however, it remained ill-housed in a redundant church which it shared with the city gaol, all thanks to the continued public misappropriation of its endowments which even a court judgment of 1737 failed to halt. Only in 1754 did the Corporation make some amends with a handsome new schoolhouse in Broad Street. The Bluecoats charity school, founded in 1711-12 under SPCK auspices for a hundred poorer children, half of them girls, came to be regarded as a model establishment with an outstanding teacher in Henry Dixon, who, as well as educating his pupils (but not above their station) in the 3Rs, grounded them in the Bible and Catechism and made them sing in the Abbey Church choir. In the 1780s educational philanthropy was extended to greater numbers of poor children through the thirty-odd Sunday schools scattered across the city; again the Anglican bias was strong, but so was the idea of inculcating the work ethic by means of an associated workshop or 'School of Industry'. Otherwise education at Bath was private and paid-for, whether at cheap dame schools, at the commercial academies designed to fit boys for business and the armed forces, or at the exclusive finishing and boarding schools for young ladies which so flourished at the spa. Many dozens of individual teachers also advertised their services, specialists in mathematics, calligraphy, drawing, embroidery, dancing, music, or languages. Besides accepting private pupils they frequently attended schools to give tuition in extra-curricular subjects and 'accomplishments'. Of governesses very little is heard, but these too were in demand.*

*282. 1711-18 On the Bluecoat Charity School*
... the Master shall make it his chief business to instruct the Children in the Principles... [of the Church of England] as they are laid down in the Church Catechism, which he shall first teach them to Pronounce distinctly and plainly... // The Master shall teach the Children the true Distinction of Syllables with the Points and Stops. As soon as the Boys can read, the Master shall teach them to write a fair legible hand, with the grounds of Arithmetick to fit them for the common affairs of life. // The Master shall bring the Children to Church twice every Lords Day and in the Morning of every other holy day and... //... shall use Prayers Morning and Evening in the School and shall teach the Children to Pray at home when they rise and go to bed, and to use graces before and after meat...

(26 Sep 1711) Agreed that a Barber be allow'd Twenty Shilling pr. Annum to Cut and Powder the Boys Hair as often as shall be necessary...

(27 Nov 1712) Order'd that those people who do not send their Children clean to school and in due time be sent for and severely reprimanded... And that those people who are able to find their Children Shoes and Stockings more than what the School allows, take care to... send them orderly to School, with their cloaths well mended and not so filthy and ragged as some of them do.

(12 Mar 1714) Some of the Childrens Parents having abus'd Mrs Bell [the Mistress] by coming up into her School and calling her Names, they were order'd to attend and were reprimanded...

(30 May 1718) Orderd that Chapman, Stilman, Margerum & Singers, or any other of ye Children who neglect their School during Mr.Dixon's [the Master's] absence, be expell'd ye School at his return from London, severely whipt, & stript of their School Cloaths in ye presence of ye other Children.

*BRO, Acc.103, Bluecoat School Trustees' Minute Book, 1711-73, pp.2-3, 23, 38-9, 47, 91*

*283. 1712 The Bluecoat pupils pass with flying colours*
That the Child[re]n of both the Ch[arity] Schools... are become the wonder of the Place. That ye Boys being now Cloathed pass'd an Examination in ye Town Hall the 9th instant with a general applause. That ye Lady Littleton, Lady Buckley, & sev[era]ll others of ye best note there, desir'd to see the Girls perform an Examination wch was accordingly done ye last Friday, and tho' Mrs.Bell had the disadvantage of a Short time to improve Her Children, and of Examining after ye Boys who had made such a wonderful Progress by ye indefatigable Diligence of Mr.Dixon, yet she made them perform to admiration, and even little ones that cannot read were able to answer their part out of ye Church Catechism broke into short Questions.

*SPCK, Abstract Letter Book (1711-12), CR1/3 no.3025, John Leasson to Mr Shute, 24 Mar 1712*

### 284. 1737 The Corporation pockets the Grammar School funds

Now we [the Charity Commissioners] ... adjudge order and decree that the mayor, aldermen and citizens of Bath, having so notoriously mismanaged, neglected, misconverted, misgoverned and misapplied the revenues of the lands... given to them or their predecessors... by... King Edward the Sixth, for the support and continuance of the... free grammar school... having only thereout paid sometimes thirty pounds, sometimes twenty pounds, and sometimes but ten pounds a year, to the masters of the said school... and... in manifest violation of the said trust, constantly applied the same to their own or other private uses... and having by their contrivance, mismanagemt or neglect, so mixt and blended the said lands and premisses with other lands... and... having absolutely refused to produce any rental or survey... pretending they had none... should be for evermore absolutely removed and displaced from the said trust...

*Charity Commissioners Reports vol.4 (Appx), 1820, pp.515-16, judgment of 14 Oct 1737*

### 285. 1748 Classics and sacred languages

At the GRAMMAR-SCHOOL, *near North-Gate*, BATH, // The LATIN and GREEK CLASSICS // Are faithfully and expeditiously Taught, // By Mr.T.ROBINS, from St.*John's College, Cambridge.* // [N.B.] Persons of ordinary Capacity (tho' ignorant of the *Greek* and *Latin* Languages) may be faithfully instructed in the true Art of Reading the *Hebrew* Bible without Points, at their own Apartments, or at my Chambers: And such as have competent Skill in this Holy Tongue, may, with the greatest Advantage, proceed to the *Syriac, Chaldec, Arabic,* &c. These being only divers Dialects of the one and the same Holy Primitive Oriental Tongue.

*Bath Journal 9 May 1748*

### 286. 1754 The Corporation's new Grammar School

On Saturday, the Anniversary of his Majesty's Inauguration... the Corporation... went in Procession, and accompanied with great Numbers of the Clergy, and Gentlemen, to the New School [in Broad Street], where the Master spoke an elegant Oration with great Applause (on the Dignity and Utility of Learning, on the Generosity of the Corporation, and the Gratitude due to it) ... [and] in the Evening, the Corporation met, and drank the Healths of the Day, and success to the School.

*Bath Journal 24 June 1754*

### 287. 1766 Costs of a daughter's polite education

After Morning-Prayers Mrs.Sewell was so kind as to go with us to Trim-Street to talk a little with Mrs.Pullaine [Pulleine], the Boarding-School-Mistress concerning her Terms: which are Sixteen Pounds a Year for Boarding, and learning to read and work [i.e. embroider], and a Guinea Entrance. Three Pounds a Year learning to dance, and Half a Guinea Entrance. Forty Shillings a Year learning Writing and Arithmetic, and Five shillings Entrance. Five shillings Entrance to each of the Teachers, which are Two. Two Guineas to be paid in

Lieu of a Silver Spoon, a Pair of Sheets, Six Napkins, and four Towels. Two Guineas at Xtmas, or once in a Year, a Present, which the Mistress divides among the several Parties concerned as she pleases. Half a Guinea to be paid at Whitsuntide, and Half a Guinea at Xtmas, if the Ladies keep the Tides at the School: but this is not insisted upon, tho' every Body pays it. One Ball in the Year, at which is paid five shillings: and five shillings a year for a Seat in the Church. They now go to the Abbey; but the Mistress has taken a Gallery for the Ladies in the Octagon Chapel, now building at the foot of Milsom Street, when it is finished. The Mistress is a well-looking Person, and we like her very well. The House is a very handsome one, very near Barton Street. All Bills to be paid every Half-year. Great care will be taken to instruct Ladies in the English Grammar. If Dolly comes here, she will soon become acquainted with Apostrophes and all the Niceties of Spelling.

*Penrose, Letters, p.146, letter of 27 May 1766*

### 288.  1770  *The schoolmistress as a friend*
ACADEMY. // MRS.BURDETT, Daughter of Lady BURDETT, late of BATH deceased, has opened an ACADEMY in a handsome House in MONTPELIER, at BELVEDERE, the most healthy Situation near that City: Boarders not to exceed 14; Young Ladies who do not board not to exceed 10. // Should any Young Ladies who have had the Misfortune to lose their Mothers, at that Age, at which the Assistance of a Parent is *most wanted,* be inclined to reside with Mrs.BURDETT as Parlour Boarders, she hopes she may be considered by such as a Friend.

*Bath Chronicle 1 Mar 1770*

### 289.  1774  *Bath itself an education*
'And yet I know a great many sensible polite people,' says Mrs.Booby, 'amongst the inhabitants of this place.' // 'Why, it would be strange indeed,' replies Rouvell, 'if the great resort of the politest company in Europe did not polish the creatures a little: for I take Bath, as a public place, to be a better school for any young fellow, than all the Universities or Colleges in the world.'

*Graves, Spiritual Quixote, vol.1 p.325*

### 290.  1775  *Only respectable spinsters need apply*
WANTED at Midsummer next, a Mistress for the Charity-School of this City, properly qualified to instruct the Girls in Reading and Plain-Work; she must be a single woman, above 30 years of age, reside in the school-house, and have an unexceptionable character. - The salary is twenty pounds per annum, forty shillings for coals, with the advantage [of selling] the children's work.

*Bath Chronicle 9 Feb 1775*

### 291.  1778  *Learning by doing*
WALKING over Claverton-Down a few days since, I saw at a distance a number of very young lads busily engaged on the turf, measuring and placing stones in various directions; as I saw they were not at play, I had the curiosity

to step to the spot; when to my surprize, I found they were making out a
*Fortification,* as regular as if they intended it for a Lilliputian Citadel, to hold
out at all events against an enemy. On enquiry, I was told by one of the most
alert, and who seemed to be the principal engineer, that they belonged to
Mr.MOORE's Academy, and were sent there by their Master, to reduce to
practice... [what] they had before been taught in theory. The dexterity with
which they carried on the work almost led me to imagine that I saw the shades
of *Uncle Toby and the Corporal* [from Sterne's *Tristram Shandy*] inspiring the
band and directing their operation...
*Bath Chronicle 10 Sep 1778*


### 292. *1778 Lessons out of the royal bedchamber*
  MISS HUDSON, Chapel-Court, Cross-Bath, takes this opportunity of
acquainting the Nobility and Gentry, that she continues to teach that peculiar
Art of EMBROIDERY, which was invented for the Queen's Bed, and which
she has studied under the celebrated Mrs.Wright. Also teaches to Embroider in
Worsted, Chenilles, Ribbons, &c. // Of whom may be had, Sets of Materials
for Embroidery, with the most fashionable patterns for Screens and Pictures;
Suits of Cloaths for Ladies, and Gentlemen's Waistcoats; Ladies' Habits, Work-
Bags, &c. - Miss HUDSON also instructs Ladies to Draw and Paint from Nature,
upon the most reasonable terms; also to draw their own Designs for One Guinea.
*Bath Chronicle 12 Nov 1778*


### 293. *1783 Latin at the Grammar School: a sample of Morgan's method*
  Q. What is the Quantity of *i*, in the Genitive Case, *alius*? Q. When is the
vowel *e* long before *i*, in the Genetive and Dative, of the fifth Declension? Q.
When is *fi* in any of the Tenses of the Verb *fio*, a long Syllable? - When a short
one? Repeat the Verse where both these Instances are exemplified. Q. What is
the Quantity of *Di*, in *Dius* - of *Di*, in *Diana*? Q. What is the Quantity of the
first Syllable, in the Interjection *ohe*? Q. You said, that a Vowel, coming before
another, in the same Word, is short; is this true with Respect to Greek Words?
- Mention an Instance or two. Q. What is the Quantity of Dipthongs? Q. But
is a Dipthong never made short? - In what Words?
*Morgan, Grammaticae Questiones, pp.107-8*


### 294. *1783 A drawing academy in prospect*
  At a meeting of the principal Artists of Bath, held at the Three Tuns tavern
yesterday evening, we hear that they began a Subscription, in conjunction with
gentlemen who are lovers of the Arts, for establishing an Academy or School
for Study from Antique Statues and the Living Model; which is to be on such
a generous plan as to extend its use not only to every class of Artists, but also
to the instruction of Youth.
*Bath Chronicle 16 Oct 1783*

### 295. 1787 Nine hundred angels

I daresay you have heard of Sunday Schools. It is but lately that we have had that institution here, and at first it went on slowly; but by joining it to a School of Industry, they now all crowd to the other [i.e. the Sunday Schools], which is a necessary step to that of industry. There is a clergyman employed for this Sunday evening service for the children alone, after the other common service is over, and it is in the great Isle [i.e. nave of the Abbey Church] where you must suppose nine hundred children in perfect order, placed on benches in long rows, so quiet that you could hardly have heard a pin drop while the Clergyman was reading. Reflect how very extraordinary this circumstance alone! when you reflect that most of them were taken out of the streets, untaught and actually almost savage, cursing, swearing, and fighting in the streets all day, and many of them without a home at night. Two girls, I myself know, slept in the street. Most of them not only ragged and starving, but without a chance of being put in the way to earn their bread. Yet here I saw them, not only in such order, but so well instructed as to have most of the service by heart; for though they had books, I observed they scarce looked at them, and yet repeated the responses perfectly, aloud. At one instant also, without direction to do so, the nine hundred dropped on their knees and rose again, which showed they knew what they were about; their little hands lifted up and joined together, looking with such innocent devotion. They sang the Psalms, all in time with the organ by heart, and notwithstanding the number, the sound was neither too loud nor too harsh, but, on the contrary, soft and affecting beyond measure. I confess, though I am no enthusiast [zealot], it drew tears from me...

*Holroyd, Girlhood, pp.17-18, Sarah Martha Holroyd to her niece Maria Josepha, Bath 4 Aug 1787*

### 296. 1789 How the Sunday schools are run

The children are divided into classes, viz. Letters, spelling, and reading. Also into two classes of perfect and imperfect catechists... // Twenty children are as many as one master or mistress can take proper care of; but it being found that in general not more than twenty attend regularly *twenty-five* are on the list... / / The masters are allowed sixpence a week more than the mistresses, not because they are better qualified as teachers, but from the difficulty of procuring them. The masters and mistresses find the apartments and forms... // ... the schools in general are seldom full till ten o'clock, which proceeds from the indolence of the parents. The different instruction the children receive, with the singing of psalms, occasions a diversity that makes the time pass without listlessness. To learn to be silent, and to bear confinement, is the foundation on which all instruction must be built. // ... By being able to repeat the verses of the Psalms they are to sing, many children who cannot read can join in singing. They begin with learning two Psalms, and are now perfect in eight, which is a sufficient number... // Those children who cannot read are ordered when they kneel to hold up their hands in a supplicating posture; it has a very good effect on the children, and has a very decent appearance.

*Plans of the Sunday Schools, pp.16-18*

### 297. 1789 A Bath language master scorns French parrots

It is a great abuse introduced in most schools to force beginners to talk nothing but French to one another; they must either speak wrong, or condemn themselves to silence. The masters... being at a loss to satisfy the expectations of the parents, presently begin by making them learn words and phrases, and labour hard to beat into their heads as many common sentences as they can, pretty near after the same manner as parrots are instructed. Those parents who are unacquainted with the language, are charmed with the supposed improvement of their children, and think them great proficients. They recommend the school as one of the best for learning... but in truth the children know nothing... // One may daily see in schools (particularly for the education of Young Ladies, where a woman teaches the French, though the grammatical knowledge has never been a business for women) pupils who have learnt French for five or six years, and who pass with some for good scholars, on account of the readiness with which they express themselves; but they observe no concord at all, cannot so much as make one part of speech agree with another, and are utterly incapable of writing four lines, or even to make sense of a common French book: In short, they know no more than the words and phrases of their own books.

*Borzacchini, Parisian Master, pp.xii-xiii*

### 298. 1794 Shades of the counting-house

GEORGE-STREET ACADEMY... // As this Academy is principally calculated for the Education of Young Gentlemen intended for a commercial life, the utmost care will be taken to render them completely qualified for that department. With this view, R.CARPENTER purposes to teach the Art of Book-keeping, according to the Italian method, in a manner seldom practised in Schools, by uniting practice with theory, in imitation of real business; so that the Young Gentlemen leaving the Academy will be able to undertake the business of the Accompting-house without that embarrassment and confusion which inevitably attend a mere theoretical knowledge of accounts. The Negotiation of Bills of Exchange will be explained, by circulating Drafts in the Academy amongst the Pupils, and a counterfeit cash will be used to practise telling. Letters will be written on different subjects of Commerce by the Pupils, in order to acquire an ease and fluency of expression, and every impropriety either in the diction or sentiment will be minutely examined and proscribed.

*Bath Chronicle 2 Jan 1794*

### 299. c.1795 New girl at the Misses Lee's establishment

On reaching the School room, all were employed in some sort of needlework - being Summer at 4 o'clock bonnets, spencers, or tippets, and walking shoes on, and attended by the 3 Teachers, we were paired off two and two, and took a walk into the country... We had to be home by 6, when those that took tea... descended to the dining room, where only Miss Mangle presided, and made tea for us. // Afterwards lessons were to be learned for the next day, and then the girls amused themselves with filligree and pasteboard trifles, &c., and the little ones with their dolls... At half past seven all went down to supper - bread, cheese and beer, by far the lesser number preferred bread and milk which I did. At 8 o'clock Miss [Sophia] Lee entered the school room and read prayers, we all kneeling, of course, after which we all went up to our bedrooms, accompanied by the three Teachers, who saw the young ladies into their rooms... // I was to belong to Mam'selle [the French mistress], and to sleep in a small bed in her room - Miss Clarke, and Miss Sanderson [other pupils] in the same room. In the large room opposite there were 8 girls... // The next morning we were called at six. At half past seven Miss Harriet [Lee] came into the School room and read prayers; at 8 Miss [Sophia] Lee opened the door. We all rose from our seats, turned towards her and curtsied. She went down to the dining room one way while we went by our own stairs... // ... After breakfast we found all the desks set up, that before had been hanging down by their hinges against the Wall, and by and by comes Mr.Perks, commonly called by the girls 'Billy Perks'. He was the Writing Master, and also taught Arithmetic. Many a warm plum, and squeezed bit of ginger bread, he has given me out of his pocket, and which I have passed onto some little one as a sort of treat. // Then I was introduced to my Music Mistress, Mrs.Oaks, tried as to my performance, and music to be brought me the next day. Music lessons three times a week, practising every day. Pianos in two Parlours, and one in the Drawing room, for the Parlour boarders, and those who were well advanced in that delightful accomplishment. // Monsieur Becker the Drawing Master came on Tuesdays and Fridays. Miss Anne [Lee] always sat with him at the Governesses' table in the School-room and we took our drawings to our desks. // Wednesday was dancing day, Miss Fleming came into the School-room, the desks being down and the day Scholars' forms put back, also the tables. Miss Fleming had a sedan chair of her own, and which she always came in. 'Simon' the Fiddler having arrived, being shown in to the School-room at the same time. The lady was very tall and stout, rather plain, but held herself very erect. She taught the Minuetts, and figure dances. Mademoiselle Le Mercier [her assistant], had the teaching of positions and steps, in the dining room. Miss Fleming used often to say, 'Now ladies, do credit to Bath', and I felt every inclination to satisfy her in that respect, for I was fond of dancing.

*Sibbald, Memoirs, pp.38-40, 44-5*

### 300.  *1796-7  De Quincey shines too much*

In my twelfth year... I entered upon the arena of a great public school - viz., the Grammar School of Bath, over which presided a most accomplished Etonian [Rev. Nathanael Morgan]... My [former] guardian was a feeble Grecian, and had not excited my ambition; so that I could barely construe books as easy as the Greek Testament and the Iliad. This was considered quite well enough for my age; but still it caused me to be placed under the care of Mr Wilkins, the second master out of four, and not under Dr Morgan himself. Within one month, however, my talent for Latin verses, which had by this time gathered strength and expansion, became known. Suddenly I was honoured as never was man or boy since Mordecai the Jew... But, unhappily, Dr Morgan was at that time dissatisfied with some points in the progress of his head class; and, as it soon appeared, was continually throwing in their teeth the brilliancy of my verses at eleven or twelve, by comparison with theirs at seventeen, eighteen, and even nineteen... young men, whom naturally I viewed with awe as my leaders... and who never had vouchsafed to waste a word on such a child as myself. The day was come, however, when all that would be changed. One of these leaders strode up to me in the public playground; and, delivering a blow on my shoulder... as a mere formula of introduction, asked me, 'What the devil I meant by bolting out of the course, and annoying other people in that manner? Were "other people" to have no rest for me and my verses, which, after all, were horribly bad?'... I was briefly admonished to see that I wrote worse for the future, or else - ... he would 'annihilate' me.

*De Quincey, Autobiographic Sketches, pp.147-50*

*301. 1798 A governess's lot*

WANTED, // A GOVERNESS, who can teach FRENCH and ITALIAN grammatically. - MUSIC enough to teach in the absence of a Master. She is expected to rise early, and will not have a maid to attend her. She is to sleep in the room with a Young Lady, and to eat with her when requested. The salary Sixty Guineas a year. - She will not visit with the Lady [of the house], as she is wanted to attend entirely to the education of two Young Ladies. A middle-aged person will be preferred, and of the Protestant Religion.

*Bath Chronicle 1 Mar 1798*

# RELIGION

At giddy Bath, according to one eyewitness about 1747, churchgoing was altogether démodé. Yet the influx of gentry inevitably did swell congregations and put pressure on the limited stock of rentable pews. Starting with St Michael's in 1734, the rather dilapidated old parish churches were successively rebuilt and enlarged, while the refurbished Abbey Church itself, so conveniently near the Pump Room, became almost fashionable in time, despite some fear of contagion from the frequent burials. For more snobbish worshippers the solution lay in private chapels-of-ease with their comfortable interiors and uncensorious preachers: St Mary's in Queen Square, the Octagon, Margaret Chapel, All Saints and Laura Chapel. Poorer people and servants (though often enough baptised, married and buried by the parish) were largely excluded from Sunday services by the cost and shortage of pews. Eventually they found a welcome at the Free Church (Christ Church), opened in 1798 after a campaign prompted by the same anxiety about working-class godlessness that also inspired the Sunday School movement or Hannah More's famous moralising pamphlets (many of them written and printed at Bath). Wesleyan Methodism, mainly of artisan appeal at this period, made rather halting progress, certainly in comparison with the Calvinistic alternative preached at the Countess of Huntingdon's high-profile chapel in Vineyards, though at times the doctrine sounded equally apocalyptic under either banner. The older Dissenting congregations remained quite small, but after 1789 the arrival of émigrés from the French Revolution notably inflated the city's traditional Catholic population which only a decade earlier had undergone a trial of its own in the Gordon Riots, when arsonists burned down their new chapel in the worst lawlessness seen at Bath for over a century.

*302. 1700 Objects of adoration*

A *Sunday* we went to Church to the *Abby*, a very Ancient Cathedral piece of *Antiquity*, and kept as badly in Repair; 'tis Crowded during *Divine Service*, as much as St.*Pauls*; in which time there is more *Billet-Deaux* convey'd to the Ladies, than Notes to desire the Prayers of the Congregation at B———'s Meeting-House: And, as the Ingenious Doctor in his Discourse, told the Audience, *He was afraid most of them came more out of Custom and Formality than in Devotion to the Sacred Deity, or a suitable Reverence to the Place of Worship.* Which was very True, I am Confident, and the Ladies were the only Saints several came there to Adore; as this *Billet-Deaux* will confirm; it was convey'd in a Candi[e]d Orange to a Lady in one of the *Galleries*, which she by accident dropt, and I had the Fortune to find.

*Ward, Step to the Bath, p.166*

*303. 1716 Chapel and church*

Went to the meeting [of Dissenters] with our company. Some thoughts of raillery came into my head during the sermon for conversation with Mrs.Marshall and put me into a gay humour... // The meeting is but a small one and that not full. Went to church in the afternoon. Heard a very indifferent charity sermon for the benefit of the charity school. The church was extremely full.

*Ryder, Diary, p.244, entry for 27 May 1716*

*304. 1739 A cold, inconvenient, impressive place of worship*

The Abbey-Church is not so much frequented by the Company as the other Congregations because Service begins here at an inconvenient time for them... The East Window over the Altar... is perfectly magnificent, very large and consisting of stained panes of Glass. The disposition of the Doors has made this Church extremely cold... The Altar-piece was given by General Wade; and it is a very handsome one of Marble, containing a good Painting of the Wise Men's offering to Christ... The Cross-Isle is quite spoiled by a Gallery and Organ-Loft erected over the Entrance of it... [But this is still] a noble Church both inside and out - it strikes one very much.

*Markham, John Loveday, pp.308-9*

*305. 1739 Field-preaching in winter: Whitefield undeterred*

Finding many in Bath were desirous to hear me, having given a short notice, about five in the evening I preached out on the town common, to a much larger audience than could reasonably be expected. It snowed good part of the time, but the people stayed very contentedly. Indeed some said (as I heard afterwards) that I spoke blasphemy; but the people of God were much rejoiced, and some, I hope, effectually wrought upon. Praised be God for opening such an effectual door here. Many adversaries must be expected in so polite a place as Bath.

*Whitefield, Journals, p.226, entry for 12 Mar 1739*

### 306. 1741 Charles Wesley embattled at Sodom

Satan took it ill to be attacked in his head-quarters, that Sodom of our land, Bath. While I was explaining the trembling jailer's question [*Acts* 16, vv.23-34], he raged horribly in his children. They went out, and came back again, and mocked, and at last roared, as if each man's name was Legion. My power increased with the opposition. The sincere were melted into tears and strong desires for salvation.

*Wesley (C.), Journal, vol.1 p.286, entry for 11 Jul 1741*

### 307. 1755 A Walcot funeral

Wednesday last a Black Girl (Servant to a Gentleman in the Square) was buried at Walcot Church: - There were six Black Men to support the Pall; and several others, of the same Complexion, attended the Corps, as Mourners.

*Bath Journal 10 Feb 1755*

### 308. 1756 Sacrilege on a solemn occasion

Yesterday, being appointed for a General Fast, was observ'd here with a suitable Solemnity, no walking in the Streets; Shops and Houses of public Resort were all shut up; Churches and Places of public Worship were so crouded, that at St.James's in particular, in Expectation of hearing Mr.Bailey, a celebrated Preacher, the Avenues were so crouded, that 'tis computed hundreds were disappointed by Want of Room. But what shall we say, when we are told, that even in the House of GOD, were some of Satan's Children, seeking like their Master to devour; for while a Gentlewoman was intent on her Devotion, her Pocket, containing two Guineas, some Silver, &c. was cut from her Side; a Thing unheard of here before, and supposed to be done by some Pickpockets returning to London from Bath Fair.

*Bath Advertiser 7 Feb 1756*

### 309. 1759 An apology to a Nonconformist congregation

WHEREAS We, PHILIP WARREN, Apprentice to Mr.Madden, Cabinet-Maker, EDWARD PONTIN, Apprentice to Mr.Axford, Jeweller, and THOMAS BURTON, Servant to Mr.Cottle, Taylor... having at several Times past contemptuously disquieted and disturbed, in an outragious Manner, the Congregation or Assembly for Religious Worship, held at the House of John Lockyer, situate in Avon-Street... and licensed for that Purpose... do hereby in this public Manner, acknowledge our Faults, and sincerely ask Pardon of all such who were there met at the Times we so disquieted and disturbed them...

*Bath Journal 5 Mar 1759*

### 310. 1766 Expensive pews, costly burials

Bath is so enlarged, that the Places of Public Worship will not contain a Tythe of the Inhabitants, and Strangers resorting hither. At the Chapel in Queen-Square, a Stranger cannot get a sitting under half a crown a Time, or a Guinea for the Season: the Inhabitants themselves, to have a Seat, must pay a Guinea

a year each Person. So numerous as the People here are, of some Sort or other, here is no Place of Burial but in the Churches... and the Fees for Breaking Ground in Churches monstrous high, Ten Pounds at the Abbey. So all the Poor, and middling People, nay all except the rich and great, are carried, when dead to the Church-yards of Widcombe or chiefly at Bathwicke, two neighbouring Parishes the other side of the river Avon, which is crossed in a Ferry-Boat; and four or five shillings are paid as a Fee for breaking the ground.
*Penrose, Letters, p.81, letter of 3 May 1766*

### 311. 1769 The Octagon Proprietary Chapel, Milsom Street
It is a handsome building, but not like a place of worship, there being fire-places in it, especially on each side of the Altar, which I cannot think at all decent, it is not liked.
*Woodforde, Diary, vol.1 p.83, entry for c.25 Jan 1769*

### 312. 1769 John Wesley's hard questions
Dear Miss Bishop,... // We have had a Society in Bath for about thirty years, sometimes larger and sometimes smaller. It was very small this autumn, consisting only of eleven or twelve persons, of whom Michael Hemmings was leader. I spoke to these one by one, added nine or ten more, divided them into two classes, and appointed half of them to meet with Joseph Harris. But if you are willing to cast in your lot with us, I had rather that those single women in both classes who desire it should meet with *you* and any others who are not afraid of the reproach of Christ... If you are determined, let me know. But consider what you do. Can you give up all for Christ? the hope of improving your fortune, a fair reputation, and agreeable friends. Can He make you amends for all these? Is He alone a sufficient portion? I think you will find Him so.
*Wesley (J.), Letters, vol.5, pp.153-4*

### 313. 1772 A service at the Countess of Huntingdon's chapel
[We were] placed in vestry just near the door (there being another one at the other end of the same side of the Chappel where Lady Fanny Shirley [the Countess's aunt] was, from whom both has a communication with her house adjoining). There were two men in our Vestry who seemed something like Deacons of the Chappel, also... a merchant or tradesman of Bristol and his wife... with their maid and child scarce a year old, who squalled and played with a rattle most of the time. The prayers read by one Mr.Sheppard (a little ugly man,) the sermon on I Philip 21 by Mr.Shirley [the Countess's ordained cousin] - an empty unmeaning discourse on a spiritual acquaintance with Christ... seemed to say good works were nothing and that this spiritual acquaintance... was not to be attained by reflection, study, reading or indeed any other means... but by some whim or caprice of God, who should (without why or wherefore) take an unaccountable predilection for some devilish sinner, or worthless prelate, and give it him. After his main discourse he concluded in giving about 20 minutes account of Mr.Adey [a converted sinner who had just

died at Bath]... However I was made amends for all the stuff [I had heard]... by
the singing. They have a book of hymns of their own composing which I perused,
the poetry very middling indeed but most sweetly sung. They chant or rather
sing the 95th Psalm and the Hundredth... [and also sang] 2 Funereal Hymns of
their own composing; the voices were sweet and the tune slow, solemn, sweet
and affecting to a great degree.
*Baker, Diary, pp.249-51, entry for 15 Nov 1772*

### 314. *1774 Advice to the Seventy Shareholders of the Upper Rooms*
You, Gentlemen, cannot plead Necessity... in keeping open your publick Rooms
on the LORD's Day for the Sale of Tea and Cakes... because the Command to
keep holy the Sabbath-Day is of universal Obligation on all Christians, high or
low, rich or poor... And may we not bear our Testimony against the Inhabitants
of this licentious City... ? Do not many of them keep their Shops open on this
Day and expose their Wares to sale? And that not so much for the Supply of the
Necessaries of Life, as the Luxuries and Superfluities of it? Add to this, the
Multitude of Hair-Dressers that swarm in the Streets, for the gratifying [of] the
unnecessary Demands made by Pride and Vanity on that sacred Time, which
ought to be employed to a better Purpose, viz. the assembling ourselves in the
House of GOD...
*Homily to the Septuagint, pp.2 and 6*

### 315. *1778 Dissenters' meetings and Anglican interments*
There is no City in *Great Britain* where Dissenters from the Established Church
may serve GOD according to their own Mode of Faith with more perfect
Freedom than in this City. The *Papist*, the *Presbyterian*, the *Quaker*, the
*Methodist*, and all the different Sects (the *Jumpers excepted)* have here their
Places of Public Worship. Mass is as publicly performed at BATH, as it is at
*Versailles.* // It is very doubtful whether the *Abbey Church* is not, on many
Accounts, a very improper Place (except to People in full Health) to attend
Divine Service at. The vast Number of Bodies buried within the Church, and
*near the Surface*, and the Frequency of the Ground being opened, before the
Effect of Putrefaction is over, the Doors and Windows not being sufficiently,
or constantly kept open, renders the confined Air perceptibly disagreeable at
first entering the Church; and, we are told, there is an Opening, or Ventilator,
in the Roof, over which if any one place their Nose, they will meet, at *all
Times*, a Stench scarce to be imagined... The malignant, sore Throat, is not
very uncommon at BATH, and who can say from what Source of Corruption it
arises?
*Thicknesse, New Prose Bath Guide, pp.30-1*

### 316. *1780 Quaker eloquence, Methodist ranting*
Large [Quaker] Meeting ... [including about] 20 Friends Strangers in Town.
Will [Matthews] Preachd on the words of David speaking of the Almighty,
'His Name shall indure for ever, as long the sun & moon remaineth'. and in a

fine strain of Gospel eloquence set forth the excellency and permanency of those Absolutes of Wisdom & Goodness which Make up his Name and are from Everlasting to everlasting. Some Gentlemen of Rank were there & sat with great attention... Afternoon Meeting Small, and dull... In coming home stepd a few Minutes into the New Methodist Chapel where one of their enthusiastic Ranters was driving all before him to Hell and destruction. He seemd to be delighted in degrading human Nature as though there were no other way of exalting the deity than by Debasing his Offspring.
*BCL, MS B920, Edmund Rack, A Disultory Journal of Events, entry for 19 Mar 1780*

### 317. 1780 Peaceable Catholics victimised in the Gordon Riots

I am the unfortunate Roman Catholic clergyman, who was hunted from place to place and pursued through several streets the evening of the Bath riot: it was with great difficulty I escaped from falling a victim to the fury of the mob. Being here the public minister for people of our persuasion I am well known and was openly attacked in the street that evening by one Butler, who is mentioned in the incendiary letter and was then servant to Mr.Baldwin, a gentleman living in this town. After pursuing me at the head of the mob he led them to my house and chapel, both which, together with all the furniture and books, were entirely destroyed. The unhappy man was afterwards tried and hanged on the spot, though from motives of delicacy I did not give evidence at his trial. // The Belltree [the old Catholic refuge in Bath], which is threatened to be first set on fire, is the house I now live in, in the upper part of which there is a long room set aside for divine worship... // I beg leave to observe that all the Catholics here, most of whom are gentlemen of family and property, chearfully took the late oaths of allegiance tendered to them by his Majesty and therefore, both on that account and for their constant peaceable behavior, flatter themselves they are entitled to his Majesty's protection.
*Williams, Post-Reformation Catholicism, vol.1 pp.198-9*

### 318. 1790ff. Rev.William Jay of the Independent Chapel, Argyle Street

When we came here [i.e. the More sisters, in 1790, to live in Gt Pulteney Street], just then the churches were, I am sorry to say, badly filled. Jay was then in all his glory, and little else talked of; his chapel was full, and half filled by people from church, I mean on a Sunday evening. I have seen great numbers of clergymen there... All this was thought nothing of by anybody; Jay's orthodoxy and talents bore everything before it, nor was the thing remarked, that ever I heard of, till the French Revolution, when Tom Paine, &c., began to show their cloven feet... // At this time the cry of the Church began to come forward, and all those harmless admirers of Jay withdrew as the prejudices of the people began to break out...
*Whalley, Journals, vol.2 pp.224-5, Martha More to T.S.Whalley, Bath 14 Jul 1802*

*319. 1792 Where are the poor to worship?*
IT has been a matter of concern to many, that the zeal, which has been so laudably manifested in this City for the religious education of the infant Poor [through Sunday schools], should not ere this have been extended to what appears to be an object of still more material consideration. As the City of Bath increases, a Chapel for the convenience of the rich is considered as a necessary appendage to each proportionate extent of other building. And so long as Chapels are permitted to be built upon a plan productive of certain emolument to the parties concerned in them, there is no reason to fear that those who can pay a guinea, and a guinea and an half for their respective sittings, will want accommodation. But it may be reasonably asked, what are they to do who have no guineas to give?... // The present Chapels, to the disgrace of this city, are, for the convenience of the rich, and the emolument of their respective builders, absolutely shut against the Poor. Some place of worship, therefore, should be provided for them.
*Bath Chronicle 1 Mar 1792, letter from 'A.B.' [William Wilberforce?]*

*320. 1793 Mourning the guillotined French King*
Sunday in several of our churches and other places of religious worship, funeral sermons were preached on the death of the unfortunate Louis; and on Monday the Catholic Chapel was hung with black, and solemn mass was said; at which all the French refugee Clergy now in Bath assisted; all the people of that nation, who have here found a shelter from the distractions in their own unhappy country, were also there. The scene was distressing - not a dry eye was within the walls of the Chapel.
*Bath Chronicle 31 Jan 1793*

*321. 1794 Hannah More's prayer*
O Lord! fit me for the duties and keep me from all the temptations of it. I thank thee that the vain and unprofitable company with which this place abounds, is a burden to me.
*Roberts, Memoir of H.More, vol.2 p.423, journal entry, Bath 15 Dec 1794*

*322. 1795 A wild success for Hannah More's* Tracts
(5 Mar) An interesting scene took place yesterday at Mr.Hazard's library in Cheap-street, the day appointed for publishing the cheap Moral and Religious Tracts, intended for general circulation by hawkers, &c. throughout the kingdom, in the laudable hope of counteracting the evils resulting from the number of wretched publications that have for many years served only to corrupt the minds and manners of the lower class of our fellow creatures. A number of hawkers attended, decently dressed, with characteristic ribbands in their hats, and an assortment of the instructive and entertaining works in poetry and prose were presented to each by a subscription of ladies and gentlemen there present... this most benevolent

plan... originated with and has been thus far carried into execution by the indefatigable zeal and abilities of that most excellent woman
- *Miss HANNAH MORE...*
(16 Apr) So great has been the demand for the cheap and entertaining tracts published under the auspices of Miss H.More, that no less than THREE HUNDRED THOUSAND have been sold since the 1st day of March!! and the sale still continues so rapid that it is with the utmost difficulty the presses employed [at Bath and elsewhere] can print off fast enough to supply calls from all parts of the kingdom.
*Bath Chronicle 5 Mar and 16 Apr 1795*

### 323. 1796 The origins of Christ Church, Montpelier

Last Sunday we were at Queens Square Chapel, being accommodated with seats by Mrs.Key, an old lady of large fortune in Queen's Square, who has a large front seat in the gallery & one for her servants behind her... There is no Organ in this chapel, but it is very neat, very well warmed, as the chapels all are here, & the service is decently perform'd. In the evening I go to prayers at the Octagon, being accomodated by Mrs.Falconer in her seat. The usual hour for eveng. prayers in the chapels is 5 o'clock. A church is now building in the upper part of the town, meant for a free church, where the poor & strangers may worship the Almighty. The idea is said to have originated with Mr.Wilberforce, who shocked to find the poor entirely excluded from the Octagon, too little room for them anywhere, & that strangers knew not where to go to church (indeed, two seats in St.James's excepted, they cannot go anywhere without paying) advertised an offer of 300£ towards a free church without mentioning his name; the plan succeeded, numbers have subscribed & a handsome building, in the gothic stile, is now in great forwardness. It is... to cost perhaps somewhat more than the 3000£. The whole body of the church is for the poor & strangers. Some seats in the gallery are to be set for a low rent, to pay a clerk, sexton &, I think, a small stipend to a clergyman...
*Wilson, Shropshire Lady, p.105, entry for 5 Nov 1796*

# CORPORATION, POLITICS AND ADMINISTRATION

*In an age of political corruption the corporation borough of Bath stood out like a beacon for its rare electoral independence and the integrity of its parliamentary representatives (Wade and Ligonier, both field-marshals, and the elder Pitt among them). It stoutly resisted infringements on its chartered privileges, defended its monopolies, and waved the constitutional flag whenever it could. But behind the display of municipal rectitude lay a self-serving, self-perpetuating oligarchy of some thirty aldermen and councillors with large powers of patronage checked only by fear of public outrage. Legal challenges by the disenfranchised freemen came to nothing. Unstable alliances within the Corporation alone, meeting in private, determined the voting for M.P.s (who might gain favour by civic donations and Guildhall feasts), for new councillors and annual office-holders, for the levying of rates, the expenditure of funds, the placing of contracts, the content of local Acts and bylaws, and all the details of routine administration, justice and policing. Benefiting from the spa's growth yet conservative-minded and deeply suspicious of every development outside its control, the Corporation was slow to reduce its debts and realise its assets, only adopting a more active role after 1750. Certain of its members had excessive influence: Ralph Allen, for instance, in the decades up to the Pitt affair in 1763; and perhaps T.W.Atwood in the early 1770s when his actions over the new market and Guildhall roused a storm of controversy. The gathering movement for political and municipal reform at Bath was, however, effectively stifled in the antiradicalism of the 1790s, though it would re-emerge after 1800. Meanwhile a hidebound Corporation also refused support to other progressive measures: the ending of discrimination against Nonconformists, for example, or the abolition of slavery.*

*324. 1703 The Corporation defends its market rights during the Queen's visit*
Whereas James Blackwell One of the Deputy Clerks of the Markett to her Majesty's household hath issued out a... Warrant directed to the Bayliff of this City... commanding him to summon twenty four honest men of this said City to appear at the Bear Inne... by two of the clock this present Afternoon then and there to hear and doe upon their severall Oaths as they shall be required Which summons is contrary to ye usuall custom of the said City... Agreed by generall consent that if any action or summons be brought or commenced against the Mayor Justices Bayliff or any other Office or Officers of this Corporation by... James Blackwell or any other person... whatsoever intending thereby to try ye validity of our Charter In ye Case of a Clark of the Markett shall be maintained & persecuted at ye whole & sole expense of ye Corporation.
*BRO, Bath Council Minutes, 28 Aug 1703*

*325. 1705-6 Bath freemen are still denied the vote*
(2 Nov 1705) A Petition of *George Dashwood* and *Richard Houblon*, Esquires, was presented to the House [of Commons], and read; setting forth, that the Petitioners, and *William Blathwaite* and *Alexander Popham*, Esquires, stood Candidates at the Election of Citizens, to serve in this present Parliament for the City of *Bath*: That Mr.*Blathwaite* and Mr.*Popham*, by several indirect Practices, did procure themselves to be returned, as duly elected, though the Petitioners had a great Majority of the legal Votes... *Ordered*, that the Consideration of the said Petition be referred to the Committee of Privileges and Elections...
(27 Jan 1706) That the Question was upon the Right of Election. // That the Petitioners Counsel insisted, that the Right of Election was [vested] in the Mayor, Aldermen, and all the Freemen, paying Scot and Lot. // The sitting Members Counsel insisted, that the Right of Election was in the Mayor, Aldermen, and Common-council, or capital Citizens, only... *Resolved*, That it is the Opinion of this Committee, That the Right of Election... for the City of *Bath* ... is in the Mayor, Aldermen, and Common Council, only.
*Journals of the House of Commons, vol.15, 1705-8 (repr. 1803), pp.12 and 255-6*

*326. 1711 Harrison's Rooms encroach on the city wall*
Whereas It is reported for a certainty that the persons of Quality & Gentry now residing in this City have threatened & are resolv'd to pull down or cause to be pull'd down the new wall that was erected upon the Burrough wall against Batts Garden [by the Corporation] pursuant to an order of the High Court of Chancery the right of wch wall hath been in dispute between the Corporation of this City and John Hall Esq, descd and Mr.Harrison And whereas the sd. Mr.Harrison hath desir'd an accommodation and acknowledged the right of the sd. wall to be [vested] in the Corporation alone, Quere [to query] therefore if (to oblige the Nobility and Gentry) a Committee shall be appointed to be chosen out of the Corporation to deal with the sd. Mr.Harrison... and... have

full power to make an end of the sd. Suit on the part of the Corporation? Agreed
that there shall be such a Committee...
*BRO, Bath Council Minutes, 7 May 1711*

### 327. *1731 Why the deficit arose - and the remedy*
By the ill Conduct of preceding Mayors, by their treating, and drinking often,
at the Chamber's Expence, the City Debts became very great, and in the Year
1731, in order to pay those Debts, it was enacted, that no Work that would
exceed 5l. [£5] Value, should be undertaken by the Mayor, or Chamberlain, at
the Chamber's Expence, without the Concurrence of the whole Body corporate,
under the Penalty of *Seventy Pounds;* that no Public Days be observ'd at the
Expence of the Chamber, except the 5th of *November,* the 29th of *May* [Oak
Apple Day], and the *Inauguration* [anniversary of the King's accession], and
that the Expence of those Days were not to exceed 20l. [£20, and] if it did, the
Overplus to be at the Charge of the Mayor; that there would be no Tavern
Scores, by the Authority of the Mayor, but on City Business; and that then the
Business be enter'd on the Tavern-Book, with the Names of the Persons present
when such Expences shall be charged; that the monies arising from the Profits
of the Pump, and all surplus Monies, in the Hands of the Chamberlain, at passing
the Accounts, be applied as a Fund to pay the City Debts; and that no Person
that has served the Office of Chamberlain shall be elected Mayor 'till he hath
passed his Accounts. // These wholesome Laws were enacted in the Mayoralty
of *Richard Ford* Esq; to whose Honor they must greatly redound...
*Bath Advertiser 6 Dec 1755, letter to Julian Alberti*

### 328. *1733 Up in arms against excise duties*
Whether Letters shall be sent by this Corporation to our Representatives in
Parliament to desire them not only to oppose themselves, but to make all the
interest they can against any New bill that may be offered to the Parliament
this Sessions for laying a duty on Merchandize Goods by way of Excise, And
to oppose any new Excise under any denomination whatsoever? Agreed that
Letters shall be sent...
*BRO, Bath Council Minutes, 19 Jan 1733*

### 329. *1743 Protecting the titled guest*
The Mayor and Corporation of Bath have published an advertisement in the
newspapers, with a reward of twenty pounds to whoever will discover some
idle people who threw dirt and cabbage stalks at the Duchess of Bedford as she
was crossing the Abbey Green there.
*Seymour, Gentle Hertford, p.261*

### 330.  1752  Municipal myopia

Narrow minds will ever have narrow views. The corporation of *Bath* seems to have forgot that the ease and plenty they now enjoy... are owing to their Waters; and that an improvement upon their Baths, would, by bringing a greater concourse of company to their town, perpetuate these blessings to them and their posterity. How little is to be expected of them, in this particular, might be guessed by their conduct to Mr.*Wood*, the architect, to whose extraordinary genius they are indebted for a great part of the trade and beauty of the place: yet they have industriously opposed his best designs, which, had they been executed, would have rendered *Bath,* in point of elegant architecture, the admiration of the whole World.

*Smollett, Essay, pp.38-9*

### 331.  1753  A raid on the dairy market

Saturday last, the Mayor ordered his Officers to go into our Market, and weigh the Butter, which they did, and took away a great Quantity (which was given to the Poor) that was under Weight; particularly twenty-five Pounds from one Woman, who, it is remarked, wore Men's Apparel 'till she was married, on Purpose to enjoy an Estate.

*Bath Journal 19 Mar 1753*

### 332.  1756  Treacherous party politics

... our Election [took place] yesterday of a Representative to fill up the Seat in Parliament, lately vacated by Mr [Robert] Henley's being made Attorney-general. The Number of Electors for Members to represent this City consists in all in Thirty, and they are the whole Corporation. Eighteen of these for a considerable Time back, were under the strongest Connections by Promise to vote in Favour of honest Mr. [Joseph] Langton [of Newton St Loe], at the next Vacancy that should happen, either by Death or Promotion. At the Day of Trial Six of our Party (the above mention'd Eighteen) prov'd Traitors, and went over to Henley's Side, so that Mr.Langton's Interest was entirely destroy'd, and this Time we cou'd do nothing for him: but to shew a just Resentment and Contempt of the six Traitors, and the whole of Mr.Henley's Party, Twelve of us absented ourselves from the Election. There were Eighteen present at the Election, Seventeen of whom voted for Henley, whom Mr.Collibee, the Mayor (who is one of us) pronounc'd to be duly elected, but, when his own Voice was ask'd, said, for such Reasons as were best known to himself, he shou'd not vote for Mr.Henley, and therefore wou'd give no Vote at all. It was observ'd there was not a Quarter Part of the Number of People as usually at the [Guild] Hall on the Occasion; that those who were present look'd highly disgusted during the Process of the Election; and that after it was all over there was not so much as One Hiss or Huzza. I must tell you it was ever a Custom with the Corporation of this Place to entertain the Member, on the Day of Election, with either a Dinner or Supper, but our honest Mayor wou'd give neither, which Occasion'd the greatest Disappointment, and no less Mortification, to our

Enemies, especially the shameful Six. I hope my Friends at Shaw will not only applaud the honest Twelve who absented, but remember them likewise in the next Bottle of October [strong ale] they shall open after this arrives.
*WRO, Cole Park MSS 161/102/2, John Lovell to Sarah Harvey, Bath 9 Dec 1756*

### 333.  1757  The Elder Pitt returned as Bath's M.P. thanks to Ralph Allen
The Part you have taken in the Honours lately done to Mr Pitt by the Corporation of Bath is understood by him as it ought to be. He has been disabled from using a Pen by the Gout in his right Arm wch he is obliged to carry in a Sling. He tells me he has made Shift to sign his Name to a Letter of Thanks, & he wishes that if that Letter shd be printed as probably it will in the Bath Papers it shd be done from a very correct Copy, as mankind are extremely alert in searching even for single Words to found some Accusation against him.
*BCL, AL 2355, Thomas Potter to Ralph Allen, 27 Apr 1757*

### 334.  1757  Pitt's popularity saps old allegiances
... at the first onset of Treaty with our Party I found the Town was canvassing in Favour of Mr Pitt - [so] Mr Langton was sent to and as his Resolutions are to offer himself a Candidate, his Friends are determin'd to serve him... [yet] I and my Friends really have the same due Sense and Regard for Mr Pitt as we have hitherto profess'd... Some of our Friends are absent, and when they return we shall have their Sentiments, which will resolve us how far we can serve Mr Pitt...
*BCL, AL 2355, Edward Bushell Collibee to Thomas Potter, Bath 23 June 1757*

### 335.  1763  Allen at odds with Pitt over the treaty to end the Seven Years' War
It is extremely painful to me to find... that the word *adequate* in the Bath address [to Parliament] has been so very offensive to you, as to hinder the sincerest and most zealous of your friends in the corporation from testifying for the future their great attachment to you. // Upon this occasion, in justice to them, it is incumbent upon me to acquaint you, that the exceptionable word does not rest with them, but with myself; who suddenly drew up that address to prevent their sending off another, which the mayor brought to me, in terms that I could not concur in... // Permit me to say, that I have not the least objection to, but feel the highest regard and even veneration for, your whole conduct; neither have I any apology to make for the expression in which I am so unfortunate as to differ from you.
*Pitt, Correspondence, vol.2 pp.225-6, Ralph Allen to William Pitt, Bath 4 Jun 1763*

### 336.  1763  Bishop Warburton tries to cool the controversy
In what followed, I dare say the concern and indignation were reciprocally equal. I mean, for the abuses thrown out against us all, by the miserable scribblers on both sides. They would not take Mr.Allen's word, but reviled me [Allen's son-in-law] in the foulest language, as instigating Mr.Allen to this offensive measure. Nay, in picture likewise (in the contrivance of which, one

Collibee, a member of the corporation, a Jacobite, and, on that account, an old inveterate, and declared enemy of Mr.Allen, is supposed to have had a hand), where the addressers of Bath are libelled in the vilest manner, your humble servant is brought in, in his episcopal habit, prompted by the Devil, to whisper in Mr.Allen's ear the word *adequate*... I, for my part, am callous to these things... But I suspect it is not altogether so well with good Mr.Allen... Yet, I believe, that which most concerned him was his ignorance, when he used the word *adequate*, that you, Sir, in a public assembly, had employed the word *inadequate*, to characterise the peace.

*Pitt, Correspondence, vol.2 pp.255-6, William Warburton to William Pitt, Bath 4 Sep 1763*

### 337.  1766  Commissioners: a new tier of local government established

And whereas the Intentions of the... Act [of Parliament for Bath] might be better carried into Execution, if the several Powers of ordering the paving, cleansing and enlightening the Squares and Streets... and of keeping a sufficient and well regulated Watch in the Night-time... were vested in a competent Number of Commissioners; Be it Enacted... That a certain Number of Commissioners, not exceeding Twenty, shall be elected, nominated and appointed...

*Acts of Parliament, 6 Geo III c.70 (1766) p.17*

### 338.  1767  Contesting a narrow election result

... mr Long [defeated 14 votes to 15] is Gon this Day [to London]; the Day of Determination in the House, Will be the ten of February, mr Long is endeavouring to make [Mr] Frederick the Booksellers vote invalid, as he had not Received the sacrament within the year he was chos[en] in to the Corporation, so then thear must be [a] new Election and we hope it will be in favour of mr Long...

*WRO, Cole Park MSS, 161/109, Sarah Lovell to her uncle John Harvey, Bath 16 Jan 1767*

### 339.  1775  Garrick canvasses on behalf of John Palmer

(15 Apr)  Palmer goes on well, & will be elected into ye Corporation, I am kissing old Women, & giving young ones ye Liberty of Drury Lane Theatre by way of Bribery & Corruption...

(20 Apr)  Palmer's Election for common councilman comes on tomorrow - he has brought down Ld C[amden, the Recorder of Bath] to insure him Success, & he will have it - what a stirring indefatigable fellow it is!

*Garrick, Letters, vol.3 pp.1002-3, David Garrick to George Colman, 1775*

### 340.  1775  City fathers deaf to advice

Having lately seen in the Bath Papers some reflections and animadversions of the Citizens on the Corporation respecting their guardianship of the city in the disposal of public monies, &c.&c. it gave me real sorrow to find they should be so well founded and true, for I believe there is scarce a man in the city out of

the body [of the Corporation] who is not ready to declare, that they have hardly
made any other use of the powers charter'd to them for our benefit, but in
opposing our inclinations and our interests; there is scarce an instance where
any one Person has endeavour'd to advise or assist them for the benefit of the
city, but they have immediately set themselves full against him, as if he had
been contriving some great mischief - and what does this proceed from? Why
to that Corporation consequence and secrecy which they affect, which will not
suffer them to inform, or be inform'd, which is eternally the reason of the
numberless blunders in their Acts of Parliament and in their carrying those acts
into execution... Surely there are as wise heads out of the body as in it, nor
would it derogate either from the wisdom or dignity of the gentlemen to get
every information, ere they determine on any business of consequence. // What
a conduct is theirs respecting the new plan that was offer'd to them for the
Town-Hall and Markets? Is it not astonishing, after it had been made appear,
that in the laying out of 7600l. [£7600] they might save 6000l. [£6000] and at
the same time adopt the most convenient and beautiful, they should turn aside
and not only prefer the plan acknowledg'd to be the worst, but thank their
surveyor and pseudo architect [i.e. T.W.Atwood], who had drawn them into
his erroneous and expensive undertaking?
*Bath Journal 24 Jul 1775, Anonymous letter*

### 341. 1775 The softly softly approach
As many severe Reflections have lately been level'd at the Body Corporation
of this City; therefore the Publication of their Charter appears the most eligible
Mode of instructing the Citizens, what to expect from those Gentlemen, who
have the Direction of the public Concerns; for have not the Inhabitants frequently
required (from the Corporation) too much? nay, as often, perhaps, as they have
done, too little; but should they at any future Time, by Supineness, neglect
their public Duty, let me recommend the Inhabitants not to treat them again
with harsh Censure and unkind Reproach, but endeavour to awake their
Attention, by humble Petition and gentle Remonstrance; then the Peace of the
City may be happily preserved, and the Corporation and Citizens mutually
enjoy, lasting Tranquillity.
*Bath: City Charter, 1775, p.[2]*

### 342. 1790 Still discriminating against Nonconformists
Resolved unanimously that the Representatives of this City in Parliament be
instructed to oppose to the utmost in their Power the Repeal of the Test and
Corporation Acts  And that this Resolution be communicated to the said
Representatives by the Deputy Town Clerk.
*BRO, Bath Council Minutes, 24 Feb 1790*

### 343. 1790 Too many dogs in Bath: time the J.P.s acted
ONE of the greatest nuisances in your city is the number of useless Dogs that
are kept there, beyond comparison more than are to be met with in any other

place of the size. Scarce a [sedan-]chairman but has his spaniel and terrier, and some of them three or four of each kind lying about his stand. When the horrid effects of canine madness is considered, and when you reflect that a quantity of provision is daily devoured by these idle animals which might serve to support many an indigent wretch and his starving family, would it not be laudable in you to reduce the number? As the chairmen are under your immediate controul, let me advise you to refuse a license to every one of them who keeps a dog.
*Bath Chronicle 29 Apr 1790, letter from 'CIVIS'*

### 344. 1790 Election fixing

The election is to come on next Monday, but the conclusion is already known, having been fixed at a meeting of the Corporation yesterday. Lord Bayham and Lord Weymouth are the fortunate candidates. Owing to Mr.Grenville declining, his votes went to Lord Weymouth, which gave him a majority over Mr.Watson, who resigned yesterday, and Mr.Morris, it is supposed, will follow his example, as he has not, I find, the least chance of success.
*HMC 35 Kenyon, p.530, James Tomkinson to Lord Kenyon, Bath 18 Jun 1790*

### 345. 1790 The reward

This day se'nnight [i.e. a week ago] our Members, Lord Bayham and Lord Weymouth, gave an elegant Ball and Supper at the Guildhall, to more than 500 ladies and gentlemen, among which were many of rank and distinction. The ball was opened by Lord Weymouth and Miss Horton (the Mayor's daughter), his Lordship danced a second minuet with Miss Anderdon, and several succeeding ones were appropriated to the sons and daughters of different Gentlemen of the Corporation. Lord Bayham and Miss Nichols graced the last minuet. Country dances then began, and tea, orgeat, cakes, and other refreshments, were plentifully served. At twelve the company sat down to a most sumptuous repast, (furnished by Mr.Philott of the Bear)... // A correspondent with some indignation notices the mighty fuss made about some poor ladies *stealing* (as it is seriously termed) a few artificial flowers at the Members' entertainment. The noble hospitable Lords must be sorry to see so unhandsome a charge brought against some of their lovely guests. If ladies did long for any of the well-made flowers to set off their diamonds to advantage, no doubt they were as welcome to use them as to pluck living flowers from their Lordships' parterre; these noblemen have more gallantry than to consider this any crime at all...
*Bath Chronicle 25 Nov 1790*

### 346. 1792 Official blessing denied the Anti-Slave-Trade Movement

A numerous and respectable meeting of the Inhabitants of Bath, and its neighbourhood, for the purpose of petitioning Parliament to abolish the African Slave Trade, was held last Friday at the Exhibition-Room, Bond-street; leave not having been granted to assemble in the Town-hall. A serious difficulty arose respecting the mode of presenting the petition, the citizens of Bath not being represented in Parliament. It was decided unanimously, that the favour could not with any propriety be requested from the Representatives of the Corporation, and that application should be made to the County Members for this purpose.

*Bath Chronicle 1 Mar 1792, report from 'VERUS'*

### 347. 1792 Would-be reformers assemble while they still can

We hear the Gentlemen who dined at the Bear Inn in this city, for the purpose of commemorating the Revolution of 1688, came to a conclusion, thenceforward to decline a particular commemoration of that event; and resolved themselves into a Society for promoting a Parliamentary reform, by procuring a more equal representation of the people.

*Bath Chronicle 15 Nov 1792*

### 348. 1799 The Town Clerk's order against scurrilous prints

WHEREAS most indecent, scandalous, and disloyal PRINTS, are daily exposed for sale in several Shops in this City:- The MAGISTRATES, in obedience to His Majesty's Proclamation, hereby declare their full determination, to indict, or otherwise prosecute, all Publishers and Venders of such illegal Prints as shall be found exposed for sale at their respective Shops or Houses, with the utmost rigour // ... more particularly as the interest of the City of Bath is immediately concerned in preventing all offences injurious to the characters of the Visitors of both sexes, who honour this place, either for their health or amusement.

*Bath Chronicle 6 Jun 1799*

## DISORDER, CRIME AND PUNISHMENT

*So much temptation, so little sin - or, for that matter, criminal activity. This frequent refrain of Bath's well-wishers had some justification, for the spa environment did seem reassuringly secure. Not that it was outstandingly well policed. It took until 1739 for the night watch to be placed on a proper legal footing; and the modest quota of constables and watchmen always needed reinforcing by sedan chairmen, specially sworn in, at times of popular unrest. This happened in the mid-1760s, mid-1790s and around 1800, all crisis points when food rioting looked likely, and again during the Gordon Riots panic of 1780. At such times and as a last resort the local militia and the troops garrisoned at nearby towns might also be called upon. But these episodes were rare, and the Corporation and parish officers were generally able to cope with the common run of drunks, brawlers, beggars, prostitutes and 'nightwalkers'. It was nonetheless a matter of much complaint that Bath, despite its burgeoning population, had no court of law able to try more serious crime which went instead to the county assizes at distant Wells, Taunton or Ilchester, a real disincentive to bringing prosecutions. The city gaol (removed in 1774 from the tower of St Mary's to a brand new building in Bathwick) consequently harboured only minor offenders and, above all, wretched debtors lingering there in quiet desperation. Poverty must have fuelled much ordinary crime: pilfering from market gardens, shop-lifting, casual theft, prostitution, and perhaps some of the resentful acts of vandalism, even arson, that were reported. Some crime was organised, as we know from the famous Poulter-Baxter gang in the early 1750s and the Barnett case forty years later, both involving the fencing of stolen property. At a more trivial level the practice of cheating and overcharging visitors and wealthy residents, often in collusion with servants, was almost endemic. The worst felonies though, such as murder, were rare - with the signal exception of infanticide. If uncommon, duels of honour, usually (like Sheridan's) fought on the neighbouring downs, were sometimes fatal and brought Bath its share of macabre notoriety.*

349. *1713 Caging night walkers*
Agreed that there Shall be a Cage or Constables Prison Erected at the Charge of the Chamber of this City on the South side of the Upper Conduit [water fountain] in the Market place... for Securing Night Walkers and other disorderly persons.
*BRO, Bath Council Minutes, 28 Dec 1713*

350. *1727 Brothel keepers in the pillory*
And [we have an account] from Bath, that one Lewis and his Wife stood in the Pillory there on Saturday last, being convicted of keeping a bad House of Repute, and procuring Young Women to be debauch'd, and forcing them so to do; for which they were severely pelted. When his Wife was mounting the Scaffold, she had the Arrogance to make the following blasphemous Comparison, saying, That she was now going to imitate the Sufferings of our S.....r, being as Innocent of the Fact she was going to suffer for, as he was when C....fied. - The chief Evidence against her, it seems, was one of her Female Servants, who having some Words with her said Mistress, would live no longer with her; and therefore demanded her Wages and her Cloaths; but she refusing to comply with her Demands, the Servant went immediately to a Magistrate, and blow'd up the whole Scene of her Mistress's way of Life; particularly, that she has danced N...d before a Number of Gentlemen; and for her Agility, had Half a Crown of each.
*Farley's Bristol Newspaper 28 Jan 1727*

351. *1730 Forthright response to the threat of arson*
This day a letter was sent to a tradesman of this city ordering him to put a sum of money under the door of St.Michael's Church before Thursday night on pain of having his house burnt and himself murdered. Hereupon the Mayor ordered fifteen constables to search and take up all vagrants and persons who would give no account of themselves, and accordingly forty were seized, and stand confined, the gates of the city were ordered to be guarded, all night-walkers examined, the fire engines drawn ready out, and all the hedge ale-houses within a mile searched for suspicious persons. A noted gaming house was also suppressed, where out[-of-work] footmen lose their time, money and honesty; one footman I am told lost a hundred pounds. This wicked practice of writing letters with desperate and damnable threats is now spread through many parts of the kingdom.
*HMC 63 Egmont, Diary, vol.1, p.117, entry for 17 Nov 1730*

352. *1731 The consequences of a gambling duel*
A duel that has been fought lately, between one Jones a gamester, and one Mr.Price (a gentleman's son but of the same profession too), has put us in great confusion. Price is kill'd, and Jones has made his escape.
*HMC 20 Dartmouth, vol.1 p.327, Earl of Orrery to Lady Kaye, Bath 3 Nov 1731*

*353. 1741-2  Alderman Ford accused of homosexuality*
(2 Feb 1741)  Whereas an Information upon the Oath of John Guiden... hath been this day made and Exhibited against John Ford one of the Aldermen and Chamberlain of this City of Bath for a Sodomiticall Attempt upon him the said John Guiden. Now it is hereby Agreed... that a prosecution shall be carryed on against the said John Ford for the above fact at the Expence of this Corporation...
(25 Oct 1742)  Whether Alderman Ford upon Consideration of the Evidence that hath been given to this Corporation of an Attempt of Sodomy and upon his neglecting to attend the Hall [Guildhall] pursuant to the Sumons that hath been given him by the two preceding mayors shall be excluded from his Office of Alderman. No 14 [votes] Yes 13.
*BRO, Bath Council Minutes, 1740-1*

*354. 1749  So much temptation, so little law-breaking*
HONESTY... has been so prevalent at *Bath*, that very little Use hath been made of any of her Prisons, notwithstanding the Opportunities and Temptations for Robbery have been greater here than perhaps in any publick Place of the Kingdom: People of Rank and Fortune rest secure in their Lodgings while the Doors of the Houses are left open to every Body; and when they appear at the Assembly-Houses their brilliant Dresses subjects them to no manner of Danger.
*Wood, Essay, 1749, vol.2, pp.318-19*

*355. 1751  How one thing leads to another*
It is hop'd this [i.e.a nearly fatal drowning], and the many Instances of the like Kind, will caution Parents and Governors of Families, to take Care (as much as in their Power lies) how their Children and their Servants spend their Time on the Sabbath-Day: For, if they are not kept under a proper Restriction, they generally run wandering into the Fields, rob Orchards, bathe in Rivers, play at Chuck, or some other Game; often Drink and keep bad Company: To support which, they pilfer from their Parent or Master: This leads them on from one Degree of Wickedness to another; when at last they commit some notorious Crime, which sentences them either for Transportation, or the Gallows.
*Bath Journal 5 Aug 1751*

*356. 1753  Criminal confessions*
I sold the [stolen] Bells, Seal, Shoe Buckles, and Girdle Buckles, all of Gold, to *J[oh]n F[or]d*, a Silversmith in *Bath*; and he melted them down before my Face, into an Ingot of Gold, not quite an ounce. I told him from whence they came, and he said he did not care if they came from the Ruffen, (that is the Devil)... We went out of *Bath*, to *Corsham* Fair, about eleven Miles from *Bath*... and we stole a silver Tankard from an Inn in *Corsham*: I brought it directly to *J[oh]n F[or]d* at *Bath*, who not being at home, I told his Wife we had stole a silver Tankard... and wanted to melt it down; I then went up Stairs with her, and she fasten'd a Pair of Sheers into a Vice, and began to cut it to Pieces, when her Husband came in... and said, *Betty* go and make a Fire in the Shop, and bring a large Crucible... and they melted it down before my Face... //

[Another time we came]... towards *Bath*, on Purpose to break open a House in *Wade's Passage*, which we look'd at several Times before. We stole in our Way... a large Iron Crow[bar] from a Sheepfold on *Salisbury Plain*, on Purpose to wrench open the Door of the said Shop: We left our horses at *Mount-Pleasant*, while we went a Milling that Swagg, that is, a Breaking open that Shop; we wrench'd open the Pad Lock, but could not open the Door, altho' we made a great Purchase with the Iron Crow; we made several Attempts, and in the mean Time the Scout came by, that is, the Watch, but *Brown* took him off, while we were at Work, which is easily done for a Quart of Drink... We tried two Shops in the Church Yard, at their Windows, the one a Toy Shop [selling jewellery and fancy goods], and the other a Watchmaker's, but was disappointed by a drunken Man's coming into the Church Yard, and setting himself down.

*Poulter, Discoveries, pp.10-11 and 13-14*

### 357. 1758 Danger on the highways

Wednesday Night a Servant of Mr.Wood's was attacked by a Footpad near the Half-Way House between Bath and Bitton; but being well mounted, avoided being robb'd. The Footpad was a thick-set Fellow; had on a long light-coloured Great Coat, a Grizzle Bob Wig; his Hat flapped before, and [he] seemed to have a hoarse hollow Voice. // And last Thursday Night a Maid Servant of Corston, near this City, returning Home, was attacked by a Footpad at the Direction-Post between Twiverton [Twerton] and Newton. He presented a Pistol to her Breast, and demanded her Money, which she not readily giving, (being greatly frighten'd) he pulled her off her Horse, swearing he would blow her Brains out if she made the least Resistance; he then rifled her Pockets, and took from her all the Money she had (being about 18s.) and made off. He had on a brown Coat, a dark Bob Wig, and had a Crape over his Face.

*Bath Journal 20 Feb 1758*

### 358. 1763 A magistrate's summerhouse robbed

Mr.Collibee's Summer-House, on the Top of Beechen-Cliff, was some Time last Week broke open, and a Mahogany Spy-Glass and a large India Tea-Board taken from thence. It appears the same was done by a Fellow in a Sailor's Habit, who has been begging about the City for some Days. He had left the above Things with a Person in Avon-Street to keep for him, saying he had brought them from Quebec. A Fellow, who was seen begging in Company with him, was taken into Custody on Tuesday; but he says he does not know where his Companion is. 'Tis supposed he is gone for Bristol.

*Bath Chronicle 14 Apr 1763*

### 359. 1771 Sentences passed at Wells assizes

On Thursday last, at the General quarter sessions of the Peace for this county, held at Wells, Jane Jarvis, otherwise Agnew, and Ann White, were convicted of keeping houses of ill fame in New King-Street, in the parish of Walcot,... and were severally ordered to remove their habitations, to pay a fine of 6s.8d. and to find sureties for their good behaviour for two years. // At the same

sessions, one Arnold, a mason, for stealing a loin of pork from the Saracen's head in this city, was sentenced either to seven years transportation, or to enlist as a soldier, the latter of which he accepted... Elizabeth Calways, for stealing worsted to the value of 2s. was sentenced to be privately whipped. - And Joseph Pike, a plaisterer, convicted of leaving his family chargeable to the parish of St.Michael in this city, was sentenced to suffer three months imprisonment, and after to be sent on board one of his Majesty's ships.
*Bath Chronicle 24 Jan 1771*

### 360.  *1771  A prisoner's plea from gaol to his fellow freemasons*
BATH PRISON,1771. Right Worshipful, - The Humble Petition of a Bro[the]r in extreme Distress, Confined almost a Twelvemonth, having no Allowance but from some Acquaintance, no bed to Lay on and often have not bread, nor victuals, nor money. Shall be Glad if my Bretherin will Consider my Deplorable Condition by Contributing something towards my Support, and as I am in a very Dissponding way hopes you will be Inclined to Reli[e]ve a Poor Unfortunate Bro[the]r.
*Norman, Masonic Lodges, p.404*

### 361.  *1772  Sheridan's second duel over Elizabeth Linley*
The last affair between Mr.Matthews and Mr.Sheridan, we are now assured, was occasioned by Mr.S's refusal to sign a paper, testifying the *spirit* and *propriety* of Mr.M's behaviour in their former rencounter. This refusal induced Mr.M to send him a challenge, which was accepted, and Kingsdown was the place appointed for the decision of their quarrel: After a few passes, both their swords were broken, Mr.S's almost to the hilt, who thereupon closed with Mr.Matthews, and they both fell. - Mr.M. having then considerably the advantage, called on S. to beg his life, which he refused (having in their former duel given M. his life;) upon which M. picked up a broken piece of his sword, gave him the wounds of which he last Wednesday lay dangerously ill, and immediately left this city... The seconds stood by quiet spectators. // 'Tis with great pleasure we inform our readers, that Mr.Sheridan is declared by his surgeon to be out of danger.
*Bath Chronicle 9 Jul 1772*

### 362.  *1777  A lamentable fall from grace*
Lawyers have been noted for cheating; but what shall we say of a physician at Bath, Dr.Schomberg, who was appointed last Sunday to hold a plate for charity at the Church door, where a large collection was expected for the Hospital, and was detected by several persons in stealing the money? Above seven pounds in guineas and half crowns were found in his coatpocket, when he was charged with the fact. Yet this man, who was base enough to attempt this uncharitable fraud, married a woman with eight hundred a year. I am heartily sorry for her and for their family: He has left Bath, and must hide his face for ever.
*Jones, Letters, vol.1 pp.256-7, William Jones to Lady Spencer, Bath 30 Dec 1777*

### 363.  1778  Inquest on a new-born baby

And first this Examinant Alexander Mortimer for himself saith that on the twentieth day of July about the Hour of Eleven oClock at Night as he this Examinant ['with a Lighted Candle in his Hand'] and... Robert Bayly were gathering worms in a Court or Lane called Ambury Lane... for the Purpose of Baiting of Hullys [wickerwork traps] for catching of fish he... saw a male Infant Child lying Dead on the Ground up near or against the west wall at the End of the said Court or Lane and immediately... called out to the said Robert Bayly saying Lord! Robert here is a young Dead Child... And this Examinant Robert Bayly for himself saith that... on being called... he immediately went to him and saw the said Child so dead in a manner aforesaid and immediately afterward called ['one Mrs Cole and several other of the Inhabitants who took up the said Child and wraped it in an Apron']... And both these Examinants... say that when they saw the said Child... it was quite naked and appeard to have been very lately Born... And this Examinant John Dodd for himself saith that... he did see and Examine the said Child and... found no marks of any Violence... And in order to Ascertain whether such Child was Born Alive or not he... opened the Body thereof and took out the Lungs of the said Child and put the same into Cold water and such Lungs swiming upon the Surface of such water he this Examinant has great reason to and verily believes that such Child was Born alive.

*BRO, Bath Coroners Examinations, 1776-98, Inquest of 21 Jul 1778*

### 364.  1780  The Gordon Riots shock Bath

Friday evening [9 June] a most alarming riot happen'd here, which was begun by a Footman and some boys breaking the windows of a house where the Roman Catholic Priest resided, adjoining to a new Chapel lately built for persons of that religion; in a very short time, as night came on, they were joined by a great number of people, most of them strangers, and armed with carpenter's tools, who broke open the chapel doors immediately and began gutting it and throwing the materials out of the window; the Magistrates and other peace officers assembled as quick as possible, but e're they could exert themselves the mob had increased to such a multitude that every effort to disperse them was ineffectual. - The riot act was read, and some persons seized, but instantly rescued; the Magistrates and many respectable Citizens used every possible exertion to prevail on the mob to disperse, but without effect. Major Molesworth with a few of the City Volunteers hastily collected, went into the chapel, to the imminent hazard of their lives, and so far prevailed upon the rioters, as to be suffered to put out the fire several times, which they repeatedly kindled for it's destruction; about twenty more of the Volunteers were soon after got together, and Capt.Duperre, at the request of the Mayor, headed them, and led them into the chapel, with their pieces not loaded, the instant they entered the building the mob rushed in upon them on all sides, and a pistol was fired at Capt.Duperre, which fortunately missed, and as fortunately destroyed an old rioter who had been once before wounded at an insurrection at Trowbridge - but it so insensed

the mob, who supposed him shot by one of the Volunteers, that they immediately
fired the chapel, and the corps having received a few wounds and finding it
utterly impossible to resist so large a body, made a slow and good retreat - The
chapel and about six or seven houses that surrounded it were entirely burnt by
about four in the morning, when this desperate rabble, by the repeated and
laudable exertions of the Magistrates and Citizens were prevailed on to disperse,
without carrying the remainder of their diabolical plan into execution, they
having declared their determination to fire the old chapel and the houses of
several Roman Catholics residing here...
*Bath Journal 12 Jun 1780*

### 365. 1780 Fanny Burney on the aftermath of the riots

We did not leave Bath till eight o'clock yesterday evening, at which time it
was filled with dragoons, militia, and armed constables, not armed with muskets,
but with bludgeons: those latter were all chairmen, who were sworn by the
mayor in the morning for petty constables. A popish private chapel, and the
houses of all the Catholics, were guarded... and the inhabitants ordered to keep
house.
*Burney (F.), Diary, vol.1 p.427, Fanny Burney to her father, 11 June 1780*

### 366. 1784 Measures to stop soliciting

It is with pleasure we congratulate the public on the active exertions of the
parish officers of St.James, in rooting out the nest of prostitutes that have for a
long time been a nuisance to the sober inhabitants in the neighbourhood of the
Cross-Bath. The method they mean to pursue is, we hear, to take them all
before the Magistrates, to send those to their respective parishes who do not
belong to the city, and to obtain warrants of commitment for the others to the
bridewell at Shepton [Mallet].
*Bath Chronicle 26 Aug 1784*

### 367. 1785 Conditions at Bath city gaol

The ascent to this prison, built in a meadow, which is sometimes overflowed
[from the river], is by a fine flight of stone steps. On the ground floor is the
keeper's kitchen, &c. and four rooms for petty offenders. Above are three stories,
five rooms on each, one or two of them used by the keeper: The rest for debtors,
one bed in a room, in which if two prisoners sleep they pay 2s. a week each; if
one has it to himself, he pays 3s. a week. Two rooms on the second story are
free wards, one for men, the other for women; on the upper floor is their workshop. There is a small court with offensive sewers. Keeper, a sheriff's officer:
No Salary: Fees, if from the court of Requests [court for small debts], 3s.6d.
Debtors for large sums, 7s.8d. Offenders Fees, 7s.8d.... Licence for beer.
Allowance to debtors, none. To offenders, 2d. a day. Clauses against spirituous
liquors; and the act for preserving the health of prisoners not hung up. - Several
Regulations will shortly be made... for the Convenience of Prisoners, by

conveying a constant stream of soft Water... [piped to the prison]. Also, it is intended that the keepers room be at the Right Hand on the entrance of the Gaol, as a Security to prevent escapes.

*Gentleman... Pocket Guide, 1785, 'Bath City Gaol'*

### 368.  1792  A very public whipping

(7 Apr)  BARNET the Baker will be made a public example to-morrow, by being whipped through the streets of the city, agreeably to a part of his sentence.

(14 Apr)  The immense croud that attended the flagellation of BARNETT, last Saturday, made a new method of punishment necessary, which undoubtedly ought to be ranked with our modern improvements. The criminal was placed in the cart, which not only gave the Beadle an opportunity of bestowing the lashings unchecked by the pressure of the croud, but at the same time made the punishment more public, as every body had a view of the offender. // The only murmur in the croud was, that our laws could not enforce a sentence more adequate to BARNETT's offences, which had reared up and encouraged a nest of young thieves, to the long annoyance of this City; - but as there was no evidence against the boy as the principal, Barnett could not be tried as the accessory, in receiving the stolen articles.

*Bath Herald  7 and 14 Apr 1792*

### 369.  1795  Crime passionnel in the schoolroom

Elizabeth Champion... who is about Seven Years and an half old... being Examined said that she went to School to... Maria Bally in Corn Street... and being in the School Room with other Scollars and the said Maria Bally between the Hours of Ten and Eleven o'Clock in the Morning... William White the Prisoner now in Custody came into the said School Room and sat down at some small distance from the said Maria Bally and continued there but a short time before this Examinant heard the Report of a pistol and saw the Smoke of the powder and the said Maria Bally immediately fell from her Chair on the Floor That she saw a Wound on the left side of her Head over her Ear That this Examinant immediately left the Room and the rest of the children followed her in order to get some assistance That she went to Fanny Greenslade an opposite Neighbour and told her that a Man had killed her Maam (meaning the said Maria Bally)... Fanny Greenslade... saith that... she saw all the children running out crying Murder in the street That she saw the said William White coming out of the Door of the said Maria Bally's House with the children whom this Examinant asked what he had done whereupon he held out a pistol in his Hand and said take me. Take me. I yield myself up That she saw the said Maria Bally lying on the Floor in her Room.

*BRO, Bath Coroners Examinations, 1776-98, Inquest of 9 Jun 1795*

### 370. 1797 The counterfeit coins trick
... it is highly necessary to caution the inhabitants of this city to beware of purchasing vegetables, fish, fruit, &c. of any of those men that cry it about the streets, as several instances have occurred this week, where, under pretence of examining the silver offered them, they have changed it, and instantly returned a base piece in its place; and after a great share of abuse to the persons for venturing to declare their suspicion of the trick, they were obliged to put up with the imposition. // It is an undoubted fact, that one Lady in particular, on buying some salmon, had no less than three bad shillings returned at one time for an equal number of good ones, and being obliged to change a half-a-guinea with him, she very incautiously took four more in the change.
*Bath Chronicle 13 Jul 1797, letter from 'Observer'*

### 371. 1797 A further case of infanticide
On Monday evening, as a dog was swimming in our river below Kingsmead, he dragged to the shore a new born female Infant, that had evident marks of wilful injury on many parts of its body. The frequency of these inhuman acts, calls aloud for Parishes to offer large rewards for the discovery of the brutal Parents, and use every means to make them suffer death as public examples.
*Bath Herald 16 Sep 1797*

### 372. 1799 Sedan chairs vandalised
WHEREAS FOUR SEDAN-CHAIRS, standing in different parts of this City, were last night wilfully CUT and DEFACED by some person or persons unknown:- // Whoever will discover the offender or offenders, so that he, she, or they may be convicted of the said offence, shall receive FIVE GUINEAS Reward, on such conviction, from the Chamberlain of Bath. // By order of the Mayor... A further Reward of FIVE GUINEAS will likewise be paid by the CHAIRMEN of this City...
*Bath Chronicle 16 May 1799*

### 373. 1799 Quis custodiet ipsos custodes?
A watchman, stationed in Gay-street, on Sunday evening last was seated in a publick-house for an hour from half past ten. From such nightly *guardians*, what are the publick to expect?
*Bath Chronicle 28 Nov 1799*

### 374. 1800 At a time of scarcity and high prices
On Wednesday symptoms of a riotous nature were manifest in our Market-place, and two or three women began to empty a sack of potatoes, and to give the owner such price for them as they thought proper. Towards the afternoon this disquietude became more general, and a large mob collected (out of the Mayor's jurisdiction) opposite Walcot-parade, and broke the windows of a man, who they were informed had lately purchased a quantity of potatoes; after committing many outrages here, they proceeded deliberately to a house

near Lark-Hall, where they beat a man, and did other mischief before the Bath Volunteers came up, who having taken a few of the most riotous into custody, the rest dispersed. It was thought necessary for the better preservation of the peace, that Captain Wiltshire's troop of Cavalry should be mounted; and a party of the horse and foot were upon guard all night. By these precautions, every thing was in a short time quiet, and has remained so since.

*Bath Herald 10 May 1800*

# POVERTY

*People begging conspicuously on the streets - or being whipped out of town by the town crier - were not in the main Bathonians, who would have forfeited any right to parish support if caught openly soliciting. Rather they were vagrants, who traditionally descended on the spa each season not for the benefit of the waters (to which all the same, as British citizens, they were in theory entitled) but to tap the philanthropy of other, more affluent, 'strangers'. It is hardly possible to quantify Bath's resident poor, but these included not merely paupers surviving on parish out-relief or accommodated in poorhouses and almshouses, but indigent inhabitants not native to the city who thereby failed to qualify for assistance, as well as anyone in low-paid and seasonal employment without a cushion of savings for times of need and old-age - building labourers, scavengers, nightsoil-men, basket-women, laundresses, sweatshop seamstresses, and many more. The humbler domestic servants (a number of them black and of near slave status) come into the same category, as perhaps should journeymen of various trades who, thanks to later-eighteenth-century inflation, found their real wages declining and their masters quite prepared to face down any talk of strikes. Even the skilled and industrious were at the mercy of events; illness, an accident, bad luck, might quickly reduce them to desperate straits. Poverty created its own culture and ways of managing. Like any other city the fashionable spa had its pawnbrokers, old clothes dealers, cheap chandlers' shops, beerhouses, gin-shops, its tattered urchins, its sifters of rubbish tips, its squatters in empty properties, its sordid backstreets and its fire-hazard lodgings. Charities alleviated some of the worst hardship: the Pauper Charity (from 1747) gave medical help, as the General Hospital did not, to Bath's own sick poor; the Lying-in Charity (1765) and Strangers' Friend Society (1790) brought some relief to outsiders. Other unfortunates benefited from private philanthropy and public appeals, but it remained very hit or miss.*

## 375. 1702 Poor creatures

We have great trouble in this city in the summer time by poor and indigent people that come to the Bath and bring with them but little money, and as soon as it is spent cannot return home because of their poverty unless they are whipt, which is very inhumane to poor creatures.

*HMC 51 Leyborne-Popham, pp.251-2, Mayor of Bath to Alex Popham, M.P., Bath 31 Jan 1702*

## 376. 1717-56 Christenings of black servants at the Abbey Church

(15 Oct 1717)     James Butler, a blackimor servant to Mr John Garner
(5 Nov 1717)      Charles Stuart, a blackmore servant to Mr Garner
(11 Sep 1720)     Richard son of James, a black
(23 Mar 1722)     Amy daughter of James, a blackmore
(19 Mar 1735)     John Heart, a black, about 18 years of age
(20 Jun 1739)     Henry Johnson, a black sarvant to Mr Loas
(10 Feb 1743)     Elizabeth Rose, a blackamore woman
(4 Jul 1743)      John Coffe, a black, aboute 15 years of age
(25 Mar 1745)     John Quashey, a black boy
(28 Sep 1754)     William Bath, a black boy, about 12 years, belonging to Mrs Hetling
(4 Feb 1756)      John Hamilton, a Negro about 29 ys. of age
(27 Apr 1756)     Agnes McBracka, Negro woman, a servant to Jacob Allen, Esq., of Jamaica

*BRO, Transcript of Abbey Church Register, Christenings*

## 377. 1734 Among the duties of the Town Crier

Agreed that John Allen Shall be Common Cryar of this City for the year ensuing on Condition he whips all Vagrants as the Mayor or Justices for ye time being shall direct.

*BRO, Bath Council Minutes, 30 Sep 1734*

## 378. 1746 A sixty-year-old in a blue coat

On Wednesday last a Man (who said his Name was Charles Floyd) was whipp'd here for begging about with a false Pass; and for endeavouring to extort Money, from People, by making dumb Motions; and holding a Knife in his Hand (when he begg'd) in order to strike greater Compassion upon People, for the Barbarity that had been exercis'd upon him. - He was (after begging here several Days) known by a Gentleman, who had seen him whipp'd before; and last Sunday he was taken up, and committed to Prison. - He has been an old Offender, and has undergone the above Punishment several Times; particularly at Cheltenham... about half a Year ago. He is a short Man about sixty Years of Age; wears a blue Coat, turn'd up with Buff; commonly wore a long grey Beard; and has the Mark [tattoo?] of a Crucifix in his Breast, done by some Grecian. - We discribe him in this Manner, in order to caution People against such Imposters; who run

about the Country, in various Disguises, with Intent to impose on mankind. - It is to be observ'd, that tho' this Man had been dumb for some Time; yet by the salutary Prescription that was applied to him (by Order of our Magistrates) he spoke very well, and extended his Voice in a loud Manner. // We hear the old Fellow has since been seen begging in Wiltshire.
*Bath Journal 3 Mar 1746*

### 379.  1749  The licensing of porters and basket-women
... whereas the Employment of poor Strangers in carrying Meat, and other Provisions for Hire, hath encouraged many such to resort to... [Bath], and has burdened the Inhabitants thereof with a great Increase of Poor, by Sicknesses, and other Accidents, before they could be duly removed to their own Parishes, where they were last legally settled, and whereas great Mistakes have been often made, in the carrying Meat & other Provisions, by such Strangers, ignorant of the Place of Abode of such Persons, to whose Houses they were directed to convey the same. To remedy such Mischeifs & Inconveniences, it is... Ordained... That, if any Person, or Persons, shall after the 11th Day of this instant Dec[embe]r, carry any Meat, or other Provisions... for Hire, unless such Person... be Licensed thereto... & unless He, or she, receives a Brass Ticket, discovering, that He, or she, is Licensed for the Purpose... [they] shall forfeit the Sum of one Shilling... & the Basket or other Implement... for every time [they offend]...
*BRO, Bath Council Minutes, 8 Dec 1749*

### 380.  1756  Testimonial for a servant
The Person whom I mention'd to you for a Servant will not, as I since find by Enquiry, be discharg'd from her present Mistress within Three Months, which I suppose will be too long for you to wait; therefore have said nothing to her: but have heard of another who has been out of Service about a Month. This last liv'd under the Character of a Sort of upper Servant at Doctor Moisey's a Physician here at Bath. She is 20 Years of Age; rather of small Stature. I ask'd Mrs.Moisey her Character, who in her Answers tells me, She is very good-natur'd, honest, and sober; not fond of gadding abroad, or scheming to bring Visitors home; can clean a Room; can wash small Things, and iron them up decently: and that she is not without some Knowledge in Cookery, which she believes was much improv'd whilst in her Service. When I talk'd with her I advis'd her to ask no Wages, but such as you gave the last Servant whither much or little; which she promises to be satisfy'd with, and expresses a great Desire to engage with you upon such Condition. I confess I wish you may either discharge, or make the general Contract with, her. If She comes to you I wish you much Satisfaction in her Services... My Man Anthony Webb tells me he knows her, and assures me that all her late Fellow-Servants speak favourably of her. He believes she will serve your Purpose very well, and wishes with me that you may take her.
*WRO, Cole Park MSS 161/102/1, John Lovell to Mrs Smith, Bath 11 Nov 1756*

*381. 1759  Echoes of the slave trade*
FOR Sale, a Negro Boy, about 13 Years old, quite black, perfectly well made
and found, has a good Capacity, been near two Years in England in a Family
where he has done the Business of a Foot-Boy, can wait at Table extremely
well, and has an Ear to Music. - For further Particulars, enquire of Mr.William
Bridgen, Coach-maker, in Bath. // N.B. He will be advertis'd only once.
*Bath Journal 31 Dec 1759*                                         ,

*382. 1765  Maternity assistance*
Amongst the great Number of useful and charitable Schemes offered to the
Consideration of the Benevolent, there is none, perhaps, more worthy public
Attention than what is now proposed, for the Relief of poor Lying-in Women...
// The great resort of poor Labourers and their Families to this City for
Employment, sufficiently evinces the Necessity of this Undertaking, and at the
same Time obviates the Objection of its being an Encouragement to Vice and
Prostitution. // It is therefore proposed to raise a Fund... to supply poor Lying-
in Women with Necessaries during the Month - such as Lodgings, Food and a
Nurse, and as this Charity will be entirely unconnected with every other Scheme,
it must necessarily incur a small Charge for Physic. Medicinal Help of every
other Kind will be administer'd gratis. It may be proper to add, that no Persons
will be deemed Objects of this Charity, but those whose extreme Poverty and
wretched Habitations deprive them of other Means of procuring such Assistance.
*Bath Chronicle 7 Mar 1765*

*383. 1766  The clandestine marriage*
[Setlement examination of] Hester Bishop (alias Vennell)... 27 years old...
About two years ago she got acquainted with John Vennell, broadweaver, of
the parish of Bradford[-on-Avon]. They agreed to be married and accordingly
put in the banns and were publicly asked in Bradford church. But John Vennell's
mother forbad the same, so she and Vennell, persuaded by Thomas Dicks, a
servant to the Revd Mr Chapman of Bradford, went to Bath where Dicks told
them they might be married. Accordingly she and John Vennell went with
Thomas Dicks to a chapel, as he told them, near the Hot Bath in Bath [St
John's?], where they were married by a man dressed in light-coloured clothes
and made use of the ring and read over the ceremony as the Church of England
directs. Thomas Dicks was very well known to the man who married them for
he went after him and brought him to that place.
*Calendar of Bradford-on-Avon Examinations. pp.26-7, no.93, 16 Aug 1766*

*384. 1776  A warning of strike action*
... at a Meeting of Journymen Carpenters Haveing Consider'd the many
hardships we labour under with our wifes and famillys in the City of Bath
Owing to the masters Giveing Low wages the Exspence of tools and high
Price of Provision &c. We hereby Gives Notise to all Masters that they Solicits
their Wages to be Advanced According to their Merrit and unless their Masters

think fitt to raise Adequet to their Workmanship three Shillings pr week -
Resolved all to Strik on Munday next.
*Bath Chronicle 22 Aug 1776*

*385.  1777  To the City Commissioners on the nastiness of Avon Street*
But who, gentlemen, that has any delicacy of taste, can survey the streets of
Bath, - the grand resort of the British Nobility and Gentry, without being
disgusted with the excrementitious filth with which some of them are spread?
- I cannot be supposed to allude so much to the new... parts of the town; but
never, surely, was censure more justly applied, than to the management of
some of the old, and in particular *Avon-street,* and the parts adjacent... Suffer
me Gentlemen, here to suggest to you the necessity, the absolute necessity, of
a particular attention to those parts of the town where the greatest number of
the labouring people are crowded together; they are ever apt to take example
by each other in degenerating into indecency: Nastiness gradually produces
sloth, and debases and corrupts both the body and the mind. // By a proper
attention to regulations, some plan might be, doubtless, formed for restraining,
not only the nasty practice of easing nature on the pavement in almost every
corner, but also the equally disagreeable one, of throwing urine and other foul
water, &c. from the windows into the streets... and the almost universal one of
throwing cinders and other refuse out before the doors... And, as some of the
owners of houses in Avon-street, have begun to do something in the long-
neglected business of repairing the pavement, it is hoped you will give proper
directions for removing all the straggling posts, raising the foot-paths, and
rendering a narrow street, in which a great number of children are frequently
seen, as secure as may be from the many horses which pass and repass to
water.
*Bath Chronicle 17 Jul 1777, letter from 'CIVIS'*

*386.  1777  Wretchedness relieved*
At this place there are so many distressed persons that no individual can think
of administering relief to them all; but the case of one man, whose family I
went to see, I will mention to your Ladyship in a few words. His name is David
Russel: he was born at Fulham, and had been able for many years to maintain
his wife and children by his industry as a musician, till the disputes at
Birmingham about the playhouses, in one of which he was employed, left him
wholly without business: he then came to Bath, where the necessities of eight
children, the eldest not fifteen years old, and a wife subject to a painful disorder,
called for more money than his utmost pains could procure; and he was himself
taken with a bad illness, which seems likely to end in a total decline: in this
situation he was thrown into prison for a debt of seven pounds contracted merely
for his children's necessary food and cloaths. Here he must have perished if a
clergyman of the place had not engaged with the creditor to collect the money
among his friends. I saw him and his children soon after he recovered his
liberty: his house was a scene of wretchedness; his wife miserably ill; and his
youngest children hungry and helpless. We propose to make, if we can, a

composition with his creditors, whose demands amount in all to near fifty pounds, including a year and a half's rent of the cottage in which he lives. He is honest, diligent, and ingenious; and all his debts were contracted for necessaries.

*Jones, Letters, vol.1 pp.255-6, William Jones to Lady Spencer, Bath 30 Dec 1777*

### 387.  1779  The badge wearers of St James's parish

On account of the increasing burden of the Poor Rates it was decided that those persons who did not really want [i.e. were not in desperate need] and who did not deserve pay from the Parish, would be prevented from applying if the Churchwardens and Overseers would enforce the Statute... to the effect that any person receiving Parish relief and the wife and children of any such person should wear a large Roman 'P' with the first letter of the name of their Parish upon their right shoulders. // In consideration of many old people who had seen better days, it was decided that they should be excused from wearing the badge, if over 60.

*BCL, St James's Parish Accounts, &c., transcr.C.W.Shickle, vestry meeting 17 Jun 1779*

### 388.  1782  Driven to extremity

Last Thursday morning, between three and four o'clock, one Elizabeth Bartlett, an old woman near seventy years of age, who has picked up a livelihood by sweeping the theatre of this city, was perceived by a watchman to walk down Avon-street, with a seeming wildness about her; he followed her at a distance, and saw her descend the steps slowly, and lay herself down in the river, shoving off from the bank. When he got to the place the stream had carried her out of his reach, but her cloaths kept the body afloat; he recollected that he had seen a long haymaker's rake the day before... which he ran for... [and] at last with difficulty he drew her into the bank, and conducted her to her lodging, a sorry garret in Avon-street. // On being asked the cause of this rash action, she gives the following account: That she can get nothing from a poor parish in the country where she was born, and being only a room-keeper here is not entitled to any thing; that her strength begins to fail her, that in the season when the playhouse is kept open, she earned three shillings per week, but that the house was to shut the next Saturday; that she has but four shillings in the world, and at quarter-day will owe ten shillings for lodging... Benefactions for the above poor woman will be received by the Printer [of this newspaper].

*Bath Chronicle 6 Jun 1782*

### 389.  1785-90  Sworn affidavits for lost pawn tickets

(20 Jun 1785) John Wheeler of... Bath Yeoman maketh Oath and saith on the Twenty fifth Day of January last he did pawn a Silver Watch a Cotton Gown a Pair of Leather Breeches two Waistcoats a Peice of Sheeting which were and are his property to Samuel Porter of... Bath Pawn broker for the Sum of One Pound Eleven Shillings and Six Pence which he received of him with a Duplicate  which is now lost or mislaid...

(10 Jul 1788) Ann Sheppard of Bath Widow... saith that on the third of October she pawned some Childrens Cloaths, that on the 8th March she pawned a Shawl, that on the 29th December she pawned an Umberralla, that on the 12th Octr. she pawned a White Shirt that on the 6th Feby she pawned two Rings... for the Sum of 19s...
(19 Jul 1789) Wm.Edwards of... Bath... saith that about three Months ago he pawned a Brown Frock[-coat] a Pair of Velveteen Breeches a buff [?] Jackat and a Cotton Waistcoat... for the Sum of fifteen Shillings and Six Pence...
(9 Aug 1790) Mary Saunders... of... Bath... saith that about two Months ago she... pawned a Chintz Gown a Muslin Apron a Linen Petticoat a Bedgown & Shift a Gold Ring a Cloth Apron a Gown and a Wais[t]coat... for the Sum of Nineteen Shillings...
*BRO, Bath Quarter Sessions, Samuel Porter's Oath Book, 1785-91*

### 390. 1786 Outside the reach of the City magistrates

The County Magistrates who reside in and near this city are at this time particularly called on to be active in their duty. The numerous beggars and vagrants that infest every field around, and every avenue to this city, have long given just cause for complaint... They are driven from our streets, but are suffered with impunity in our suburbs. Now is the season for night-robbers; prevention is the best remedy; we hope therefore... the Justices... will rid us of any fears from this unhappy people, who by their idle and unprofitable lives render themselves real pests to society.
*Bath Chronicle 2 Nov 1786*

### 391. 1786 The victims of a terrible Avon Street fire

On Thursday morning last about three o'clock, a fire, the most fatal in its consequences that ever happened in this city, broke out in the house of Charles Hayward, in Avon-street; every apartment in which was occupied by poor persons. Before any of the wretched lodgers were alarmed, the fire had got to such a height, that only seven out of fourteen were saved, two of whom jump'd from the window of the attic story. - The names of those who perished were, Eliz Yapp (the widow of a razor-grinder) and her daughter who sold matches; Mary Hayward, daughter of the keeper of the house; Catherine Woolley, (a basket-woman, whose husband had left her) and her two children; and a travelling boy who was sick. - Hayward and his wife, and Eliz.Prestly, were among those that escaped; the latter was so much hurt in her knee by the fall, that it is feared an amputation must take place, if her life can be preserved. - Every article in the house was consumed; and the poor creatures, reduced to the greatest distress, are humble supplicants for the benevolence of the humane. // The fire began in the ground floor, and was first discovered by the lodgers under-ground - Hayward procured water with a design of putting it out, but on opening the door the flames were so fierce as to scorch him considerably, and the stair-case instantly taking fire, prevented the escape of his daughter who had run up stairs to alarm the lodgers above. // The screams of the miserable

sufferers were dreadful beyond description, and the situation in which they were found [was] truly affecting; - Elizabeth Yapp, kneeling at the foot of her bed with one arm round he[r] daughter's neck; the daughter lying on the bed, with her arm's round her mother's waist. Catharine Woolley, with her two children, under the bed. The young man who was ill of the small-pox, lying by the bed side: and Hayward's daughter lying across the bed, with her legs hanging over, and almost burnt off. Hayward was burnt in attempting to save his daughter. // The Directors of the Fire Offices, or the Vestries of the several parishes in this city, would do well to have ladders placed in safe and convenient situations in cases of fire; these being as conducive to the preservation of lives and property, as engines are to stop the progress of the flames.
*Bath Chronicle 14 Dec 1786*

### 392. 1790 Obituary of a pensioner
A few weeks since died Wm.Arkel, the poor old pensioner with two wooden legs that for many years sat under a shed in the [Orange].Grove knitting purses to his support. He was well known to the Company frequenting this City and Cheltenham.
*Bath Chronicle 25 Feb 1790*

### 393. 1790 A concert on behalf of John Prynn
... the Band of Musick beg permission to invite the Benevolent to a // CONCERT of Vocal and Instrumental MUSICK, // Which they intend *gratuitously* to perform // For the BENEFIT OF JOHN PRYNN, // Late a JEWELLER, of this City; // A young man who began life with all the hopes that a good trade, and a pleasing address could inspire; but Providence has thought fit to blast those views by a severe stroke of the palsy - rendering him at once an object of horror, poverty, and commiseration. Betwixt two and three years has he laboured under this awful dispensation, the assistance that the waters of this, his native city, might have afforded him, has been thwarted by extreme indigence - nay often by the want even of food! That he has met with many friends it is true, and a most affectionate Brother has supplied him with the scanty savings of hard-earned wages, but repeated calls have drained all the sources of support, - and he is now *miserably destitute*. This is no exaggerated account, the object lingers on the spot - and the truth may be easily known.
*Bath Chronicle 9 Sep 1790*

### 394. 1799 Calamity for a journeyman's family
About one o'clock on Tuesday morning two unfinished houses in Weymouth-street, near Walcot-terrace, built by James Franklin, a bankrupt, suddenly gave way and fell down. The family of Thomas Fido, an industrious journeyman carpenter, who inhabited some of the unfinished rooms, providentially were awake, and had just time to save their lives by running naked into the street, but the whole of the poor man's goods and furniture were buried in the ruins and totally destroyed.
*Bath Chronicle 14 Feb 1799*

*395. 1799 The Strangers' Friend Society, estab. Bath, 1790*
This Society is formed on the most benevolent and disinterested plan, *Protestants, Roman Catholics, Strangers, Foreigners, and all such as have no helper*, have an equal right to be relieved by it; and no other recommendation is required than *a sufficiency of evident Distress.* // As the concerns of the *Soul* are beyond comparison the most important, the strictest attention will be paid to the eternal interests of all those who are, or may be objects of this institution... // Should this institution meet with the encouragement and support it deserves, we shall... be able to procure food, clothes, coals, and medical assistance, for multitudes who are utterly destitute of these things, and hereby lives, profitable to the Publick, will, under the blessing of GOD, be recued from *untimely* death.
*Bath Chronicle 18 Apr 1799*

ҡ҉ ҡ҉ ҡ҉ ҡ҉ ҡ҉ ҡ҉ ҡ҉ ҡ҉ ҡ҉ ҡ҉ ҡ҉ ҡ҉ ҡ҉ ҡ҉ ҡ҉

## ROYALTY AND LOYALTY

Court patronage still counted enormously, and Queen Anne's extended stays in 1702 and 1703 had a tonic effect on the whole spa. But suspicions that it remained a Jacobite stronghold lingered on, gaining fresh currency with the abortive Western rising of 1715 and the continuing reports of the Old Pretender's sympathisers congregating and plotting there. Orange and purple, the loyal colours of Hanover, may have been worn in 1716 but two years later Stuart badges were again being openly flaunted. The Corporation, however, took a strong Hanoverian line in 1722 by electing Wade to represent the city, and in 1727 and 1728 it supported the ultraloyalist celebrations of George II's accession and coronation. The formation on that occasion of a company of militia captained by a local jeweller may have offered a useful precedent for Ralph Allen to raise a uniformed troop at the time of the 1745 rebellion. By then Bath was utterly behind the dynasty. Royal anniversaries, wartime victories and glorious conclusions of peace were greeted with effusive displays of flags, bell-ringing, bonfires, fireworks, the drinking of loyal toasts at the Guildhall, and grand celebratory balls. If the reigning monarch was hard to tempt to Bath, at least the royal offspring were not shy of bestowing their favours: Princess Amelia repeatedly from 1728, Frederick, Prince of Wales, in 1738, Princess Caroline in 1746, and later in the century George III's disrespectful sons. In 1788, the centenary of William III's landing, orange symbolism was again much in evidence, but Bathonians harked still further back, to the Restoration, in continuing to mark Oak Apple Day every 29 May. The downside of excessive attachment to King and Constitution was that it blinded upright citizens to the need for democratic reform. Hence the alarmism of the 1790s about the threat of subversion and revolution, which did not entirely stem from patriotic zeal against the French.

### 396. 1702 Queen Anne returns to Bath as monarch

Her Majesty is going to the Bath, and will set out from Windsor on Wednesday, lodge at Oxon [Oxford] that night and dine there on Thursday and then to Cirencester; so to Bath on Friday, where she designs to continue about a month.

*CSPD 1702-03 (Anne), p.217, Sir Charles Hedges to Sir George Rooke, 21 Aug 1702*

### 397. 1702 A civic gift to the Queen

Whether a peice of plate of the vallue of 40l. [£40] or thereabo[u]ts Shall be presented to her Maj[es]ty at her coming to ye Bath - Agreed by gen[er]all consent...

*BRO, Bath Council Minutes, 22 Aug 1702*

### 398. 1716 Hanoverian loyalism in the wake of the 1715 rising

To-day being King George's birthday the gentlemen here... subscribed for a ball and entertainment to-night... There was very good company and good clothes... There was my Lord Conway [i.e. Francis Seymour], in scarlet velvet. He is a great Tory, but it is thought appeared there on purpose to clear himself from suspicion of being concerned in the rebellion which he lies under. There were several officers... There was Mrs.Walpole and her sister Mrs.Shorter danced there very well. I gave my sister and Mrs.Marshall a favour of purple and orange knots, such as Mrs.Walpole wore herself as being the colours of Hanover and the Prince of Orange. And I wore one of the same myself in my hat. A great many gentlemen and ladies wore the same, though there were several that wore none at all, but some were gold ones.

*Ryder, Diary, pp.245-6, entry for 28 May 1716*

### 399. 1717 Jacobite sympathisers at Bath

... when the Parliament meets... God knows what temper they will be in... there is no better intelligence... between the present and the late ministry, and itt has been said that some of the latter who are now at the Bath seem to be afraid of being taken up [i.e. arrested], for the writers for the court have accused them of being in Plots with the Jacobites.

*Wentworth Papers, p.445, Lord Bathurst to the Earl of Strafford, 28 Sep 1717*

### 400. 1718 And Jacobite symbolism on display

The D[uke] of Ormond's birthday about the beginning of this month was observed in a very extraordinar[y] manner in several places of England, particularly at Bath, where the gentry as well as commonalty wore white roses and other badges.

*HMC 55 MSS Various, vol.5 p.262, Charles Dickson? to the Laird of Balinshoe, 12 May 1718*

### 401. 1728 *Captain Goulding demonstrates Bath's innocence*

... the Company of Volunteers ... were of absolute necessity for the service of
the Town in general; and farther, to convince the whole World, that it was a
barbarous, base, malicious Report, to the great Prejudice of all the Inhabitants
here, that *Bath* was a disaffected Place to his late Majesty, ever since the
Rebellion in *Scotland*; because, unfortunately for the Town, some Arms were
found at the Carriers, which are now in the Tower of *London*. But having a real
Value for the Happiness of this City, I could not avoid making a strict Inquiry...
And I never could hear... that any one single Inhabitant of the Town knew any
one Secret, or had any Knowledge of the Arms coming to *Bath*, or any other
Proceeding against the Government... And I am well assured, that there is not
one place in all the King's Dominions, better affected to his present Majesty
King GEORGE, than the Inhabitants of the City of Bath; and by our making
such publick Acclamations of Joy, it brought in all the Western Subjects for
about forty Miles round, to be Eye-witnesses of our Affections to his present
Majesty, to whom we were reported to be a very disaffected People. // *Bath*
being the Capital and most publick and gay Place in *Europe*, and from whence
all Examples almost are taken, you saw in the Rebellion we were made the
Butt of the World... without deserving it. So that no body can deny, but there
was an absolute Necessity of our Procession on his Majesty's publick Rejoicing-
days; and I think it was the only indefatigable Method that could be taken, in
raising Volunteers, and roasting of Oxen. It was a new thing in these Parts, and
which assembled such numberless and vast surprizing Crouds together; and
then 'twas you saw we took the Opportunity to declare our Innocence to the
Princess AMELIA, in as handsome and respectful a Speech as I could make.
And afterwards I had it cry'd and spread amidst the Country People, to
strengthen their Affections... And I think it ought to be kept up every Year.
What are Rejoicing-days for, but to triumph and convince the Disaffected, and
shew that we have a superiour Number; and that we could, if there was an
Occasion, crush all Enemies and Villainy, intended against the King and
Government?

*Goulding, Essay, pp.3 and 6-7*

### 402. 1734 *Royal visitors promote the spa*

The Prince of Orange was of great advantage to Bath and his great Cure will
give the Waters the Reputation it deserves, his behaviour gained the Esteem of
every body and the Respect that was shewn him by the People here, has so
Established this Town in the favour of the King & Queen that on the slightest
illness of any of the Royal Family they will be directly sent here. And there is
talk (with a very good foundation) that the King will have a House built here.
The Princess Amelia came here on Tuesday night and was Received in a very
handsome manner, we are very full of Company & shou'd have much more
was it not for the Elections.

*BCL, AL 1265, John Wood I to William Brydges, Bath 27 Apr 1734*

### 403. 1745 Spying out the Young Pretender's man

Here is lately come to this place, a Scotch Gentleman, who is not known by any Person here, as far as I can find... yet, it's generally believed he came from ye Rebels Army. Consequently is not come hither on any good designe. I shall be always ready, to detect any Person, that is an Enemy to my King and Country; and heartily wish that the rascally Banditti may be soon Waded [i.e. dealt with as General Wade did during the 1715 Rising] according to their demerits. // In this, or any other occurrence of this Nature I hope my name will be conceal'd...
*Williams, Two suspected Jacobites, James Grist? to the Duke of Newcastle, Bath 11 Dec 1745*

### 404. 1746 Bath saved from Popery and dictatorship

I know of no Bath news worth sending only that the princess [Amelia] was Last Sunday attended by the Mayor to the Abbey Church and heard a Sermon preachd by Dr.Coney. The Text was the two first verses of the 9th Psalm; the Heads of the Discourse was our happiness in being deliv[er]ed from a Rebellion which was disign'd to bring in Popery and Arbitrary Government which after compareing with that we at present enjoy'd goes on to say that tho' this was owing in a great measure to the Behaviour of the Duke [of Cumberland, at the battle of Culloden], yet (as his expression was) we are not to Neglect to return God thanks as the Real author of our Deliverence; The Ladies... [were dressed] very fine and vast crouds of all sorts of People at the Church. Her Highness leaves this place to morrow.
*BCL, AL 662, T.Brasier to Fernando Fairfax, Bath 27 May 1746*

### 405. 1749 Fireworks, but no Handel

Next Wednesday Evening the Fireworks are to be play'd off here, on Occasion of the Thanksgiving for the Peace; a Stage, with a Pyramid, being erected for that Purpose in the vacant Spot of Ground, facing the Parade. Amongst other Things, there will be Two Hundred Sixty-four Pumps, Two Hundred Sky-Rockets, Four Catherine-Wheels, and One Horizontal Wheel, Six Balloons, Four Mines, Two Fountains, and One Sun, which is to be plac'd on the Top of the Pyramid, &c. - As many Persons, from all Parts of the County, are gone to London to see the Fireworks play'd off there; so a great Concourse of People are expected here, who have not Time, nor Opportunity, to go so far.
*Bath Journal 24 Apr 1749*

### 406. 1749 Patriot Allen's troops

Tuesday being the Day appointed for the General Thanksgiving for the Peace... the Soldiers, whom Ralph Allen, Esq; cloath'd and arm'd at the Time of the Rebellion [1745], met about Ten o'Clock, and went to Mr.Allen's Chapel to hear Divine Service; after which, they were all order'd to partake of a Dinner which was provided for them: In the Evening, they were drawn up, and fir'd three Vollies. Mr.Allen's House was finely illuminated, and there was a great Bonfire near it.
*Bath Journal 1 May 1749*

### 407.  1752  How Princess Amelia passes her time

Her Royal Highness... comes every morning to the Pump-room between 7
and 8 for her first glass of the smallest size, & about a quarter after 8 for her
second glass, which is all she drinks in publick. She has no doctor with her, nor
makes use of any here... By what I can learn, her deafness is much as it was. It
is not fixt; some days she hears tolerably, & others not so... She is very affable
& civil, comes to the room at noon lately, & sometimes at nights, & plays at
cards there, chiefly at commerce. She takes all opportunitys when fair of getting
on horseback, & amuses herself almost every day some hours in angling in the
river, in a summer house by the river side in the garden, formerly known by the
name of Harrison's walks, which has two fire-places in it, & to second her
against cold, puts on a riding habit, & a black velvet postillion cap, tied under
her chin.
*Harris, Life of Hardwicke, vol.2 p.472, Hutton Perkins to Hardwicke, Bath 17 Sep
1752*

### 408.  1758  A victory bonfire near the unfinished Circus

As my brother [the Elder Pitt] has a great many friends at the Bath, I employed
one to ask Mr.Mayor if he would approve of my indulging myself in doing
what little I could to add to the public rejoicings for the success of his majesty's
arms [at the taking of Louisborough]. He sent me word he should take it as a
compliment. So I ordered a bonfire, so placed as to be sure no bonfire ever was
for the beauty, upon a rising ground before the Circus (where my brother's
house is), ten hogsheads of strong beer round it, which drew all the company I
could desire, and enabled them to sing 'God bless great George our king' with
very good success, with the help of all the music I could get in the Circus. The
whole town was illuminated; which, as it is the prettiest in the world, was the
gayest thing I ever saw.
*Henrietta, Letters, vol.2 pp.249-50, Anne Pitt to the Countess of Suffolk, 26 Aug 1758*

### 409.  1760  The accession of George III

Monday Night last the Deputy Sheriff of the County brought to this City the
Proclamation of his Present Majesty King GEORGE the Third, and delivered
it to the Worshipful the Mayor, who immediately sent a general Invitation to
all the Nobility, Clergy, Gentry, and Inhabitants to attend the Corporation the
next Morning in the Procession, and in the Evening to celebrate the Day by
drinking his Majesty's health, &c. The Procession was as follows: First, the
several Companies of Trade with their Flags flying, after them the City Music
and the greatest Part of Mr.Nash's Band playing before the Mayor and
Corporation, and the... Nobility, Clergy, and Gentry, &c. who with the
Corporation, subscribed their Names at the [Guild] Hall, to testify their Loyalty
and Attachment to his Majesty. - The Proclamation was made by the Town
Clerk in six different Places of the City to a crowded Audience, who seconded
every reading of the same with great Shouts and Acclamations of their Joy on
the Occasion: The Bells of every Church in the City ringing, and the Guns at

Mr.Simpson's [Assembly Rooms] firing. The Guildhall was not large enough to contain the Company that appeared in the Evening...
*Bath Journal 10 Nov 1760*

### 410. 1779 The true militia spirit

To the Royal Volunteers of Bath. // HEARING that there are some amongst you who do not entirely understand how it is intended you are to act in your Military Character, I think it incumbent upon me to explain this matter. // ... You are not by any means on the footing of the Hired Soldier. YOU CANNOT BE COMPELLED TO ANY THING. You are not to be subject to the Articles of War, or to any kind of Punishment but such Fines as you may hereafter agree to for Neglect of Duty, for Drunkenness, Rioting, or different Behaviour from the Character which you ought to support. All Crimes are to be tried by Seven of the Corps, and the greatest Punishment that can be inflicted is EXPULSION... You are not to march out of your County without you are willing. Yet should it become absolutely necessary, by our Enemies daring to attempt their threatened Invasion, I cannot believe there is a Man amongst you would decline it. No! The Royal Volunteers of Bath will exert themselves to the utmost in so glorious a Cause as endeavouring to defend the Country, their Liberties, their Properties, their tenderest Connections, and all they hold dearest to them... A.MOLESWORTH [Commander of the Bath Volunteers]
*Bath Chronicle 23 Sep 1779*

### 411. 1788 George III is invited over from a rival spa

The Report of the Mayor Chamberlain Sheriffs and Town Clerk... that in Pursuance of the Resolution of the Corporation for addressing the King - they went to Cheltenham and had Audience of him on Tuesday the Fifth instant and the Town Clerk read to his Majesty the following address.- // Your Majesty's most Dutiful and Loyal subjects, the Mayor, Chamberlain and Sheriffs of the City of Bath, beg leave to approach your Royal Person, and for the Corporation to Congratulate your Majesty, on your own, the Queen's and Princesses Safe Arrival at Cheltenham; - To assure your Majesty of their unalterable Loyalty, and Affection to your Person and Government; - and respectfully to invite your Majesty, with your Royal Consort, and such of your Royal Family, as are at Cheltenham, to the City of Bath; and hope that your Majesty's health is perfectly restored.- // To which address his Majesty most Graciously condescended to return thanks for their kind Invitation and was extremely sorry that he could not consistent with his health pay them a visit at this Juncture, but at some future Period he assured them that he would take the earliest opportunity of gratifying their wishes, upon which after being most graciously received they had the Honor of Kissing his Majesty's Hand.
*BRO, Bath Council Minutes, 11 Aug 1788*

*412.  1788  On the anniversary of William of Orange*
It so happened that this year being the centenary of the arrival of King William,
not a lady was to be seen [at Bath] without streaming orange-coloured ribbons,
or gentlemen without rosettes of the same in their button-holes.
*Hankin, SchimmelPenninck, vol.1 p.80*

*413.  1792  Stirred up by the French Revolution*
(10 Nov)  On Tuesday last, two foreigners in this city made an itinerant street
musician play their favourite [revolutionary] air *Ca [Ça] ira,* which they
appeared to enjoy with a degree of extacy. An English officer passing by, gave
the fellow a severe reprimand and *commended* 'God save the King.' - The
Frenchmen vociferated *Ca ira! Ca ira! Ca ira!* A large mob assembled on the
occasion, and joined the loyal burthen with their huzzas for upward of an hour,
to the great mortification of the foreigners: who certainly acted imprudent, at
least... whilst so many of their unhappy [*émigré*] countrymen experience the
benevolence and hospitality of British generosity.
(22 Dec)  The Mayor of this city having been informed that some persons had
prepared an effigy of [Thomas] Paine in order to hang and burn it, very prudently
ordered that no such exhibition should take place here, as it was particularly
incumbent on the inhabitants of Bath, for the sake of its infirm and sick visitors,
to prevent every kind of disorder; and the intent of the Bath Association [see
*414* below] was to promote peace and to suppress tumult; and by every legal
means destroy faction. The populace however, were determined to show their
abhorrence of the culprit, and they took it up to Beechen Cliff (out of the Mayor's
jurisdiction,) where it was filled with combustibles and consumed amidst the
loudest plaudits, the firing of cannons, &c.
*Bath Herald 10 Nov and 22 Dec 1792*

*414.  1792  The wild doctrine of equality*
GUILDHALL, BATH, Dec.8,1792. ASSOCIATION FOR PRESERVING
LIBERTY, PROPERTY, AND THE CONSTITUTION OF GREAT-BRITAIN
AGAINST REPUBLICANS AND LEVELLERS... // 1st. We declare our firm
and loyal Attachment to his Majesty's Person and Government, and the present
Constitution of KING, *Lords,* and *Commons.* // 2dly. We declare our Detestation
and Abhorrence of all Publications and Associations, by whatever Name
distinguished, wherein Principles or Doctrines are, or hereafter may be published
or recommended, which may in any wise tend to alienate the minds of his
Majesty's Subjects from their due Allegiance; and resolve, that we will use our
utmost endeavours to discourage and suppress the same. // 3rdly. That the
wild Doctrine of EQUALITY, newly propagated, is unknown to the English
Constitution, is incompatible with Civil Society, and only held forth as a
Delusion to mislead the lower Ranks of the People, to poison the Minds of his
Majesty's Subjects, to subvert all Distinction [between classes], to destroy
Subordination between Man and Man, and to substitute Anarchy in the place
of our present mild and happy Government.
*Bath Chronicle 20 Dec 1792*

### 415. 1798 Hero of the General Thanksgiving

This loyal City shone away [i.e. was all illuminated] on the Rejoicing night I find - The Laurels have not yet been taken away from the Doors; and a *Nelson Flag* is now a fashionable Head Dress. By a Nelson Flag is meant a Handkerchief of those Colours fancifully disposed as it looks very pretty.

*Piozzi, Letters, vol.2 p.539, Hester Lynch Piozzi to Lady Williams, Bath 18 Dec 1798*

### 416. 1799 Royal ennui: the Prince of Wales suffers at Bath

... of all the dull séjours I have experienc'd, this certainly at the present moment is the dullest. Perhaps my having been a good deal indispos'd since I have been here... makes me consider this place as stupider than it really is. However, I understand that in the opinions of most people it really *is* so, & perhaps the more so, from the comparative very gay & crowded winter which has fallen to the lot of this water-drinking place during the last three or four months, the like of which I am inform'd has never before been known. As to myself... I certainly am better & gradually getting better every day, my spasms, from the good effect of the waters... I go as little out as I possibly can; to avoid singularity one must occasionally go to the Rooms, or, properly speaking, to the Balls, for half an hour, which is the utmost time I have staid, as there is hardly a creature I ever saw before in my life that go there, & the two Balls that I have hitherto been at so crowded, so hot, & so stinking, that I was absolutely gasping for fresh air, & dying to get away from the moment I came into the Rooms.

*George, Prince, Correspondence, vol.4, letter 1444, the Prince to the Queen, Bath 10 Apr 1799*

### 417. 1799 Overdoing Oak Apple Day

It is with much regret that for some years past we have remarked considerable injury to have been suffered by the woods and young timber around this city, in consequence of wearing oaken sprigs in the hat, and decorating shop-windows and apartments of houses with oaken branches, on the 29th of May [to commemorate the Restoration of Charles II]. If the practice alluded to be meant as an expression of *Loyalty*, we would just suggest that this is a very improper display of it; since it would never sanction that injury to individuals and loss to the publick, which are produced by these annual depredations on private property.

*Bath Chronicle 30 May 1799*

# BEAU NASH AND HIS SUCCESSORS

*Nash resists easy summing up. Perceptions of him gradually altered during that unprecedented 54-year career when he single-handedly created the role of full-blown master of the spa ceremonies, legislator, arbitrator, organiser, publicist, figurehead and representative of the fashionable company as the Mayor was of the citizens. A commoner, but with a patrician's affability and assurance, Nash financed his way via the gaming tables and owed his position to no-one. Assiduous to the private interests of his clients, he also encouraged them to socialise, polish their manners, and show off at the balls - a status-enhancing message that spread well beyond the confines of Bath. Civic recognition of Nash's signal importance came as early as 1716 with his honorary freedom, and at his death in 1761 with a ceremonious funeral. Embittered, tyrannical, impoverished, even scorned he may have been towards the end, but this was still a towering act to follow, as indeed his successors soon discovered. Collett, a sprightly Frenchman, left within two seasons; Derrick, the Irish lobby's choice, survived six; but neither possesssed anything like Nash's authority. On Derrick's death a major contest blew up over rival candidates for the post, only settled by electing a compromise figure, the famously elegant William Wade. In 1774 he too was embroiled in controversy as the proprietors of the new Upper Assembly Rooms tried to restrict his sphere of influence. The eventual solution in 1777 was to split the M.C.'s responsibilities and make separate appointments for Upper and Lower rooms. On his own not even Nash could now have managed the much-enlarged spa. The M.C.s from this point on - Dawson and Brereton, later Tyson and King - worked sensibly together to avoid friction, though the superiority of the Upper Rooms as a venue did threaten the Lower Rooms' viability until the personable James King restored their popularity. Over at the Guildhall yet another M.C. by now officiated, the city élite having pointedly inaugurated its own series of assemblies.*

### 418.  1716  The indispensable, inescapable Nash
Gnash is the man here that is the life and soul of all their diversions. Without
him there is no play nor assembly nor ball and everybody seems not to know
what to do if he is absent. He has the privilege of saying what he pleases and
talking to the ladies as his fancy leads him and no affront is to be taken, though
he sometimes puts modest women to the blush. His conversation and sayings
seem to make a great part of the conversation of others and the repeating of
what he does or says helps to fill up the conversation very much. Upon this
account, though he is a very ugly man in his face, yet he is very much beloved
and esteemed by the ladies as a witty and genteel man.
*Ryder, Diary, p.240, entry for 22 May 1716*

### 419.  1723  Flatterer's portrait
Your *Word* is the Law; and whatever Mr.N. pleases to order, every one submits
to with the same Pleasure and Resignation, as if done by his own private
Authority. This, Sir, before your Time no one could think would ever happen,
nor is it likely that after your Demise we shall ever see it again. It deserves
therefore to be more particularly noted that we see it actually so in our Days;
and that you have that singular Art to preserve Decency and Order in such a
mix'd Society of Persons of all Rank, Orders, and Sexes, as compose the general
Resort to *Waters*, notwithstanding two such *Makebates* [mischief-makers] stand
in your way, I mean *Play* and *Women*... I desire then that *Posterity* would be
pleas'd to be inform'd, that Mr.NASH was a Man about five Foot eight Inches
high; of a Diameter exactly proportion'd to your Height, that gives you the
finest Shape. Of a black brown Complexion, that gives a Strength to your
Looks... You have Strength and Agility to recommend you to your own Sex,
and great Comeliness of Person to keep you from being disagreeable to the
other. You have heighten'd a great degree of natural good Temper with the
greatest Politeness, which, improv'd with your natural good Wit, makes your
Conversation as a private Person as entertaining and as delightful, as your
Authority as a Governor is respectful. With these happy Accomplishments,
with the fine Taste you discover in whatever Habit you please to appear, and
great Gracefulness with which you dance our Country Dances, it will be no
great Wonder that you support your Empire when once you obtain'd it. I don't
mention your Dexterity in *French* Dances, because you don't affect dancing
them [any more], in which I think you shew your Judgment; though, no doubt,
you might as well excel in a Minuet or Riggadoon , as in [country dances like]
*Bartholomy Fair*, or *Thomas I cannot*. To conclude, I write this near about the
18th Year of your *Reign*, and eight and fortieth of your Age.
*Whatley, Characters, pp.vi-vii and xiv-xv*

### 420.  1725  Good reasons for promoting the rooms
Beau Nash a man of great Gallantry, and of uncommon assurance, tho' no[t]
young but a batter'd old Beau turned of fifty years and not at all handsome, is
the greatest promoter of the diversions at Harrison's, and one of the greatest

Gamesters, and the first man in the Ladys good Graces, tis thought that he shares with Harrison in the good profitts arising from these rooms.
*BCL, MS 914.238, Diary of a Tour by Three Students from Cambridge, 1725, pp.117-18*

### 421. 1728 Sancho and Peepo milk the visitors

... the Plan was drawn, and to Building they go; and a very fine House and Garden was compleated, fit for *Sancho* [Nash] and *Peepo* [Harrison] to carry on their weighty Affairs in; and a great Trade they had, and without doubt a great many Battels were fought there, insomuch that *Peepo* grew very rich, and *Sancho* very great; *Peepo* very covetous, and *Sancho* very extravagant... *Sancho*'s Business was to look out sharp, and bring Persons down to the place; and *Peepo* welcom'd them in. Then away *Sancho* set out for more, and, by this vertuous and fair Proceeding, without Villainy or Covetousness, *Sancho* and *Peepo* ruined all the poor Souls in that publick Business there, who used to live very handsomely; or at least ruin'd them so, that what little Business they got, they were oblig'd to beg for, or not eat. 'Twas then *Peepo* was satisfied, and *Sancho* not displeas'd: And all the Money that the Gentry brought to Town, was spent in that Place. The Inhabitants of the Town got nothing but a little Money for their Lodgings and Provisions... They did observe there were a great many noble Families used the Springs at the Season... and a great deal of Money spent in the Year; but they did not consider what *Sancho* and *Peepo* shar'd, and that *Sancho* by his Share kept a Coach and Six, several Saddle-horses, a great many Servants, and a Seraglio of Whores, besides twenty Bastards; and sometimes he would fool away four or five hundred Pounds in a Week, at a Game he was infatuated to, call'd *Pharo*; besides Surgeons for Salivations, great Presents, and a hundred other Extravagances, and no Man... could guess within several thousand Pounds, what these two shar'd.
*Goulding, Essay, pp.20-2*

### 422. c.1730 Nash repentant

Madam! I have heard that a sincere confession with a hearty repentance merits absolution! if you give an example of the truth of the... [proposition?] I shall own you as good a Catholique as I am a bad Christian; a Gamester neither knows by his own resolutions or hapinesse, both which I forfeited last night by engaging att deep play, wch tho a sorry excuse is the only one that lays a claim to yo[ur] goodness. I durst not see Lady Jerningham, till I had confest the Impertinence of Madam yo[ur] most humble servt R:Nash.
*BCL, AL 658, Richard Nash to Lady Jerningham, Bath c.1730*

### 423. 1731 Nash obliging

I suppose Lett told you how humane and good Mr.Nash was to me when I left Bath; he carries it on still and is prodigious good and obliging.
*HMC 78 Hastings, vol.3 p.6, R.Delves to the Countess of Huntingdon, 22 Mar 1731*

### 424. 1731 Nash despondent

Nash seems dejected and oppressed at heart; I suppose he has not yet recovered his losses of last year, and the malicious part of us say that his taxes and contributions are much lessened, and that upon application to his Parliament for a vote of credit the majority was against it. What, Madam, can be more abject than a despised King? But in my mind, he seems to labour under the unconquerable distemper of old age, and tho' he attends the balls as usual, his dancing days are over.

*HMC 20 Dartmouth, vol.1 p.327, Earl of Orrery to Lady Kaye, Bath 3 Nov 1731*

### 425. 1738 Host and go-between

Yesterday about Four in the Afternoon their Royal Highnesses the Prince and Princess of Wales arriv'd here, amidst the loud Acclamations of Thousands, having had a delightful Journey. Mr.Nash, the generous Sir Clement of this Place [Sir Clement Corterel, the Court M.C.], went some Miles, in his Chariot and Six, to meet the Royal Pair and return'd a Quarter of an Hour before their Royal Highnesses Arrival to acquaint the Mayor of their Approach. Their Royal Highnesses were receiv'd at the City Gates by the Mayor and Corporation in their Formalities...

*Gloucester Journal 24 Oct 1738*

### 426. 1748 A superior critique in Oxford Latin

Sed eccum! gregaria inter capita longe spectabilis eminet *albescens Galerus*. Procul, O procul este, cordati, & quicquid est sapientiae severioris! En Theatrum ingreditur Archichoragus ipse...

[But see yonder, conspicuous among the flocking heads there looms *a great white hat*. Men of sound judgment, leave now; leave, if you are of a sober turn of mind. Behold, the great orchestrator of events enters on the stage in person, that distinguished judge of morals, the arbiter of good taste and manager of frivolities. // Here he is then, the very person visitors so love to have pointed out. // But seriously, you don't mean that feeble, toothless old man? Whatever sort of fellow is that? Where on earth is the famous elegance of language and regal charm? Where is that well-bred ease and affable politeness we expect of Bath's Master of the Ceremonies? Heavens! how grim he looks, his face lit with a ruddy glow, fixed in a shameless blush, and on top of that a kind of ill-tempered vacancy coupled with coarse jocularity. - Yet such a master has many fair followers, and what in that case am I to say of *you*? However let me avoid being malicious or charged with treason against the King of Bath!]

*Burton, Epistolae, pp.22-3*

### 427. 1748 Nash defends his stewardship of the funds

I Think it hard, after above Forty Years being a Fool, and Slave to the Publick, I should be accus'd of getting Money by the Publick *SUBSCRIPTIONS*; I now appeal to the Publick Rooms, who receive the Money; to the Musick, who are

constantly paid by the Receivers, if ever they were defrauded of a Shilling, or that I ever touch'd a Six-penny Piece of it. Indeed, when there was any small Surplus left, those that think I got any of it, may find it in the Hospital Charity-Book. To this I call GOD and Man to witness, *RICHARD NASH*. N.B. It has cost me more Money annually, on the Publick Account, than any Ten that ever came to Bath; and if it was not for the Sake of the Bath, and Company, I would leave 'em to the Confusion I found them in.
*Bath Journal 25 Apr 1748*

### 428.  1755  The grand arbitrator takes sides

WHEREAS I, RICHARD NASH, Esq., to oblige the City of BATH, and the Quality and Gentry resorting thereto, have for these fifty Years used my constant and steady Endeavours to keep all the Diversions of the said Place on the most proper Footing; and the Decency and Regularity of the publick Diversions, and the present flourishing Condition of the Place, is entirely owing to my Care and Management: BE IT KNOWN, that in Pursuance of the same Plan to regulate the publick Diversions, and zealous to remedy the many Mischiefs arising from the having two Play-Houses [i.e. competing theatres], tending to disturb the Company in their Amusements, and ruin the City; I sent to Mr.Simpson (on the Death of his Father) and likewise to Mr.Brown [the two theatre managers]; and as Mr.Simpson, notwithstanding all my Threats and Entreaties, cou'd not be prevailed upon to come into any Measures whatsoever towards an Accommodation; and as Mr.Brown declar'd his Readiness to come into any Measures that I thought proper, and actually made Mr.Simpson the most advantageous Offer he could wish for; I hereby declare, that I think Mr.Brown has a just Claim to the *Favour* and *Protection* of the Company, for the *Readiness* he shewed to oblige them, and that *his Play-House* ought to be encouraged; and I *readily* and *solemnly* assure him, that I will use my best Endeavours to serve him, and to influence the Quality that may come here to declare themselves for his Play-House, and desire that House may be supported.
*Bath Journal 17 Nov 1755*

### 429.  1761  End of an era

On Tuesday Evening the Remains of RICHARD NASH, Esq., were interred in the Abbey Church, after being carried from his House in St.John's Court, in Funeral Procession... 1st, the Children of the Charity-Schools, singing a solemn occasional Hymn: 2nd, Mr.Nash's, and the City Music, sounding at proper Intervals a Dead March: 3rd, three Clergymen: 4th, the Body, covered with a black Velvet Pall, adorned with Plumes of Feathers, and supported by the six senior Aldermen: Messrs.Wiltshire and Simpson, Masters of the Rooms, followed as chief Mourners, accompanied by several of the Corporation, and many other Gentlemen... When the Ceremony was over, the Bells being muffled, a Funeral Peal was rung, and 88 Minute Guns were fired [i.e. once a minute, for each of Nash's years] on Mr.Simpson's Platform.
*Bath Journal 23 Feb 1761*

### 430.  1761  A unique man of parts

... View *him* in every various Station,
You'll find none like *him* in the Nation;
GARRICK himself wou'd scarce have ventur'd,
To play the Parts in *him* concenter'd:
The *Beau*, the *Scholar*, *Courtier*, *Cit*,
The *Man of Honour*, and the *Wit*:
Though not a *Bully*, bravely blunt,
Nor apt to give, nor take Affront!
The *Moralist*, the *Man of Pleasure*,
But not.... a *Hoarder up of Treasure*.
There ne'er was such a Contradiction;
He seem'd both *real*, and a *Fiction*...

*Bath Chronicle 12 Mar 1761*

### 431.  1761  The first attempt to fill Nash's shoes
Collet is an old Frenchman, who has lived here many years, and assumed the
office of director and arranger of all entertainments, after the death of Richard
Nash... [He] is nearly seventy years old, but still very active and diligent. He
dances like the youngest, and is civility itself to every one, but more especially
to foreigners; so that we and others could not find praise enough for him as he
rushed about with us for hours, showing us everything that was in the slightest
degree worth noticing.
*Kielmansegge, Diary, pp.116-17, entry for Oct-Nov 1761*

### 432.  1763  Diminishing respect for the M.C.'s rulings
... my sister went to the Queen's birthday ball at Wiltshire's rooms, which
was in general esteemed a very good one; but at the close of it they cooked up
a little sort of a riot... Collet had carried himself off before upon some affront
he had received, of which he has had plenty this winter, and since that night
hath resigned his office to one Derrick, a little Irishman, to whom they say the
rooms are to allow fifty pounds a year. If that is the case, it is no hard matter to
prognosticate what authority he will gain, and how far it will be attended to.
*HMC 47 Shrewsbury &c., p.97, A.Hollier to Mrs Carr, 31 Jan 1763*

### 433.  1767  A plot to overthrow Derrick
When I left Bath, I thought your throne as solidly established as any throne in
Europe. You ruled with lenity, and your subjects obeyed with cheerfulness.
But... it seems a conspiracy has broke out, to distress, and even subvert, your
government... There is a committee, you say, formed against you; form a counter
committee of your most considerable friends, not forgetting two or three of our
tough [Irish] countrymen... The profit is the real cause of discord, and therefore
I am afraid... [lest] some man of quality and fortune should avail himself of

those civil dissensions, and come and swallow the oyster, and leave you and
your antagonist only the shells.
*Stanhope, Letters, vol.6 letter 2479, Lord Chesterfield to Samuel Derrick, 6 Feb 1767*

### 434. c.1767 Derrick charms the innocent Lydia Melford

As soon as we were settled in lodgings, we were visited by the Master of the
Ceremonies; a pretty little gentleman, so sweet, so fine, so civil, and polite,
that... he might pass for the prince of Wales; then he talks so charmingly, both
in verse and prose, that you would be delighted to hear him discourse; for you
must know he is a great writer, and has got five tragedies ready for the stage.
He did us the favour to dine with us, by my uncle's invitation; and next day
'squired my aunt and me to every part of Bath; which, to be sure, is an earthly
Paradise.
*Tobias Smollett, Humphry Clinker (1st ed. 1771), the fictional Lydia's letter of 26 Apr*

### 435. 1769 The polite company in uproar

Never was such a Scene of anarchy and confusion remembered in this city, as
happened on Tuesday night last at one of the public rooms; when the friends of
Mr.Brereton and Mr.Plomer met mutually to support their choice of each of
the above Gentlemen as Master of the Ceremonies. - A written Paper was
produced by a Gentleman in the interest of Mr.Plomer, which he requested to
be permitted to read; but a general hiss of disapprobation from the other party
ensuing, an universal confusion of course followed: - Scandalous epithets and
blows were the consequence; and the Mayor was sent for to appease the tumult;
who attended with proper officers, and the riot act was read three times by the
Town Clerk. Where this affair will end, is much to be dreaded. - No less than
eight writs were issued yesterday morning; and a subscription, it is said, is
open to support the suits; so that it will be at least a pleasing circumstance to
the Gentlemen of the Gown... The Magistrates have suppressed both the public
and private Balls for a time.
*Bath Chronicle 13 Apr 1769*

### 436. 1774 An open letter to the current M.C., William Wade

HAVING been a constant visitor at Bath for twenty years, I am exceedingly
hurt when I compare the present disorderly state of your amusements, with
those I enjoyed during the reign of your illustrious predecessor Mr.Nash, who
absolutely directed them all. I am informed you are not invested with any such
power, and that the amusements at present are chiefly conducted by the Masters
of the Rooms, in which case it is impossible the harmony of the place can be
restored to us. // When I reflect on the services done this city by so distinguished
a character as Field-Marshall Wade, your uncle, I feel much that his nephew
should fill the station of Master of the Ceremonies at Bath *in part only*; for I
am informed that in the regulation of many principal parts of the amusements,
you have not even a negative voice. - You are allowed, Sir, to be well qualified
for your office; do, therefore, exert yourself, and feel your proper consequence,

in order that the amusements may be justly arranged, and equally divided between the New and Old Assembly-Rooms; for till that is done, and they are opened alternately as usual, it is impossible for the company to mix in that pleasing manner which heretofore rendered Bath so agreeable to every one.
*Bath Chronicle 20 Oct 1774, letter from 'An Old Subscriber...'*

### 437. *1777 A man of the world the ideal candidate*
The present contest for the office of *Master of the Ceremonies* to this polite city, has given an opening for a troop of dark assassins to aim their envenomed shafts at the individual who seems likely to foil his various competitors... // The scurrilous writers I allude to... have represented the office of Master of the Ceremonies at Bath, as a trust of so sacred a nature, that if we credit their description of it, none but the most rigid *Stoic*, or hypocritical *Archbishop*, is qualified for the employment. That this is not absolutely the case, let the delightful annals of *King* NASH declare!... I do not urge this in support of the libertinism of the Master of the Ceremonies, - but to prove that the office does not require a total seclusion from the pleasures and enjoyments of the world. The present candidate [William Brereton], whom they are so anxious to run down, has, undoubtedly, been addicted to play; but has he not pledged himself to the public, totally to renounce it, if he be elected. Let us look back... on our former Masters of the Ceremonies... *Nash* was never happy but with the *bottle* in one hand, and the *dice-box* in the other. As for *Derrick*, he was too extravagant a satire on *pleasure*, as well as *decorum*, to merit a moment's attention. But if I am rightly informed, his successor, even the *immaculate* Capt.*Wade*, devoted more of his time to *gaming* of every denomination, than he did even to *gallantry*, or the other *duties* of his regency. Mr.*B[rereto]n*, therefore, in my opinion, stands now upon fairer ground than either of them... // His private character stands as unimpeached as that of any man who has mixed in so long with the pleasurable circles of the world, - though invention... has dragged an innocent amour of five and twenty years standing from the grave of oblivion, and represented it as the basest seduction of yesterday!... let his adversaries enquire... at Bath, his place of residence of many years; there they will be informed, that he has strictly supported the character of a good husband, - an affectionate parent, - a warm friend, - a man punctual in the discharge of his debts, - and beloved by all ranks of people with whom he has been connected...
*Bath Chronicle 25 Sep 1777, letter from 'A Scrutineer'*

### 438. *1780 A rule is a rule*
Capt Dawson Master of the ceremonies [at the Upper Rooms] & the Bishop of Worcesters Lady had lately a dispute on a Dress Ball night. The Lady came in with her hat on, which is contrary to the established rules. Capt D politely remonstrated - the Lady would not obey. The Capt insisted - She would not, but retird into the Tea Room. The Capt followd her; and told her that if she would not comply, He must be obligd to take her Hat off Himself. She was still obstinate and ordering her Chair left the rooms. The conduct of Capt D. was

highly applauded; but the Bishop has been silly enough to resent it, & some
abusive letters have appeard in the London papers on the Occasion.
*BCL, MS B920, Edmund Rack, A Disultory Journal of Events... at Bath, entry for 22
Jan 1780*

### 439.  1781  The Guildhall's own Arbiter Elegantiarum

IT having been reported to some of the Subscribers to the Assemblies at the
Town-Hall, Bath, that I had no intention to continue officiating as Master of
the Ceremonies; I beg leave to assure [them]... that after the very respectable
manner in which I was solicited to accept that office... and the... approbation I
have had the satisfaction to experience during the two years I have already
held it... I shall esteem myself honoured by a continuance of their protection...
// Simeon Moreau
*Bath Chronicle 18 Oct 1781*

### 440.  1782  Decorum in the country dances: Dawson's new ruling

To prevent the frequent disagreeable and alarming disputes which arise from
Ladies suffering their acquaintance to stand above them in a Country-Dance, it
is most humbly requested of the Company to comply with the following
regulation: - // 'That no person shall allow a Couple to take place above them,
unless they choose to go to the bottom themselves.' // It is hoped this will
effectually put a stop to the disorder and confusion which never fails to begin
the moment the Company stand up to dance Country-Dances, and restore that
order and decorum so absolutely necessary to be preferred in all polite
assemblies. // WM.DAWSON, Master of the Ceremonies
*Bath Chronicle 17 Jan 1782*

### 441.  1786-90  During the reigns of Tyson and King

(9 May 1786) ... several Ladies exhibited in minuets tho' the Men have so
great an aversion to them that only one Gentleman except the Masters of the
Ceremonies of both Rooms danced with them - Tyson is promoted to the upper
Rooms and a Mr King, a very genteel fashionable looking young Man officiates
at the lower.

(5 Jan 1790) Last night I was again at the Ball, quite dissipated you see, but
the truth is it was Tyson's Benefit, and as he is my acquaintance, independant
of being M:C:, it was but decent that at least one of us should appear there.
There were near twelve Hundred people there as fine as Sattins and feathers
could make them.
*Sheridan (E.), Journal, pp.82 and 192*

*442. 1794 Panegyric on James King, M.C. at the Lower Rooms*

Oui, je l'ai vu cet aimable Roi,
Dans la brillante Assemblée,
Où nous avons passé, je crois,
La plus agréable soirée.

Qu'il me paroissoit charmant,
Ce Roi, rempli de politesse,
Avec son air doux & galant
Aux Bourgeois comme à la Noblesse.

Quand aux Dames il offroit sa main,
Sur son front brilloit la candeur;
Les Graces étoient dans son maintien,
Son sourire annonçoit le bonheur.

Recevant d'un accueil affable
Tout le monde sans exception;
Chacun se croyoit redevable
De ses soins & de son attention.

Heureux qui a l'art de plaire
Il est comblé de mille faveurs,
Quand il sait par ses manières,
Comme JAMES KING, gagner les coeurs.

[Yes, I have seen this obliging King in the glittering assembly where I think we spent a most pleasant evening. // How charming and urbane this King seemed - as gentle and attentive to commoners as he was to the nobility. // As he handed out the ladies, his brow was bright with innocence; the Graces were in his bearing; his smile presaged happiness. // No-one was denied his kindly welcome; all felt obliged to him for his notice and consideration. // Happy the person with the talent of pleasing; favours are heaped on him when, like James King, he can win hearts by courteous behaviour.]
*Bath Herald 1 Feb 1794, anonymous verses [by an émigré?]*

# SOURCES AND ACKNOWLEDGMENTS

*Manuscripts, ephemera, etc.*
I am grateful to the following institutions for permission to quote:
BCL (Bath Central Library): items 2, 4, 12, 38, 44, 52, 61-2, 72, 75, 114, 122, 149, 166, 177, 204, 208, 231, 275, 316, 333-4, 382, 402, 404, 420, 422, 438
BL (British Library, Dept of Manuscripts): items 9-10
BRO (Bath Record Office): items 39, 74, 92, 98, 142, 164, 175, 248, 282, 324, 326, 328, 342, 349, 353, 363, 369, 376-7, 379, 389, 397, 411
BrRL (Bristol Reference Library): item 242
BrRO (Bristol Record Office): items 6, 48
SPCK (Society for Promoting Christian Knowledge): item 283
WRO (Wiltshire Record Office): items 202, 332, 338, 380

*Newspapers (in original or microfilm)*
*Bath Advertiser; Bath Chronicle; Bath Herald; Bath Journal* - Bath Central Library
*Farley's Bristol Newspaper; The Oracle or Bristol Weekly Miscellany* - Bristol Reference Library
*Gloucester Journal* - Gloucester Central Library

*Books, pamphlets, periodicals, etc.*
Permission to reprint has been sought from all owners of material still in copyright. Where owners could not be traced and permissions proved unobtainable, the publisher will be pleased to hear from those controlling publication rights.

Anstey, New Bath Guide, 1766: item 172. Christopher Anstey, *The New Bath Guide* (Bath, 1766)
Art of Thriving at Bath: item 63. *The Art of Thriving at Bath, or, A Display of Poundage*, 2nd ed. (Bath? post-1737)
Austen, Letters: items 118, 161, 256. *Jane Austen's Letters to her Sister Cassandra and Others*, ed. R.W.Chapman. 2 vols. (Oxford, Clarendon P., 1932). By permission of OUP
Baker, Diary: item 313. *The Diary of John Baker*, ed. P.C.Yorke (London, Hutchinson, 1931)
Bath: City Charter, 1775: item 341. *Bath: the City Charter, containing the Original Institution of Mayors...* (Bath, J.Salmon, 1775)
Bath General Hospital, Vindication: item 105. Bath General Hospital, *A Short Vindication of the Proceedings of the Governors... in relation to Mr.Archibald Cleland* (Bath, 1744)
Bayly, Sermon: item 108. Edward Bayly, *A Sermon Preach'd...for the Support of the General Hospital...* (Bath, 1749)
Bemrose, Life of Wright: item 272. William Bemrose, *The Life and Works of Joseph Wright, ARA* (London, 1885)

Borzacchini, Parisian Master: item 297. M.Guelfi Borzacchini, *The Parisian Master, or, A New Method for... the French Language* (Bath, 1789)

Bradley, General Treatise: item 163. Richard Bradley, *A General Treatise on Husbandry and Gardening*. 3 vols. (London, 1724)

Burney (C.), Letters: item 229. *The Letters of Dr Charles Burney*, ed. A.Ribeiro. Vol.1- (Oxford, Clarendon P., 1991-). By permission of OUP

Burney (F.), Diary: item 365. *Diary and Letters of Madame d'Arblay [Fanny Burney], 1778-1840*, ed. C.Barrett. 6 vols. (London, 1904)

Burney (F.), Early Diary: item 225. *The Early Diary of Frances Burney, 1768-1778*, ed. A.R.Ellis. 2 vols. (London, 1889)

Burton, Epistolae: item 426. John Burton, *Epistolae altera Peregrinantis altera Rusticantis* (Oxford, 1748)

Calendar of Bradford-on-Avon Examinations: item 383. *Calendar of Bradford-on-Avon Settlement Examinations and Removal Orders, 1725-98*, ed. P.Hembry (Wiltshire Record Society, 46, 1990). By permission of the Society

Charity Commissioners Reports: item 284

Cheyne, Essay: item 241. George Cheyne, *An Essay of Health and Long Life* (London, 1724)

Clarke, Tour in 1791: items 24, 207. Edward Daniel Clarke, *A Tour through the South of England, Wales, and... Ireland... Summer of 1791* (London, 1793)

Cowper (Countess), Diary: item 121. *Diary of Mary, Countess Cowper, Lady of the Bedchamber... 1714-1720* (London, 1864)

Cowper (Spencer), Letters: items 106, 145, 243. *Letters of Spencer Cowper, Dean of Durham, 1746-64*, ed. E.Hughes (Durham, Surtees Society 165, 1956). By permission of the Society

CSPD=Calendar of State Papers Domestic: item 396

Curwen, Journal: item 50. *The Journal of Samuel Curwen, Loyalist*, ed. A.Oliver. 2 vols. (Cambridge, Mass., Harvard University P. for Essex Institute, Salem, Mass., 1972). By permission of Harvard U.P.

Delany, Autobiography: item 266. *The Autobiography and Correspondence of Mary Granville, Mrs Delany*, ed. Lady Llanover. 6 vols. (London, 1861-2)

De Quincey, Autobiographic Sketches: item 300. *De Quincey's Works*, vol.14, *Autobiographic Sketches* (Edinburgh, 1863, repr. 1886)

Dibdin, Tour: item 20. Charles Dibdin, *The Musical Tour of Mr.Dibdin* (Sheffield, 1788)

Diseases of Bath: item 97. *The Diseases of Bath; a Satire* (London, J.Roberts, 1737)

Dodsley, Correspondence: item 222. *The Correspondence of Robert Dodsley, 1733-1764*, ed. J.E.Tierney (Cambridge, Cambridge University P., 1988). By permission of CUP

Draper, Brief Description: items 7, 144. Joseph Draper, *A Brief Description of Bath in a Letter to a Friend* (London? 1747)

Eaves and Kimpel, Richardson: item 128. T.D.Eaves and B.D.Kimpel, *Samuel Richardson* (Oxford, Clarendon P., 1971). By permission of OUP

Elwin, Noels and Milbankes: items 151, 203, 247, 271. Malcolm Elwin, *The Noels and the Milbankes: their Letters... 1767-1792* (London, Macdonald, 1967). By permission of Little, Brown & Co. (UK) Ltd

Farington, Diary: item 162. *The Diary of Joseph Farington*, ed. K.Garlick et al. 16 vols. (New Haven, Conn., Yale University P. for the Paul Mellon Center, 1978-84). By permission of Yale U.P.

Forbes, Life of Beattie: item 25. William Forbes, *An Account of the Life and Writings of James Beattie LLD*, 2nd ed. 3 vols. (Edinburgh, 1807)

Frampton, Journal: item 140. *The Journal of Mary Frampton... 1779... 1846*, ed. H.G.Mundy, 2nd ed. (London, 1885)

Gainsborough, Letters: item 15. *The Letters of Thomas Gainsborough*, ed. M.Woodall, rev.ed. (Ipswich, Cupid P., 1963)

Gale, Tour: items 1, 90. Samuel Gale, 'A Tour through Several Parts of England... 1705', *Bibliotheca Topographica Britannica*, ed. J.Nichols, vol.3 (London, 1780?)

Garrick, Letters: items 42. 339. *The Letters of David Garrick*, ed. D.M.Little and G.M.Kahrl. 3 vols. (London, Oxford University P, 1963). By permission of Harvard U.P.

Garrick, Private Correspondence: items 199, 230, 264. *The Private Correspondence of David Garrick*. 2 vols. (London, 1831-2)

Gentleman... Pocket Guide, 1785: item 367. *The Gentleman, Merchant, Tradesman. Lawyer, and Debtor's Pocket Guide in Cases of Arrest* (Bath, W.Gye, 1785)

*Gentleman's Magazine*: item 265

George, Prince of Wales, Correspondence: item 416. *The Correspondence of George, Prince of Wales, 1770-1812*, ed. A.Aspinall. 8 vols. (London, Cassell, 1963-70)

Goulding, Essay: item 401. Thomas Goulding, *An Essay against Too Much Reading* (London, 1728)

Goulding, Fortune-Hunter: item 125. Thomas Goulding, *The Fortune-Hunter, or, The Gamester Reclaim'd* (London? 1736)

Graham, New Treatise: item 117. James Graham, *A New, Plain and Rational Treatise on the... Bath Waters* (Bath, 1789)

Graves, Spiritual Quixote: item 289. Richard Graves, *The Spiritual Quixote*. 3 vols. (London, 1774)

Gray, Correspondence: item 17. *Correspondence of Thomas Gray*, ed. P.Toynbee and L.Whibley. 3 vols. (Oxford, Clarendon P., 1935). By permission of OUP

Hankin, SchimmelPenninck: items 136, 412. Christiana C.Hankin, *Life of Mary Anne SchimmelPenninck*. 2 vols. (London, 1858)

Harris, Life of Hardwicke: item 407. George Harris, *The Life of Lord Chancellor Hardwicke*. 3 vols. (London, 1847)

Hearne, Reliquiae: item 193. *Reliquiae Hearnianae: the Remains of Thomas Hearne, M.A.*, ed. P.Bliss. 3 vols. (London, 1869)

Henrietta, Letters: item 408. *Letters to and from Henrietta, Countess of Suffolk... 1712 to 1767*. 2 vols. (London, 1824)

Herschel, Scientific Papers: item 274. *The Scientific Papers of Sir William Herschel.* 2 vols. (London, 1912)

Hervey (J.), Letter-books: items 93, 141, 190. *Letter-Books of John Hervey, First Earl of Bristol.* 3 vols. (Wells, 1894)

Hervey (W.), Journals: item 276. *Journals of the Hon.William Hervey... 1755 to 1814.* (Bury St Edmunds, 1906)

HMC=Historical Manuscripts Commission

HMC 8 pt.1: item 107. Reports, vol. 8, part 1

HMC 20 pt.1: items 352, 424. Reports, Dartmouth, part 1

HMC 29 pt 4: item 119. Reports, Portland, part 4

HMC 35: items 95, 124, 344. Reports, Kenyon

HMC 38: item 99. Reports 14 appx.part 9, Buckingham, etc.

HMC 42: item 123. Reports, Carlisle

HMC 47: item 432. Reports, Shrewsbury and Coventry Corporations

HMC 51: item 375. Reports, Leybourne-Popham

HMC 55 pt 5: item 400. Reports, MSS. in Various Collections, part 5

HMC 63, Diary, pt.1: items 259, 351. Egmont, Diary, part 1

HMC 78, pt 3: items 95, 124, 344. Reports, Hastings, part 3

Holroyd, Girlhood: items 279, 295. *The Girlhood of Maria Josepha Holroyd... 1776 to 1796,* ed. J.H.Adeane (London, 1896)

Homily to the Septuagint: item 314. *A Homily to the Somersetshire Septuagint, or, A Letter... to the Seventy Proprietors of the New Assembly Rooms, in Bath* (Bristol, 1774)

Ibbetson et al., Picturesque Guide: item 26. J.C.Ibbetson et al., *A Picturesque Guide to Bath, Bristol Hot-Wells, the River Avon...* (London, 1793)

Jesse, Selwyn: items 130, 250, 269. John Heneage Jesse, *George Selwyn and his Contemporaries,* new ed. 4 vols. (London, 1882)

Jones, Letters: items 248, 362, 386. *The Letters of Sir William Jones,* ed. G.Cannon (Oxford, Clarendon P., 1970). By permission of OUP

*Journals of the House of Commons*: item 325

Kelly, Reminiscences: item 236. *Reminiscences of Michael Kelly.* 2 vols. (London, 1826)

Kielmansegge, Diary: items 45-6, 129, 267, 431. Friedrich Kielmansegge, *Diary of a Journey to England in the Years 1761-1762* (London, 1902)

Landon, Haydn in England: items 27, 138. H.C.Robbins Landon, *Haydn in England, 1791-1795* (London, Thames & Hudson, 1976). By permission of Thames & Hudson

Lucas, Essay on Waters: item 110. Charles Lucas, *An Essay on Waters.* 3 vols. (London, 1756)

Madden, Bath Macaroni: item 134. William Madden, *The Bath Macaroni* (Bath, 1781)

Markham, John Loveday: item 304. Sarah Markham, *John Loveday of Caversham, 1711-1789* (Wilton, Michael Russell (Pub.) Ltd., 1984). By permission of Michael Russell (Publishing) Ltd

Mavor, British Tourists: item 30. William Mavor, *The British Tourists.* 6 vols. (London, 1800)

Montagu (Mrs E.), Letters: item 100. *The Letters of Mrs.Elizabeth Montagu*, ed. M.Montagu, 3rd ed. 4 vols. (London, 1809-13)

Montagu (Mrs.E.), Queen of the Blues: item 133. *Mrs. Montagu, 'Queen of the Blues': the Letters and Friendships... 1762 to 1800*, ed. R.Blunt. 2 vols. (London, John Murray, 1923). By permission of John Murray (Publishing) Ltd

Montagu (Lady M.W.), Letters: item 192. *The Complete Letters of Lady Wortley Montagu*, ed. R.Halsband. 3 vols. (London, Oxford University P., 1965-7). By permission of OUP

More, Letters: item 139. *The Letters of Hannah More*, ed. R.B.Johnson (London, John Lane, 1925)

Morgan, Grammaticae Questiones: item 293. Nathanael Morgan, *Grammaticae Questiones* (Bath, 1783)

Morris, Diary: items 60, 215. *The Diary of a West Country Physician [Claver Morris], A.D. 1684-1726*, ed. E.Hobhouse (London, Simpkin Marshall, 1934)

Narrative of What Passed: item 196. *A Narrative of What Passed at Bath upon Account of the Late Earthquake... 18th of March Last* (London. 1750)

New Bath Guide, 1762: item 112. *The New Bath Guide* (Bath, C.Pope, 1762)

New Bath Guide, 1764: item 170. *The New Bath Guide* (Bath, C.Pope, 1764)

Nichols, Literary Anecdotes: item 101. John Nichols, *Literary Anecdotes of the Eighteenth Century*. 9 vols. (London, 1812-15)

Norman, Masonic Lodges: item 360. George Norman, 'The Masonic Lodges of Bath: Minute Book VII of the Lodge Meeting at the White Hart, No.49', *Trans. Somerset Masters Lodge*, No.3746 (Bath, 1922)

Nuttall, Calendar: item 103. Geoffrey F.Nuttall, *Calendar of the Correspondence of Philip Doddridge DD, 1702-51* (Northampton?, Northamptonshire Record Society 29, 1979). By permission of the Society

Oliver, Practical Essay: item 89. William Oliver, *A Practical Essay on Fevers... [and] Dissertation on the Bath-Waters* (London, 1704)

Orrery Papers: item 260. *The Orrery Papers*, ed. Countess of Cork and Orrery. 2 vols. (London, 1903)

Osborn, Letters: item 191. Sarah Osborn, *Political and Social Letters of a Lady of the Eighteenth Century, 1721-1771*, ed. E.F.D.Osborn (London, 1890)

Pembroke Papers: items 155, 252. *Pembroke Papers, 1780-1794: Letters and Diaries of Henry, Tenth Earl of Pembroke and his Circle*, ed. Lord Herbert (London, Jonathan Cape, 1950)

Penrose, Letters: items 148, 173, 287, 310. John Penrose, *Letters from Bath, 1766-1767*, ed. B.Mitchell and H.Penrose (Gloucester, Alan Sutton, 1983). By permission of Alan Sutton Publishing Ltd.

Piozzi, Letters: items 28, 212, 280, 415. *The Piozzi Letters: Correspondence of Hester Lynch Piozzi, 1784-1821 (formerly Mrs Thrale)*, ed. E.A. and L.D.Bloom. Vol. 1- (Newark, University of Delaware, 1989-). By permission of Associated University Presses

Piozzi, Thraliana: item 21. *Thraliana: the Diary of Mrs Hester Lynch Thrale (later Mrs Piozzi), 1776-1809*, ed. K.C.Balderston. 2 vols. (London, Oxford University P, 1942). By permission of OUP

Pitt, Correspondence: items 245, 335-6. William Pitt, Earl of Chatham, *Correspondence*, ed. W.S.Taylor and J.H.Pringle. 4 vols. (London, 1838-40)

Plans of the Sunday Schools: item 296. *Plans of the Sunday Schools and School of Industry Established in... Bath* (Bath, R.Cruttwell, 1789)

Pococke, Travels: items 8, 128, 244. *The Travels through England of Dr.Richard Pococke*, ed. J.J.Cartwright. 2 vols. (London?, Camden Society, new series 42 and 44, 1888-9)

Poulter, Discoveries: item 356. *The Discoveries of John Poulter, alias Baxter... by Himself*, 6th ed. (Sherborne, R.Goadby,1753)

Powys, Diaries: items 13, 239. *Passages from the Diaries of Mrs.Philip Lybbe Powys of Hardwick House, Oxon., A.D. 1756 to 1808*, ed. E.J. Climenson (London, 1899)

Roberts, Memoir of H.More: items 116, 321. William Roberts, *Memoirs of the Life of... Mrs.Hannah More*. 4 vols. (London, 1834)

Ryder, Diary: items 34, 120, 214, 303, 398, 418. *The Diary of Dudley Ryder, 1715-1716*, ed. W.Matthews (London, Methuen, 1939). By permission of Routledge

SANHS=Somersetshire Archaeological and Natural History Society

Selection of Catches, Glees, &c.: item 234. *A Selection of Favourite Catches, Glees, &c. as Sung at the Bath Harmonic Society*, 2nd ed. (Bath, R.Cruttwell, 1799)

Seymour, Gentle Hertford: item 329. Frances Seymour, Duchess of Somerset, *The Gentle Hertford*, ed. H.S.Hughes (New York, Macmillan Co., 1940)

Shaw, Tour: items 22, 81, 254. Stebbing Shaw, *A Tour to the West of England in 1788* (London, 1789)

Sheridan (E.), Journal: items 232, 253, 441. *Betsy Sheridan's Journal: Letters from Sheridan's Sister, 1784-1786 and 1788-1790*, ed. W.LeFanu (London, Eyre & Spottiswoode, 1960). By permission of Reed Books

Sheridan (R.B.), Letters: items 131, 224. *The Letters of Richard Brinsley Sheridan*, ed. C.Price. 3 vols. (Oxford, Clarendon P., 1966). By permission of OUP

Sibbald, Memoirs: items 180, 299. *The Memoirs of Susan Sibbald, 1783-1812*, ed. F.P.Hett (London, John Lane, 1926)

Smollett, Essay: item 330. Tobias Smollett, *An Essay on the External Use of Water* (London, 1752)

Smollett, Humphry Clinker: item 434. Tobias Smollett, *The Expedition of Humphry Clinker* (1st pub., London, 1771)

Smollett, Letters: item 113. *The Letters of Tobias Smollett*, ed. L.M.Knapp (Oxford, Clarendon P., 1970). By permission of OUP

Southey, Life: item 251. *The Life and Correspondence of Robert Southey*, ed. C.C.Southey. 6 vols. (London, 1849)

Stanhope, Letters: items 47, 111, 194, 433. *The Letters of Philip Dormer Stanhope, 4th Earl of Chesterfield*, ed. B.Dobrée. 6 vols. (London, Eyre & Spottiswoode, 1932). By permission of Reed Books

Stukeley, Itinerarium: item 258. William Stukeley, *Itinerarium Curiosum*, 2nd ed. 2 vols. (London, 1776, based on 1724 ed.)

Stukeley Family Memoirs: items 94, 263. *The Family Memoirs of the Rev.William Stukeley, M.D. and... Correspondence...* 3 vols. (Durham, Surtees Society 73, 76, 80, 1882-7)

Sutherland, Attempts: item 14. Alexander Sutherland, *Attempts to Revive Antient Medical Doctrines* (London, 1763)

Swift, Correspondence: item 96. *The Correspondence of Jonathan Swift*, ed. H.Williams. 5 vols. (Oxford, Clarendon P., 1963-5). By permission of OUP

*The Tatler*: item 213

Thicknesse, New Prose Bath Guide: items 132, 154, 315. Philip Thicknesse, *The New Prose Bath Guide, for the Year 1778* (Bath, 1778?)

Trigg, Correspondence: item 126. W.B.Trigg, 'The Correspondence of Dr.David Hartley and Rev.John Lister', *Trans.Halifax Antiquarian Society*, 1938-40, pp.231-78. By permission of the Society

Verney Letters: item 188. *Verney Letters of the Eighteenth Century*, ed. Lady Verney. 2 vols. (London, Ernest Benn, 1930)

Walpole, Correspondence: item 85. *The Yale Edition of Horace Walpole's Correspondence*, ed. W.S.Lewis. 48 vols. (New Haven, Conn., 1937-83). By permission of Yale U.P.

Warburton, Letters: item 268. *Letters from the Reverend Dr.Warburton... to the Hon.Charles Yorke... 1752 to 1770* (London, 1812)

Ward, Step to the Bath: items 31, 187, 302. Ned Ward, *A Step to the Bath, with a Character of the Place* (London, 1700)

Wedgwood, Letters: item 76. *The Selected Letters of Josiah Wedgwood*, ed. A.Finer and G.Savage (London, Cory, Adams & Mackay, 1965)

Wentworth Papers: items 189, 399. *The Wentworth Papers, 1705-1739... from the... Correspondence of Thomas Wentworth, Lord Raby*, ed. J.J.Cartwright (London, 1883)

Wesley (C.), Journal: item 306. *The Journal of the Rev.Charles Wesley*, ed. T.Jackson. 2 vols. (London, 1849)

Wesley (J.), Journal: item 23. *The Journal of the Rev.John Wesley, A.M.*, ed. N.Curnock. 8 vols. (London, 1909-16)

Wesley (J.), Letters: item 312. *The Letters of the Rev.John Wesley, A.M.*, ed. J.Telford, standard ed. 7 vols. (London, Epworth P., 1931). By permission of Epworth Press.

Whalley, Journals: item 318. *Journals and Correspondence of Thomas Sedgewick Whalley, D.D.*, ed. H.Wickham. 2 vols. (London, 1863)

Whatley, Characters: item 419. Robert Whatley, *Characters at the Hot-Well, Bristol... and at Bath, in... 1723* (London, 1724)

Whitefield, Journals: item 305. *The Journals of George Whitefield*, ed. W.Wale. (London, 1905)

Whitehead, Original Anecdotes: item 150. Thomas Whitehead, *Original Anecdotes of the Late Duke of Kingston and Miss Chudleigh* (London, 1792)

Wilkes, Letters: items 53, 153, 176. *Letters from... 1774 to... 1796 of John Wilkes, Esq., Addressed to his Daughter.* 4 vols. (London, 1804)

Williams, Post-Reformation Catholicism: item 317. J.Anthony Williams, *Post-Reformation Catholicism in Bath*. 2 vols. (London? Catholic Record Society, Record Series 65-6, 1975-6). By permission of the Society

Williams, Two Suspected Jacobites: item 403. J.Anthony Williams, 'Two Suspected Jacobites at Bath in 1745', *Notes & Queries for Somerset & Dorset*, vol.28 (1968) pp.55-8. By permission of *NQSD*

Wilson, Shropshire Lady: items 159, 182, 323. Ellen Wilson, 'A Shropshire Lady in Bath, 1794-1807', *Bath History*, vol.4 (1992) pp.95-123. By permission of *Bath History*

Wood, Essay, 1742-3: items 3, 64, 104, 262. John Wood, *An Essay towards a Description of... Bath*. 2 vols. (Bath, 1742-3)

Wood, Essay, 1749: items 167-8, 354. John Wood, *An Essay towards a Description of Bath*, 2nd ed. 2 vols. (London, 1749)

Woodforde, Diary: items 158, 311. James Woodforde, *The Diary of a Country Parson*, ed. J.Beresford. 5 vols. (London, Oxford University P., 1924-31). By permission of A.P.Watt Ltd.

Yonge, Journal: item 32. *The Journal of James Yonge, 1647-1721, Plymouth Surgeon*, ed. F.N.L.Poynter (London, Longmans, 1963). By permission of Longman Group

Young, Tour: item 16. Arthur Young, *A Six Weeks Tour through the Southern Counties of England and Wales* (London, 1768)

*Acknowledgments*

I am indebted to Michael Bishop for help over item 426, though the version printed is my own, and to both Alan Summers and John Wroughton for much practical advice on publishing. More generally I am grateful for information, ideas and stimulus over the years from many past and present members of the History of Bath Research Group, Bath Archaeological Trust and other bodies. An anthology of this kind could not be compiled without much application to libraries and record offices. In this respect I must particularly thank Elizabeth Bevan and her team at Bath Central Library, and Colin Johnson and Mary Blagdon at Bath Record Office. I wish too to acknowledge my gratitude to the various editors, publishers and keepers of manuscripts who have freely given me leave to print extracts in this book. Finally my special thanks go to my son Adrian for his assistance on computer matters and to my wife Mary for her support and encouragement at all times.